Reading STREET

Grade 5

# Scott Foresman
# ELL Teaching Guide

**Editorial Offices:** Glenview, Illinois • Parsippany, New Jersey • New York, New York
**Sales Offices:** Needham, Massachusetts • Duluth, Georgia • Glenview, Illinois
Coppell, Texas • Sacramento, California • Mesa, Arizona

ISBN: 0-328-14603-X

4 5 6 7 8 9 10 V004 14 13 12 11 10 09 08 07

# Contents

## Unit 1:   Meeting Challenges

## Unit 2:   Doing the Right Thing

## Unit 3:   Inventors and Artists

## Unit 4: Adapting

## Unit 5: Adventurers

## Unit 6: The Unexpected

# Scott Foresman Reading Street
## Overview of Weekly Support for English Language Learners

The ELL Teaching Guide provides weekly lesson materials to support English language learners with scaffolded comprehension instruction and vocabulary development. It builds on the Student Edition and on literacy instruction in the Teacher's Edition. Support for English language learners and teachers is based on the Three Pillars, developed by Dr. Jim Cummins:

Activate Prior Knowledge/Build Background
Access Content
Extend Language

Scott Foresman Reading Street provides these resources:

- **Student Edition** that builds every student's reading and language skills
- **Decodable Readers** for practicing emergent literacy skills (grades K–3)
- **Leveled Readers** for differentiated instruction
- **Teacher's Edition** with ELL instructional strategies built into the lesson plans
- **ELL Readers** that develop English language learners' vocabulary and comprehension skills
- **ELL Posters** with high-quality illustrations and five days of activities supporting key vocabulary and concepts
- **Ten Important Sentences** to focus on comprehension while expanding English
- **ELL and Transition Handbook** that supports teachers' professional development and students' transition to advanced levels of English proficiency
- **ELL Teaching Guide** see below

## E L L Teaching Guide Features

**"Week at a Glance" Lesson Planners** offer a quick reference to the ELL support materials for each lesson of the year.

**"Picture It!" Comprehension Lessons** provide teaching strategies for each comprehension skill. A reproducible "Picture It!" student practice page helps students learn the key comprehension skill through illustrations, graphic organizers, sheltered text, and ELL-friendly activities.

**Vocabulary Activities and Word Cards** stimulate language production and reinforce target vocabulary. Small-group and partner activities use reproducible Word Cards to practice listening, speaking, reading, and writing. Home-language activities allow students to connect their prior knowledge to key vocabulary and concepts in English.

**Multilingual Summaries** of each main reading selection provide a brief, accessible summary in English and translations of the summary in the next most common five languages among the U.S. school population: Spanish, Chinese, Vietnamese, Korean, and Hmong. Students and parents can use the summaries to prepare for reading, build comprehension, support retellings, and strengthen school-home connections.

**ELL Reader Lessons and Study Guides** support every ELL Reader with scaffolded instruction to help students understand and respond to literature. The reproducible Study Guides support students' comprehension and provide writing and take-home activities for learners at various English proficiency levels.

**Multilingual Lesson Vocabulary** provides translations of the target vocabulary in Spanish, Chinese, Vietnamese, Korean, and Hmong.

# Frindle
### Student Edition pages 22–33

| Week at a Glance | Customize instruction every day for your English Language Learners. | | | | |
|---|---|---|---|---|---|
| | **Day 1** | **Day 2** | **Day 3** | **Day 4** | **Day 5** |
| **Teacher's Edition** | Use the ELL Notes that appear throughout each day of the lesson to support instruction and reading. | | | | |
| **ELL Poster 1** | • Assess Prior Knowledge<br>• Develop Concepts and Vocabulary | • Preteach Tested Vocabulary | • Word Builders | • Spelling Bee | • Monitor Progress |
| **ELL Teaching Guide** | • Picture It! Lesson, pp. 1–2<br>• Multilingual Summaries, pp. 5–7 | • ELL Reader Lesson, pp. 212–213 | • Vocabulary Activities and Word Cards, pp. 3–4<br>• Multilingual Summaries, pp. 5–7 | | |
| **ELL Readers** | | • Teach *Hana Gets Serious* | • Reread *Hana Gets Serious* and other texts to build fluency | | |
| **ELL and Transition Handbook** | Use the following as needed to support this week's instruction and to conduct alternative assessments:<br>• Phonics Transition Lessons<br>• Grammar Transition Lessons<br>• Assessment | | | | |

**Picture It!** Comprehension Lesson
## Plot and Character
Use this lesson to supplement or replace the skill lesson on pages 18–19 of the Teacher's Edition.

### Teach
Distribute copies of the Picture It! blackline master on page 2.
• Tell students that they are going to read a story and that the pictures go with the story.
• Share the Skill Points (at right) with students. Have students describe each picture. Invite them to make a guess about the problem at the beginning of the story, based on the pictures.
• Read the story. Ask: *What was the problem? What was the solution?*

### Practice
Read aloud the directions on page 2. Have students complete the chart at the bottom of the page. Have students keep their organizers for later reteaching.

**Answers for page 2:** *Characters*: Mr. Lopez, Clarissa, other students. *Problem*: The star of the play is sick. *Solution*: Clarissa, the stage manager, will play the role.

> ## Skill Points
> ✓ The **plot** of a story is what happens. A story usually starts with a problem or conflict. The problem builds to a climax. The resolution of the problem comes at the end of the story.
>
> ✓ **Characters** are the people in the story. You can tell what characters are like from what they do and say.

**Look** at the pictures. **Read** the story.

- **Think** about the characters. **Think** about the plot. What is the problem? What is the solution?

- **Complete** the chart at the bottom of the page.

## Last-Minute Drama

It was the night of the school play. Clarissa had worked hard. Everything was ready. Then Mr. Lopez told her the bad news. Amy was sick! And she was the star of the show!

"What will we do?" Clarissa cried. "Who can learn Amy's part right now?"

"I think I know one person who can play the part," Mr. Lopez said. "You."

She did know the lines by heart. "But who will be the stage manager?" she wondered. "I will," he replied. "You already did most of the work. It will be easy."

Mr. Lopez was wrong about one thing: his job was not easy. But he and Clarissa made it through. The play was saved!

| **Characters** | **Problem** | **Solution** |
|---|---|---|
| | | |

# Vocabulary Activities and Word Cards

Copy the Word Cards on page 4 as needed for the following activities.
Use the blank cards for additional words that you want to teach.
Also see suggestions for teaching vocabulary in the ELL and Transition Handbook.

| Write a Dialogue | Where's the Stress? | Related Words |
|---|---|---|
| • Give pairs of students sets of Word Cards. Ask them to make up a dialogue between two people. You may choose to give the students a context for their dialogue. For example, they may be two inventors speaking in an advertisement for their invention, an automatic pizza maker. They should include each of the vocabulary words in their dialogue, if they can.<br><br>• Ask students to write down their dialogue. Encourage correct use of capitalization and punctuation. Ask volunteers to perform their dialogues for the class. | • Give each student a set of Word Cards, and have them arrange the cards on their desks face up.<br><br>• Read each word aloud one by one. As you do so, emphasize the stressed syllable, telling students to underline the stressed syllable on their Word Cards.<br><br>• When you are finished, write the following list on the board, and have students use it to check their work: ac*quaint*ed, as*sign*ment, es*sen*tial, ex*pand*ed, guar*an*teed, pro*ce*dures, rep*u*tation, *wor*shipped. | • Give pairs of students these Word Cards: *acquainted*, *assignment*, *expanded*, *guaranteed*, *procedures*, and *worshipped*.<br><br>• Explain that each of these words has an added ending, either an inflection or a suffix. Explain that inflections are verb endings such as *-ed*, *-ing*, and noun endings such as *-s* or *-es*. Suffixes are word parts such as *-ment*, *-ly*, *-ness*, *-ful*.<br><br>• Ask pairs to look up each word and find its root word. Have them fold each card so that only the root word shows. Check their foldings.<br><br>• Point out that the root word in *procedures* is spelled with double *e*: *proceed*. Explain that the *d* in the word *guaranteed* is like *-ed* in many verbs. |

# acquainted

# assignment

# essential

# expanded

# guaranteed

# procedures

# reputation

# worshipped

# Multilingual Summaries

## Frindle

Nick was nervous about starting the fifth grade. The language arts teacher was known for being strict. Mrs. Granger made long vocabulary lists and gave a lot of homework. She loved the dictionary. Mrs. Granger liked to have her students look up words in the dictionary.

The first six classes on the first day of school went well for Nick. But Mrs. Granger's class was much harder. Nick asked a question about dictionaries at the end of class. He hoped Mrs. Granger would spend a long time answering the question. Then she might forget to give homework.

She told Nick to write a report about his question. She gave homework too. Everything Nick had heard about Mrs. Granger was true.

## Frindle

Nick estaba nervioso porque comenzaba el quinto grado. Todos decían que la profesora de la clase de lenguaje era muy estricta. La Sra. Granger preparaba listas de vocabulario muy largas y daba muchísima tarea. Ella amaba el diccionario. A la Sra. Granger le gustaba que los estudiantes buscaran palabras en el diccionario.

El primer día, a Nick le fue muy bien en las primeras seis clases. Sin embargo, la clase de la Sra. Granger fue la más difícil. Nick hizo una pregunta sobre los diccionarios al final de la clase. Tenía la esperanza de que la Sra. Granger se demorara mucho respondiendo a la pregunta. Así, se le olvidaría darles tarea.

Ella le pidió a Nick que hiciera un escrito sobre la pregunta. También les dio tarea. Todo lo que Nick había escuchado sobre la Sra. Granger era verdad.

# Multilingual Summaries

Chinese

## 尼克的新字

尼克升上五年級了，他心情好緊張，因為聽說五年級的國文老師一格蘭傑老師很嚴格，她很喜歡列一大堆生字要學生背，家庭作業也好多。她最愛字典了，很愛叫學生查字典。

尼克升上五年級後第一天上課，前六堂課他都覺得不難，老師上課他都聽得懂，可是一遇到格蘭傑老師就不同了，她的課好難喔。要下課的時候，尼克問老師一個有關字典的問題，他希望格蘭傑老師花很多時間回答問題，然後可能就會忘記要出家庭作業了。

可是尼克的如意算盤打錯了，老師竟然叫他寫一份有關字典的報告，而且她也沒忘記要出家庭作業。天呀！原來所有關於格蘭傑老師的傳說都是真的！

Vietnamese

## Frindle

Nick hồi hộp khi bắt đầu lên học lớp năm. Cô giáo dạy văn nổi tiếng là nghiêm khắc. Cô Granger viết những bản ngữ vựng dài và cho nhiều bài tập về nhà làm. Cô ấy yêu thích từ điển. Cô Granger thích cho học sinh của mình tra cứu những chữ trong từ điển.

Sáu giờ học đầu tiên của hôm đầu nhập học diễn ra tốt đẹp cho Nick. Nhưng giờ lớp của Cô Granger thì khó hơn nhiều. Vào cuối buổi học, Nick hỏi cô một câu hỏi về từ điển. Cậu bé hy vọng là Cô Granger sẽ mất nhiều thời giờ để trả lời câu hỏi. Rồi cô ấy có thể quên không cho bài tập về nhà làm.

Cô ấy kêu Nick viết một bài tường trình về câu hỏi của cậu. Cô cũng cho bài tập về nhà làm nữa. Mọi điều mà Nick từng nghe về Cô Granger là có thật.

# Multilingual Summaries

## 프린들

닉은 5학년이 되는 것이 초조하다. 국어 과목 선생님이 엄격하기로 유명한 분이기 때문이다. 그레인저 선생님은 외울 단어 목록을 길게 만들고 숙제 또한 아주 많이 내준다. 선생님은 사전을 너무 좋아해서 학생들에게 사전에서 단어 찾아오기를 시키는 것을 좋아한다.

학교 첫날 첫 여섯 과목은 순조로웠지만 그레인저 선생님의 수업은 훨씬 어렵다. 닉은 수업이 끝날 때 사전에 대한 질문을 하나 한다. 그레인저 선생님이 질문에 긴 시간동안 대답해 주다가 숙제 내주는 걸 잊어버렸으면 하고 바랬던 것이다.

선생님은 닉에게 그 질문에 대한 보고서를 써 오라고 할 뿐만 아니라 숙제까지 내준다. 그레인저 선생님에 대한 소문이 사실이었던 것이다.

## Frindle

Nick nyuaj siab pib kawm ntawv qib tsib. Tus xib hwb qhia ntawv Miskas qhia nyaum nyaum li. Mrs. Granger hais kom nws cov tub ntxhais kawm cov lus tshiab ntau ntau thiab nqa ntaub ntawv ntau mus tsev. Nws nyiam phau ntawv txhais lus heev. Mrs. Granger nyiam kom nws cov tub ntxhais nrhiav cov lus tshiab uas nyob rau hauv phau ntawv txhais lus.

Thaum hnub pib kawm ntawv mas thawj rau hoob kawm ntawv los mus zoo heev rau Nick. Tab sis, Mrs Granger hoob kawm ntawv mas nyuaj zog. Sij hawm kawm ntawv yuav luag tas, Nick nug ib qhov txog phau txhais lus. Nws cia siab tias Mrs. Granger yuav hais lus ntau ntau teb nws lus nug thiab tsis nco qab muab ntaub ntawv rau lawv nqa mus tsev.

Nws hais kom Nick sau ib daig ntawv txog nws cov lus nug ntawd. Nws kuj muab ntaub ntawv rau lawv nqa mus tsev thiab. Nick xav tias tag nrho txhua yam nws twb hnov txog Mrs. Granger muaj tseeb tiag.

# Thunder Rose
Student Edition pages 46–63

| <br>**Week at a Glance** | Customize instruction every day for your English Language Learners. | | | | |
|---|---|---|---|---|---|
| | **Day 1** | **Day 2** | **Day 3** | **Day 4** | **Day 5** |
| **Teacher's Edition** | Use the ELL Notes that appear throughout each day of the lesson to support instruction and reading. | | | | |
| **ELL Poster 2** | • Assess Prior Knowledge<br>• Develop Concepts and Vocabulary | • Preteach Tested Vocabulary | • Weather Watchers | • Review Cause and Effect | • Monitor Progress |
| **ELL Teaching Guide** | • Picture It! Lesson, pp. 8–9<br>• Multilingual Summaries, pp. 12–14 | • ELL Reader Lesson, pp. 214–215 | • Vocabulary Activities and Word Cards, pp. 10–11<br>• Multilingual Summaries, pp. 12–14 | | |
| **ELL Readers** | • Reread *Hana Gets Serious* | • Teach *Tommy and the Tornado* | • Reread *Tommy and the Tornado* and other texts to build fluency | | |
| **ELL and Transition Handbook** | Use the following as needed to support this week's instruction and to conduct alternative assessments:<br>• Phonics Transition Lessons<br>• Grammar Transition Lessons<br>• Assessment | | | | |

**Picture It!** Comprehension Lesson
## Cause and Effect
Use this lesson to supplement or replace the skill lesson on pages 42–43 of the Teacher's Edition.

### Teach
Distribute copies of the Picture It! blackline master on page 9.
• Have students compare the two pictures. The pictures show a pond before and after a drought. Explain that a drought is a long period of time without water. Then read the paragraph aloud.
• Share the Skill Points (at right) with students.
• Ask: *What effects did the drought have on the pond?*

### Practice
Read aloud the directions on page 9. Tell students to read the paragraph to see how causes and effects are linked together. Discuss an effect of drought that can be the cause of another effect. Then have the students complete the table at the bottom of the page. Have students keep their organizers for later reteaching.

**Answers for page 9:** *Cause:* The rain stops. *Effect:* Insects and plants die. *Cause:* There is no more food.

> ### Skill Points
> ✓ A **cause** makes something happen. The **effect** is what happens.
> ✓ An effect may become the cause of another effect.

Name _____

**Look** at the pictures and **read** the paragraph. Then **complete** the table.

- For each effect shown, **write** its cause.
- For each cause shown, **write** its effect.

# The Terrible Effects of a Drought

When the rain stops for a long time, a drought happens. Water dries up and disappears. Without water, plants begin to die. Insects and fish can't live without plants and water. They disappear too. When that happens, there is no more food for the birds. Soon, the birds move away. A drought has a long chain of effects.

| Cause | Effect |
|---|---|
|  | A drought happens. |
| The water in the pond dries up. |  |
|  | Birds move away. |

# Vocabulary Activities and Word Cards

Copy the Word Cards on pages 10–11 as needed for the following activities.
Use the blank card for an additional word that you want to teach.
Also see suggestions for teaching vocabulary in the ELL and Transition Handbook.

| Group Story | Definition Game | Word Mix |
|---|---|---|
| • Put all the Word Cards into a paper bag. Have students sit in a circle.<br><br>• Draw a word out of the bag, and make up a story starter using it, for example: *A mysterious young woman stepped daintily through the herd of cattle*. Then, invite a student to draw a card and create the next sentence of the story, using the new word. Explain to students that the story need not be realistic.<br><br>• Continue in this way until all the words have been used. | • Divide students into pairs, and give each pair a set of Word Cards. Tell partners to work together, writing a definition for each word on the back of the card. Provide dictionaries for reference.<br><br>• Students can then quiz each other by playing a game. One student reads aloud a definition (making sure the word on the other side isn't visible) and challenges his or her partner to guess what the word is, based on the definition. | • Display a set of Word Cards. Ask students to study the words. Ask one student to leave the room.<br><br>• The rest of the group should choose one word to remove from the set. Have them think of several clues about the word and plan who will say them.<br><br>• When the student returns, students take turns giving clues about the missing word until it is guessed. The student who gives the final clue is the next one to leave the room. The winner is the student who guesses with the fewest clues. |

# branded | constructed

# daintily

# devastation

# lullaby

# pitch

# resourceful

# thieving

# veins

# Multilingual Summaries

English

## Thunder Rose

Rose was born in a thunderstorm. She could sit up and talk the day she was born. Rose had the power of thunder in her. She drank milk straight from the cows. She could bend metal when she was two years old. When Rose was twelve, she stopped a herd of cattle from stampeding. She jumped on the biggest bull's back. She grabbed his horns, and she stopped him.

Rose decided to take the herd to market. She rode on the big bull. There was no rain on the trail. The cattle were tired and thirsty. Rose tried to lasso the clouds. She tried to squeeze rain out of them.

But a tornado came instead. Rose tried to tame it. The tornado became two tornadoes. Rose began to sing. Her voice sounded like thunder. Rose's song calmed the tornadoes. It began to rain.

Spanish

## Rosa Trueno

Rosa nació en medio una gran tormenta. Ella podía hablar desde el día que nació. Rosa tenía el poder de los truenos dentro de ella. Bebía leche directamente de las vacas. A los dos años podía doblar metales. Cuando cumplió doce años, detuvo una manada de ganado que salía en estampida. Saltó sobre el lomo del toro más grande. Sujetó sus cuernos y lo hizo detener.

Rosa decidió llevar la manada al mercado. Iba montaba sobre el toro grande. No se vislumbraba lluvia en camino. El ganado estaba cansado y sediento. Rosa trató de enlazar las nubes. Trató de exprimirles algo de lluvia.

Pero lo que llegó fue un tornado. Rosa trató de amansarlo. El tornado se convirtió en dos tornados. Rosa comenzó a cantar. Su voz era como el sonido de los truenos. La canción de Rosa logró que los tornados se calmaran. Entonces comenzó a llover.

# Multilingual Summaries

## 雷之女羅絲

　　羅絲出生的那一天，外頭正下著大雷雨。她一出生就會坐起來講話，她擁有雷所賜予的超能力，可以直接從母牛身上喝牛奶，兩歲的時候可以把金屬弄彎，十二歲時能夠使驚慌亂竄的牛群安靜下來，她跳上那隻體積最大的公牛背上，抓住他頭上的角，成功地讓牠停了下來。

　　羅絲決定把牛群趕到市場上賣。她騎在大公牛身上，一路上都沒有下雨，每隻牛都又累又渴。羅絲試著召來一些雲，想從雲裡面擠出一點雨來。

　　結果，雲沒有來，反而是龍捲風出現了。羅絲想把龍捲風平息下來，但是沒想到龍捲風竟然從一個變成兩個。羅絲看到情況不對，於是開始唱歌，她的歌聲聽起來就像雷聲。羅絲的歌聲平息了龍捲風，天空這時候也開始下雨了。

## Nàng Rose Sấm Sét

　　Rose sanh ra trong một cơn mưa bão. Cô ấy có thể thức cả đêm để kể chuyện ngày cô ra đời. Rose có sức mạnh sấm sét trong mình. Cô bé uống sữa trực tiếp từ những con bò. Cô bé có thể uốn cong kim loại khi mới hai tuổi. Khi Rose mười hai tuổi, cô ngăn được đàn bò không cho chúng chạy tán loạn. Cô nhảy lên lưng con bò đực to lớn nhất. Cô nắm lấy sừng của nó và làm nó phải dừng lại.

　　Rose quyết định đưa đàn bò ra chợ. Cô cõi con bò đực to. Trên đường đi không có mưa. Đàn bò mỏi mệt và khát nước. Rose cố bắt những cụm mây bằng dây thòng lọng. Cô bé cố vắt mây để lấy mưa.

　　Nhưng một cơn lốc xoáy đến. Rose cố gắng làm cho nó thuần phục. Cơn lốc xoáy trở thành hai. Rose bắt đầu hát. Tiếng hát của cô nghe giống như sấm vang. Bài hát của Rose làm lắng dịu những cơn lốc. Trời bắt đầu mưa.

# Multilingual Summaries

## 천둥 로즈

폭우 속에서 태어난 로즈는 태어나자마자 일어나 앉고 말을 할 수 있었다. 로즈는 천둥의 힘을 갖고 있었고 젖소로부터 직접 우유를 마셨다. 로즈가 두 살이 되었을 때는 쇠를 구부릴 수 있었고 열두 살이던 때에는 달아나던 소떼를 멈추기도 했다. 덩치가 가장 큰 소의 등에 뛰어올라 뿔을 움켜잡고 소를 멈춘 것이다.

로즈는 소떼를 시장으로 몰고 가기로 하고 큰 소 위에 올라탄다. 가는 길에 비가 오지 않아 소떼가 피곤해하고 목말라하자 로즈는 올가미 밧줄로 구름을 낚아채 비를 짜내려 한다.

하지만 비 대신 회오리바람이 불어 온다. 로즈는 회오리바람을 꺾으려고 애쓰지만 회오리바람은 두 개가 되어 버린다. 그러자 로즈가 천둥 같은 목소리로 노래를 부르기 시작한다. 로즈의 노래는 회오리바람을 잠재운다. 그리고 곧 비가 내린다.

## Xob Quaj Rose

Rose yug los thaum los nag xob nag cua. Hnub nws yug los ntawd nws sawv hais lus. Rose muaj xob quaj lub hwj chim nyob rau hauv nws. Nws haus kua mis nyuj. Thaum nws muaj ob xyoo xwb, nws muab hlau chom kom nkhaus li. Thaum Rose muaj kaum ob xyoo, nws ua kom ib pawg nyuj kom txhob khiav lwj khiav liam ub no. Nws dhia mus rau saum tus txiv nyuj loj tshaj nruab qaum. Nws tsuab tus txiv nyuj kub txwm kom nws tsum kiag.

Rose txiav txim siab tias nws yuav coj pawg nyuj nawd mus tom kiab khw. Nws caij tus txiv nyuj loj. Lawv mus kev ntev heev mas nag tsis los li. Cov nyuj nkeeg heev thiab nqhis dej. Rose sim muab txoj hlua ntes huab cua. Nws sim nyem huab cua ntawd kom los nag.

Tab sis ua cas muaj khaub zeeg cua tuaj xwb. Rose sim tua khuab zeeg cua ntawd tab sis khaub zeeg cua faib ua ob qhov. Rose pib hu nkauj. Nws lub suab zoo li xob quaj. Qhov Rose hu nkauj no ua kom khaub zeeg cua tus tus lawm. Ces nws pib los nag.

# Island of the Blue Dolphins   Student Edition pages 72–83

| Week at a Glance | Customize instruction every day for your English Language Learners. | | | | |
|---|---|---|---|---|---|
| | **Day 1** | **Day 2** | **Day 3** | **Day 4** | **Day 5** |
| **Teacher's Edition** | Use the ELL Notes that appear throughout each day of the lesson to support instruction and reading. | | | | |
| **ELL Poster 3** | • Assess Prior Knowledge <br> • Develop Concepts and Vocabulary | • Preteach Tested Vocabulary | • Survival Strategies | • What Will You Do? | • Monitor Progress |
| **ELL Teaching Guide** | • Picture It! Lesson, pp. 15–16 <br> • Multilingual Summaries, pp. 19–21 | • ELL Reader Lesson, pp. 216–217 | • Vocabulary Activities and Word Cards, pp. 17–18 <br> • Multilingual Summaries, pp. 19–21 | | |
| **ELL Readers** | • Reread *Tommy and the Tornado* | • Teach *Finding Home* | • Reread *Finding Home* and other texts to build fluency | | |
| **ELL and Transition Handbook** | Use the following as needed to support this week's instruction and to conduct alternative assessments: <br> • Phonics Transition Lessons <br> • Grammar Transition Lessons <br> • Assessment | | | | |

**Picture It!** Comprehension Lesson

# Theme and Setting

Use this lesson to supplement or replace the skill lesson on pages 68–69 of the Teacher's Edition.

## Teach

Distribute copies of the Picture It! blackline master on page 16.
- Tell students they are going to read a short story and that the picture goes with the story.
- Share the Skill Points (at right) with students. Remind students that pictures often help tell part of the story.
- Ask students to guess when and where the story takes place, based on the picture. Then read the story aloud.

## Practice

Read aloud the directions on page 16. Have students read the story. When they are finished, tell them to answer the questions by circling the letter of each correct answer. Have students keep their work for later reteaching.

**Answers for page 16: 1: C.** in a forest; **2: B.** during a storm;
**3: A.** the challenges of survival

> ### Skill Points
> ✓ The **setting** of a story is when and where it happens.
> ✓ The **theme** is the message or underlying meaning of the story. Often the theme is not stated. You can figure out the theme from events in the story.

**Look** at the picture and **read** the story. Then **answer** the questions that follow.

## Emergency!

The pilot was in trouble. He was flying over the wilderness when, suddenly, a storm hit. The winds were too strong. It was dangerous to keep flying. So the pilot made an emergency landing. The plane was wrecked. What could the pilot do now? How would he stay alive?

Read each question. Circle the letter of the correct answer.

1. Where does the story take place?
    **A.** in a desert
    **B.** over the ocean
    **C.** in a forest
    **D.** in the mountains

2. When does the story take place?
    **A.** during a drought
    **B.** during a storm
    **C.** in the middle of the night
    **D.** in the future

3. What is the theme of the story?
    **A.** the challenges of survival
    **B.** the beauty of nature
    **C.** the fun of traveling
    **D.** the pleasures of everyday life

# Vocabulary Activities and Word Cards

Copy the Word Cards on page 18 as needed for the following activities.
Use the blank card for an additional word that you want to teach.
Also see suggestions for teaching vocabulary in the ELL and Transition Handbook.

| Fishing Game | Poster Matching | Survival Stories |
|---|---|---|
| • Use one or more sets of Word Cards. Attach a metal paper clip to each card. Put the words in a bucket. Then tie a string to a short stick and a magnet at the end of the string to make a "fishing pole."<br><br>• Have students take turns "fishing" for words. When they "catch" a word, students should make a sentence using that word. If they use the word correctly in a sentence, they keep the "fish." If they cannot, they must return the word to the bucket. The student who has the most "fish" at the end of the game wins. | • Have students take turns choosing a card without showing it to the other students.<br><br>• Display the ELL Poster. The student will use it to make up clues about his or her word. For example, "I see some of this on the beach." (kelp)<br><br>• The student who correctly guesses the word chooses the next card and uses the Poster in the same way. | • Form small groups of students, and give each group a set of Word Cards. Tell groups to make up a survival story using all the vocabulary words.<br><br>• Give each group a sheet of chart paper. Tell them to write their story on the paper, using tape to attach the Word Cards at the appropriate places.<br><br>• When they are finished, invite groups to read their stories aloud to the class. |

# gnawed

# headland

# kelp

# lair

# ravine

# shellfish

# sinew

# Multilingual Summaries

## Island of the Blue Dolphins

Karana lived alone on the Island of the Blue Dolphins. She needed to find a place to build a shelter. One place was too close to the wild dogs. Another place was too noisy. The sea elephants' barking would keep her awake. Then Karana found a safe place near some big rocks.

First, Karana used branches to make a place to sleep. Then, she used whale ribs to build a fence next to a big rock. The fence would keep animals away from the food she gathered.

Then, she gathered wooden poles and big leaves. She tied these together to make the walls and roof of her house. Karana made bowls for cooking and shelves to hold her food. Now she had food and shelter. She was alone but she had what she needed.

Spanish

## La isla de los delfines azules

Karana vivía sola en la isla de los delfines azules. Necesitaba encontrar un lugar para construir su refugio. Uno de los lugares estaba muy cerca de los perros salvajes. En otro había mucho ruido. Los ladridos de los elefantes marinos la despertarían. Luego, Karana encontró un lugar seguro cerca de unas rocas grandes.

Primero usó ramas para hacer un lugar donde dormir. Luego, usó costillas de ballena para hacer una cerca al lado de una roca grande. La cerca mantendría a los animales alejados de la comida que recolectara.

Después buscó palos y hojas grandes. Amarró todas esas cosas juntas para hacer las paredes y el techo de su casa. Karana hizo ollas para cocinar y armarios para guardar su comida. Ya tenía comida y refugio. Estaba sola, pero tenía lo que necesitaba.

# Multilingual Summaries

## 藍色海豚島

卡拉娜自己一個人住在藍色海豚島上。她需要找個可以遮風避雨的地方住，原本她找到兩個地方，但是一個太接近野狗，而另一個又太吵了，海象的叫聲老是把她吵醒。後來，卡拉娜終於在一堆大岩石旁邊找到了一個安全的地方。

剛開始的時候，卡拉娜用樹枝鋪了一個地方睡覺，後來，又用鯨魚肋骨在一塊大岩石旁邊建了圍欄，這樣動物就不能偷吃她辛苦採集的食物。

然後，她又收集很多木樁和大片樹葉，把它們綁在一起，當作房子的屋頂和外牆。卡拉娜還做了煮東西的大碗和放食物的架子。現在，她有吃的東西，也有住的地方。她還是一個人，不過所有需要的東西她都有了。

## Đảo Cá Heo Xanh

Karana sống một mình trên Đảo Cá Heo Xanh. Cô cần tìm một nơi để làm một chỗ ẩn náu. Một nơi thì quá gần với những con chó hoang. Một nơi khác thì quá ồn. Tiếng sủa của những con voi biển làm cô không ngủ được. Rồi Karana tìm được một nơi an toàn gần những hòn đá lớn.

Đầu tiên Karana dùng những cành cây để làm chỗ ngủ. Rồi cô dùng xương sườn của cá voi để làm hàng rào bên cạnh một hòn đá lớn. Hàng rào sẽ ngăn không cho các con thú đến gần thức ăn mà cô đã thu nhặt được.

Rồi cô đi lượm gậy gọc và những chiếc lá to. Cô cột chúng lại để làm vách và mái nhà. Karana làm tô chén để nấu ăn và ngăn kệ để giữ thức ăn. Bây giờ cô có thức ăn và chỗ ở. Cô ấy chỉ có một mình nhưng cô có những thứ mình cần.

# Multilingual Summaries

## 푸른 돌고래 섬

　푸른 돌고래 섬에 혼자 살고 있는 카라나는 집 지을 장소를 찾아 다니는데 어떤 곳은 야생 개들과 너무 가까이 있고 어떤 곳은 너무 시끄럽다. 바다 코끼리 가 내는 소리 때문에 계속 잠을 못 잘 것 같기도 하다. 곧 카라나는 큰 바위들 근 처에 있는 안전한 장소를 찾아낸다.

　카라나는 먼저 나뭇가지를 이용해 잠잘 곳을 만들고 나서 고래 갈비뼈로 큰 바위 옆에 울타리를 만든다. 이 울타리는 카라나가 모아둔 음식을 동물들이 가 져가지 못하게 할 것이다.

　다음에 카라나는 나무 막대기와 큰 잎사귀들을 모은 다음 이것들을 함께 묶 어 벽과 지붕을 만든다. 요리할 그릇과 음식을 넣어둘 선반도 만든 카라나는 이 제 음식도 있고 집도 있다. 카라나는 혼자이지만 필요한 것들을 가지고 있다.

## Pov Txwv Ntses Ntov Fis Xim Xiav

　Karana nyob nws ib leeg xwb nyob ntawm Pov Txwv Ntses Ntov Fis (Dolphin) Xim Xiav. Nws nrhiav ub nrhiav no ib qhov chaw ua tsev nyob. Ib qhov chaw nyob ze ze ib pawg dev qus. Lwm qhov chaw nrov nrov heev. Cov dej hiav txwv ntxhwv tsem heev ces nws pw tsis tau li. Ces nws ho nrhiav ib qhov chaw zoo nyob ze ib co pob zeb loj loj heev.

　Karana xub thawj siv ceg ntoo los ua ib thaj chaw pw. Tom qab ntawd nws siv ib tug ntses whale loj loj cov tav los xov laj kab nyob ze ib lub pob zeb loj. Txoj laj kab no yuav tiv thaiv cov tsiaj txhu kom lawv cuag tsis tau cov mov nws sau lawm.

　Ua li ntawd tas ces nws nrhiav cov ncej ntoo thiab nplooj loj loj. Nws muab cov no los khi ua ke los ua phab ntsa thiab lub ru tsev. Karana ua lub ntim los ua mov noj thiab txua txee los khaws cia nws cov mov. Ces nws thiaj li muaj mov noj thiab muaj tsev nyob. Nws haj tseem nyob nws ib leeg xwb tab sis nws muaj txhua yam nws xav tau.

# Satchel Paige

| Week at a Glance | Customize instruction every day for your English Language Learners. | | | | |
|---|---|---|---|---|---|
| | **Day 1** | **Day 2** | **Day 3** | **Day 4** | **Day 5** |
| **Teacher's Edition** | Use the ELL Notes that appear throughout each day of the lesson to support instruction and reading. | | | | |
| **ELL Poster 4** | • Assess Prior Knowledge<br>• Develop Concepts and Vocabulary | • Preteach Tested Vocabulary | • Reporting Live | • Personal Challenges | • Monitor Progress |
| **ELL Teaching Guide** | • Picture It! Lesson, pp. 22–23<br>• Multilingual Summaries, pp. 26–28 | • ELL Reader Lesson, pp. 218–219 | • Vocabulary Activities and Word Cards, pp. 24–25<br>• Multilingual Summaries, pp. 26–28 | | |
| **ELL Readers** | • Reread *Finding Home* | • Teach *Roberto Clemente* | • Reread *Roberto Clemente* and other texts to build fluency | | |
| **ELL and Transition Handbook** | Use the following as needed to support this week's instruction and to conduct alternative assessments:<br>• Phonics Transition Lessons<br>• Grammar Transition Lessons<br>• Assessment | | | | |

## Picture It! Comprehension Lesson
# Sequence

Use this lesson to supplement or replace the skill lesson on pages 90–91 of the Teacher's Edition.

### Teach

Distribute copies of the Picture It! blackline master on page 23.
• Tell students to look at the picture of Wilma Rudolph. Explain that Wilma Rudolph is a famous American athlete. Build background by telling students that Wilma competed in track and field. She ran races and won three gold medals at the Olympics in 1960.
• Share the Skill Points (at right) with students. Read the paragraph aloud.

### Practice

Read aloud the directions on page 23. Have students complete the time line. Explain that they can count to find missing information: Wilma was born in 1940 and became very ill when she was five, so she became ill in 1945. Have students keep their time lines for later reteaching.

**Answers for page 23:** 1940: Wilma Rudolph is born; 1945: Wilma becomes ill; 1956: Wilma wins bronze medal; 1960: She wins three gold medals.

> ## Skill Points
> ✓ The **sequence of events** is the order in which events happen.
> ✓ The author does not always describe the events in the order they happen.
> ✓ You can keep track of events by making a time line.

**Read** the story of Wilma Rudolph's life. **Write** an important event from her life at each year listed on the time line.

### Wilma Rudolph

Wilma Rudolph was a great athlete. In 1960, she won three gold medals. But Wilma started life as a sickly child. She was born in 1940. When she was five, she became very ill. It was hard for her to walk. But she kept trying. In 1956, she won a bronze medal at the Olympic games. People called her "the fastest woman alive."

| 1935 | 1940 | 1945 | 1950 | 1955 | 1960 | 1965 |
|------|------|------|------|------|------|------|

1940            1945                                    1956

_____    _____    _____

_____    _____    _____


1960

_____

_____

# Vocabulary Activities and Word Cards

Copy the Word Cards on page 25 as needed for the following activities.
Use the blank card for an additional word that you want to teach.
Also see suggestions for teaching vocabulary in the ELL and Transition Handbook.

| Sports Headlines | Contrasting Words | Identifying Compound Words |
|---|---|---|
| • Show students the sports section of a newspaper, and read aloud some of the headlines. Then form groups of students and give each group a set of Word Cards.<br><br>• Tell groups to create headlines using all the Word Cards. Students may use more than one vocabulary word per headline. Have students write their headlines on sentence strips, taping the Word Cards on the strips at the appropriate places. | • Give pairs of students sets of Word Cards. Ask them to write a contrasting word for each vocabulary word on the back of the cards. Encourage students to use a thesaurus or dictionary.<br><br>• Make suggestions if students get stuck: *confidence/shyness; fastball/slow ball; mocking/ praising; outfield/infield; unique/ordinary; weakness/ strength; windup/pitch.*<br><br>• Students then take turns reading the contrasting word to the partner. The partner should identify the vocabulary word it is paired with. | • Explain to students that a compound word is a word that is made up of two words. *Daylight*, for example, is made up of *day* and *light*.<br><br>• Give pairs of students sets of Word Cards. Have them determine which of the words are compounds. If a word is a compound word, students should show this by drawing a vertical line between the two words. If it is not a compound word, they should leave the card as it is.<br><br>• Ask students to display their compound words and tell what the component words are. Correct any discrepancies or incorrect breaks. |

confidence

fastball

mocking

outfield

unique

weakness

windup

# Multilingual Summaries

## Satchel Paige

Satchel Paige was a great baseball pitcher. He started playing on professional teams when he was nineteen. Many people came to see him strike batters out. After one year, he started playing in the Negro major leagues. He played on different teams for seventeen years.

Satchel got married in 1941. He thought he would stay home and not play baseball. But he could not stay away from baseball. After a year, he was playing again.

In 1942, Satchel's team was in the league championship. Satchel had to pitch to Josh Gibson. Gibson was the best batter in the league. Satchel said he would strike him out, and he did.

## Satchel Paige

Satchel Paige fue un gran lanzador de béisbol. Comenzó a jugar en equipos profesionales cuando tenía diecinueve años. Mucha gente iba a los partidos a verlo ponchar bateadores. Después de un año, comenzó a lanzar en las Ligas Mayores Negras. Jugó en diferentes equipos por diecisiete años.

Satchel se casó en 1941. Pensó que podría quedarse en casa y no jugar más béisbol. Pero no podía mantenerse lejos de este juego. Después de un año, estaba jugando de nuevo.

En 1942, el equipo de Satchel estaba en el campeonato de la liga. Satchel tenía que lanzarle a Josh Gibson. Gibson era el mejor bateador de la liga. Satchel dijo que podía poncharlo y así fue.

# Multilingual Summaries

## 薩裘・派吉

　　薩裘・派吉是個偉大的棒球投手。他在 19 歲時加入職業棒球隊開始了棒球生涯，很多人都專程來看他投出使擊球員連續出局的好球。一年後，他又轉到黑人大聯盟裡打球。他在那裡總共待了 17 年，期間換過幾次球隊。

　　薩裘在 1941 年結婚，他覺得自己要多點時間跟家人共處，所以決定不打棒球了。但是他實在沒有辦法抵抗棒球的誘惑，一年後，他又開始打了。

　　1942 年，薩裘在聯盟冠軍賽中遇上了喬許・吉布森，他是棒球聯盟裡最厲害的擊球手。薩裘說他要使吉布森出局，結果，他真的辦到了。

## Satchel Paige

　　Satchel Paige là một cầu thủ ném bóng chày xuất sắc. Ông bắt đầu chơi cho những đội chuyên nghiệp khi ông mười chín tuổi. Nhiều người đến xem ông đánh bại những cầu thủ đánh bóng chày. Sau một năm, ông bắt đầu chơi cho các liên đoàn bóng chày quan trọng của Người Mỹ Đen. Ông ấy chơi cho nhiều đội khác nhau trong 17 năm.

　　Satchel lập gia đình vào năm 1941. Ông ấy nghĩ là mình sẽ nghỉ ở nhà và không chơi bóng chày nữa. Nhưng ông không thể không chơi bóng chày. Sau một năm, ông trở lại chơi tiếp.

　　Vào năm 1942, đội của Satchel tranh giải vô địch liên đoàn. Satchel phải ném bóng chày cho Josh Gibson. Gibson là người đánh bóng chày giỏi nhất trong liên đoàn. Satchel nói là sẽ đánh bại ông ấy, và ông đã làm vậy.

# Multilingual Summaries

## 사첼 페이지

사첼 페이지는 훌륭한 야구 투수로 열 아홉 살에 프로 야구팀에서 뛰기 시작했는데 많은 사람들이 그가 타자를 삼진 아웃시키는 것을 보러 왔다. 1년 후 그는 니그로 메이저리그에서 뛰기 시작했으며 그 후 17년 동안 여러 팀에서 선수 생활을 했다.

1941년에 결혼한 사첼은 야구를 하지 않고 계속 집에서 지내겠다고 생각했지만 야구를 떠나서 살 수 없었던 그는 결국 1년 후 다시 야구를 시작했다.

1942년 사첼의 팀이 리그 결승전에 올랐는데 경기 중에 사첼은 리그 최고의 타자인 조시 깁슨을 상대로 공을 던져야 했다. 사첼은 그를 삼진 아웃시키겠다고 말했고 사첼의 말대로 이루어졌다.

## Satchel Paige

Satchel Paige txawj pov pob baseball. Nws pib ua si rau cov pawg uas them nyiaj thaum nws muaj kaum cuaj xyoo xwb. Neeg coob coob tuaj saib nws pov pob dhau cov neeg uas sim ntaus pob. Nws ua si ib xyoo xwb ces nws pib ua si rau hauv ib lub koom haum ua si rau cov Miskas Dub. Nws ua si 17 xyoo nrog ntau pawg.

Satchel yuav poj niam xyoo 1941. Nws xav zoj tias nws yuav tso baseball tseg thiab nyob tsev xwb. Tab sis nws tso tsis tau tseg kiag. Tom qab ib xyoo, nws rov ua si dua.

Xyoo 1942, Satchel pawg yog ib lub pawg ntawm ob lub uas zoo tshaj nyob rau hauv koom haum ua si baseball. Yog li ntawd ob lub pawg ntawd yuav ua si ua ke seb leej twg mam li yeej. Satchel tau pov pob baseball rau Josh Gibson. Gibson yog tus ntaus baseball zoo tshaj nyob hauv koom haum ua si ntawd. Satchel hais tias nws yuav pov peb lub pob dhau Gibson kom nws ntaus tsis tau, ces nws ua li ntawd thiab tiag.

# Shutting Out the Sky   Student Edition pages 116–127

| Week at a Glance | Customize instruction every day for your English Language Learners. | | | | |
|---|---|---|---|---|---|
| | **Day 1** | **Day 2** | **Day 3** | **Day 4** | **Day 5** |
| **Teacher's Edition** | Use the ELL Notes that appear throughout each day of the lesson to support instruction and reading. | | | | |
| **ELL Poster 5** | • Assess Prior Knowledge<br>• Develop Concepts and Vocabulary | • Preteach Tested Vocabulary | • Immigration Challenges | • Immigration Interviews | • Monitor Progress |
| **ELL Teaching Guide** | • Picture It! Lesson, pp. 29–30<br>• Multilingual Summaries, pp. 33–35 | • ELL Reader Lesson, pp. 220–221 | • Vocabulary Activities and Word Cards, pp. 31–32<br>• Multilingual Summaries, pp. 33–35 | | |
| **ELL Readers** | • Reread *Roberto Clemente* | • Teach *Love, Enid* | • Reread *Love, Enid* and other texts to build fluency | | |
| **ELL and Transition Handbook** | Use the following as needed to support this week's instruction and to conduct alternative assessments:<br>• Phonics Transition Lessons<br>• Grammar Transition Lessons<br>• Assessment | | | | |

**Picture It!** Comprehension Lesson
## Cause and Effect

Use this lesson to supplement or replace the skill lesson on pages 112–113 of the Teacher's Edition.

### Teach

Distribute copies of the Picture It! blackline master on page 30.
• Tell students that the picture shows a young man named Emilio. Tell students the paragraph is about Emilio. It tells about Emilio's education.
• Share the Skill Points (at right) with students.
• Ask students to think about the causes and effects of studying. Ask: *Why do people study hard? What happens if you study hard?* (Possible answers: to succeed in life; I do better on tests.)
• Read the paragraph aloud.

> ### Skill Points
> ✓ A **cause** makes something happen. The **effect** is what happens.
> ✓ An effect may have more than one cause, and a cause may have more than one effect.

### Practice

Read aloud the directions on page 30. Have students read the paragraph and complete the diagrams. Have students keep their organizers for later reteaching.

**Answers for page 30:** *Cause*: Emilio wanted to learn English. *Cause*: He studied and practiced. *Effect*: He graduated at the top of his class. *Effect*: He is going to college next year.

Name _____

**Read** the paragraph. **Complete** the diagrams.

## Emilio's Road to Success

When Emilio came to the United States, he didn't understand English. But he wanted to learn. He studied and practiced. In a few years, he could speak English very well. In high school, Emilio got good grades. He graduated at the top of his class. Next year, Emilio is going to college.

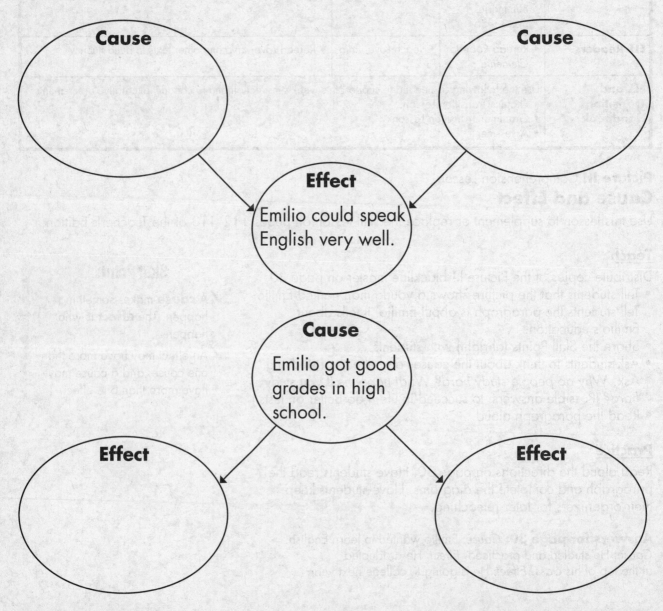

**Cause**

**Cause**

**Effect**
Emilio could speak English very well.

**Cause**
Emilio got good grades in high school.

**Effect**

**Effect**

# Vocabulary Activities and Word Cards

Copy the Word Cards on pages 31–32 as needed for the following activities.
Use the blank card for an additional word that you want to teach.
Also see suggestions for teaching vocabulary in the ELL and Transition Handbook.

| Synonym Match | Do or Draw | An Immigrant's Story |
|---|---|---|
| • On blank cards, write a synonym for each of the vocabulary words, for example: *suggestion, suggested, situation, push, bargained, newcomers, extra, immigrant, street vendor.*<br><br>• Shuffle these synonym cards with a set of Word Cards, and then arrange them face down in a grid.<br><br>• Form two teams. Ask Team 1 to choose a pair of cards. If they are synonyms, the team keeps the pair. Teams take turns choosing pairs of cards until all have been matched. The team holding more cards wins. | • Give each student a set of Word Cards. Review what nouns and verbs are.<br><br>• Ask a student to come to the front of the class and choose a Word Card without showing it to anyone. Explain that the student will either act out or draw to demonstrate the word. If the word is a noun, the student will draw. If it is a verb, he or she will act it out. The rest of the class should try to guess the word.<br><br>• The first person to correctly guess the word is next to choose a word and either draw it or act it out. | • Give pairs of students sets of Word Cards. Have them shuffle the cards and place them face down.<br><br>• Students take turns drawing cards and saying sentences using the words until all cards are used. The student who is listening should verify that the sentence uses the word correctly. If not, pairs should work together to make corrections.<br><br>• If appropriate for some pairs, challenge them to tell a continuous story with their sentences. Suggest that students tell a story about an immigrant to the United States. |

advice | advised

circumstances

elbow

hustled

immigrants

luxury

newcomer

peddler

# Multilingual Summaries

## Shutting Out the Sky

Marcus left Romania in 1900 when he was sixteen years old. He went to live with relatives in New York City. He was allowed to stay for free for a few days. Then he needed to get a job to pay rent.

Marcus could not find a job. His relative gave him a dollar. She told him to be a peddler and sell things on the street. He did not want to do that but needed money.

He bought two boxes of chocolates. He opened the boxes and put the chocolates on a tray. No one was buying from him. Another peddler helped Marcus make a sale. Soon Marcus had sold all the chocolates. He bought dinner in a restaurant that night. Then he counted the money that he had earned.

**Spanish**

## Fuera del cielo

Marcus dejó Rumania en 1990 cuando tenía diecisiete años. Se fue a vivir con unos parientes a Nueva York. Ellos le permitieron quedarse gratis por unos días. Después, tenía que conseguir un trabajo para pagar el alquiler.

Marcus no podía encontrar trabajo. Su pariente le dio un dólar y le dijo que trabajara como mercachifle y vendiera productos en la calle. Él no quería hacerlo pero necesitaba el dinero.

Compró dos cajas de chocolates. Abrió las cajas y puso los chocolates en una bandeja. Nadie le compraba. Otro mercachifle ayudó a Marcus a hacer una venta. Rápidamente, Marcus vendió todos los chocolates. Esa noche compró la cena en un restaurante. Después contó el dinero que había ganado.

# Multilingual Summaries

## 生存的奮鬥

　　馬庫斯在 1900 年離開了羅馬尼亞，當時他才 16 歲。他去紐約投靠親戚，不過只能免費住幾天，之後就必須找工作賺錢付房租。

　　馬庫斯找不到工作，他親戚給了他一塊錢，叫馬庫斯當小販，去街上賣東西。馬庫斯其實不想這麼作，但是他需要錢，所以只好乖乖聽親戚的話。

　　他買了兩盒巧克力，把巧克力從盒子裡拿出來放在托盤上賣，可是沒有一個人來跟他買。有個小販很好心，幫馬庫斯賣巧克力，很快地，就把所有巧克力都賣出去了。晚上，馬庫斯就去餐廳裡吃頓豐盛的晚餐，然後算他當天到底賺了多少錢。

## Che Khuất Bầu Trời

Marcus rời nước Romania vào năm 1900 lúc cậu mười sáu tuổi. Cậu đến sống với thân nhân ở Thành Phố New York. Cậu được phép ở vài ngày mà không phải trả tiền. Sau đó cậu phải có việc làm để trả tiền thuê nhà.

Marcus không tìm được việc làm. Thân nhân cho cậu một đồng đô-la. Bà ấy kêu cậu làm nghề bán hàng rong, và bán hàng ngoài đường. Cậu không muốn làm nghề đó nhưng cậu cần có tiền.

Cậu mua hai hộp kẹo sô-cô-la. Cậu mở hộp và để kẹo vào một cái khay. Không ai mua kẹo của cậu. Một người bán hàng rong khác giúp Marcus bán. Chẳng mấy chốc Marcus bán hết kẹo sô-cô-la. Tối hôm đó, cậu mua thức ăn ở nhà hàng. Rồi cậu đếm số tiền mình đã kiếm được.

# Multilingual Summaries

## 살 곳을 찾아

마커스는 1900년 16살이던 때 루마니아를 떠난다. 뉴욕에 있는 친척과 함께 살려고 했던 그는 그곳에서 며칠만 공짜로 머물 수 있었고 그 이후에는 방세를 내기 위해 일자리를 찾아야 했다.

일자리를 찾을 수 없던 마커스에게 친척은 1달러를 주며 거리에서 물건을 팔아보라고 한다. 그는 그 일을 하고 싶지 않았지만 돈이 필요했다.

그는 초콜릿 두 상자를 사서 상자를 열고 초콜릿을 접시에 놓았지만 아무도 그 초콜릿을 사지 않는다. 다른 행상인이 도와준 덕분에 곧 마커스는 초콜릿을 다 팔게 된다. 그날 저녁 그는 음식점에서 저녁을 사먹고 자신이 번 돈을 세어본다.

## Thaiv Lub Ntuj

Thaum nws muaj kaum rau xyoo, Marcus tawm lub teb chaws Romania xyoo 1900 mus txog lub nroog New York. Nws mus nrog nws kwv tij nyob dawb ob peb hnub xwb ces nws yuav tsum nrhiav hauj lwm them nyiaj hli.

Marcus nrhiav tsis tau hauj lwm li. Nws ib tug kwv tij pub ib duas rau nws. Nws hais kom nws muag khoom nyob ntawm txoj kev rau cov neeg mus mus los los. Nws tsis xav ua li ntawd tab sis nws yuav tsum khaws tau nyiaj.

Nws yuav ob lub thawv khob noom. Nws qhib ob lub thawv ntawd ces nws muab txhua lub khob noom rau saum ib lub phaj. Tab sis mas tsis muaj leej twg yuav nws cov khob noom ntawd. Ib tug neeg muag khoom pab nws muab ib lub khob noom. Tsis ntev ces, nws muag nws cov khob noom tas. Hmo ntawd, nws mus tsev ua mov noj mus yuav ib rooj mov. Noj tas ces nws suav nws cov nyiaj tas.

# Inside Out

| Week at a Glance | Customize instruction every day for your English Language Learners. | | | | |
|---|---|---|---|---|---|
| | **Day 1** | **Day 2** | **Day 3** | **Day 4** | **Day 5** |
| **Teacher's Edition** | Use the ELL Notes that appear throughout each day of the lesson to support instruction and reading. | | | | |
| **ELL Poster 6** | • Assess Prior Knowledge<br>• Develop Concepts and Vocabulary | • Preteach Tested Vocabulary | • Acts of Kindness | • Dramatic Conversations | • Monitor Progress |
| **ELL Teaching Guide** | • Picture It! Lesson, pp. 36–37<br>• Multilingual Summaries, pp. 40–42 | • ELL Reader Lesson, pp. 222–223 | • Vocabulary Activities and Word Cards, pp. 38–39<br>• Multilingual Summaries, pp. 40–42 | | |
| **ELL Readers** | • Reread *Love, Enid* | • Teach *Butterfly Garden* | • Reread *Butterfly Garden* and other texts to build fluency | | |
| **ELL and Transition Handbook** | Use the following as needed to support this week's instruction and to conduct alternative assessments:<br>• Phonics Transition Lessons<br>• Grammar Transition Lessons<br>• Assessment | | | | |

## Picture It! Comprehension Lesson
## Compare and Contrast

Use this lesson to supplement or replace the skill lesson on pages 142–143 of the Teacher's Edition.

### Teach

Distribute copies of the Picture It! blackline master on page 37.
• Direct students' attention to the two pictures. One shows San Francisco. The other shows Chicago. Invite students to describe the two cities, based on the pictures.
• Share the Skill Points (at right) with students.
• Tell students they are going to compare and contrast San Francisco and Chicago. Explain how a Venn diagram is used to record similarities and differences. Read the paragraph aloud.

### Practice

Read aloud the directions on page 37. Have students read the paragraph and then complete the Venn diagram. Have students keep their organizers for later reteaching.

**Answers for page 37:** *San Francisco:* along a bay, TransAmerica Building; *Both:* near body of water, have tall buildings; *Chicago:* next to a lake, Sears Tower

> **Skill Points**
>
> ✓ When writers **compare and contrast**, they show how things are similar and how they are different.
>
> ✓ You can use a chart or diagram to keep track of similarities and differences.

Name _____

**Look** at the pictures and **read** the paragraph. Then **complete** the diagram.

- **Write** features that both cities have in the center of the diagram.
- **Write** information that only applies to one city in the section for that city.

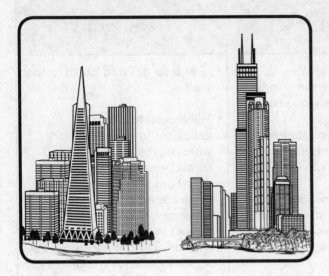

## Two American Cities

Chicago and San Francisco are similar in many ways, but they are also different. For example, they are both next to a body of water. However, San Francisco is along a bay, and Chicago is next to a lake. They both have very tall buildings. San Francisco has a building shaped like a pyramid. It is called the TransAmerica Building. Chicago has the Sears Tower. It is one of the tallest buildings in the world.

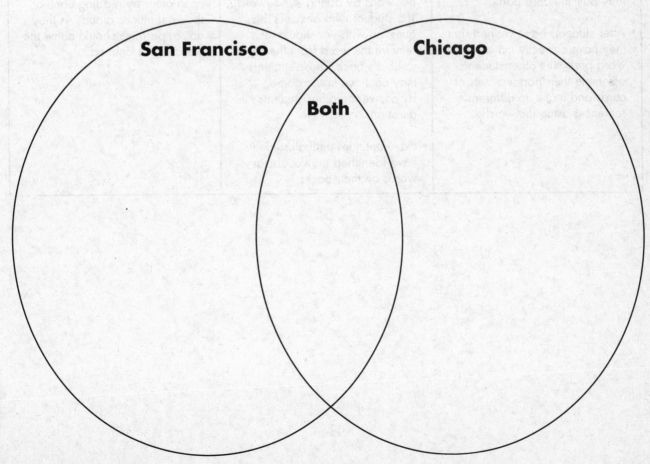

**San Francisco**

**Both**

**Chicago**

# Vocabulary Activities and Word Cards

Copy the Word Cards on page 39 as needed for the following activities.
Use the blank card for an additional word that you want to teach.
Also see suggestions for teaching vocabulary in the ELL and Transition Handbook.

| Matching Word Halves | What Am I? | Definitions |
|---|---|---|
| • Distribute a set of Word Cards and a pair of scissors to each student.<br><br>• Tell students to cut each card in half. The division need not be precise as long as students cut between letters.<br><br>• Have students shuffle their decks. Each student then gives his or her deck to a partner. That student should then match all the word parts to reassemble the Word Cards. Tell students to create an oral sentence for each word as they pair the card parts.<br><br>• After students have verified that they have correctly matched the word parts, the other students assemble their partners' sets of cards and make up different sentences using the words. | • Write the vocabulary words on the board where everyone can see them. Then tape each of the Word Cards to the back of a student. Not all students need to have words in order to participate in the activity.<br><br>• Ask students to circulate, asking each other yes-or-no questions to determine what word is on their backs. For example:<br>*Am I a verb?*<br>*Am I a present-tense verb?*<br><br>• The student finally identifies his or her word by asking *Am I [word]?* The student who answers this question with *yes* should then remove the word from the other student's back. These students may continue in the game by answering other students' questions.<br><br>• Play continues until all students have identified the vocabulary words on their backs. | • Give a set of Word Cards to each student.<br><br>• Tell students to write the definitions for the vocabulary words on the backs of the cards. Remind students that the definitions must correspond to the correct parts of speech. *Disrespect,* for example, is a verb as used in this unit, and *migrant* is an adjective. If necessary, ask students to consult a dictionary to check for meanings.<br><br>• Pair students and have them test each other by reading each of their definitions aloud. As they do so, partners should name the word that is defined. |

caterpillar

cocoon

disrespect

emerge

migrant

sketched

unscrewed

# Multilingual Summaries

## Inside Out

Francisco moved to the United States from Mexico. He did not speak or understand English. School was hard.

In his classroom, Francisco sat near a caterpillar in a jar. Francisco watched the caterpillar and brought it leaves to eat. During art class, Francisco drew pictures of birds and butterflies. The teacher put one of his drawings on the board.

Francisco had no jacket. Mr. Sims noticed that he was shivering. He gave Francisco a jacket from a box of old jackets. The next day, Francisco wore the jacket. Curtis started a fight with him and said that the jacket was his. Both boys were punished. Francisco stayed inside during recess. He noticed the caterpillar had made a cocoon.

At the end of the year, Francisco got a prize for his drawing. Curtis liked the drawing. Francisco gave it to him. That day, the butterfly came out of the cocoon. The class watched as Francisco let it fly away.

Spanish

## Por dentro y por fuera

Francisco se mudó de México a Estados Unidos. No hablaba ni entendía inglés. La escuela era difícil para Francisco.

En la clase, Francisco se sentaba al lado de un frasco donde había una oruga. Francisco observaba a la oruga y le traía hojas para que comiera. En la clase de arte, Francisco dibujó pájaros y mariposas. La maestra puso uno de los dibujos en el tablero de anuncios.

Francisco no tenía chaqueta. El señor Sims observó que el niño estaba titiritando de frío. Le dio a Francisco una chaqueta de una caja de chaquetas viejas. Al día siguiente, Francisco llevaba puesta la chaqueta. Curtis comenzó a pelearse con Francisco y le decía que la chaqueta era de él. Los dos niños fueron castigados. Francisco se quedó dentro de la escuela en el recreo. Observó que la oruga había echo un capullo.

Al final del año, Francisco recibió un premio por su dibujo. A Curtis le gustaba el dibujo. Francisco se lo regaló. Ese día, la mariposa salió del capullo. La clase observaba a Francisco cuando la dejó salir y volar.

# Multilingual Summaries

## 意料之外

弗朗西斯科從墨西哥搬到美國。他一點不懂英語，功課學習非常困難。

在教室裏，弗朗西斯科看見，座位旁的瓶子裏關著小毛蟲。弗朗西斯科常盯著看，用新摘的葉子喂養它。藝術課時，他畫了小鳥與蝴蝶。老師把他的一幅畫貼在黑板上。

弗朗西斯科沒有夾克。西蒙斯先生看他冷得發抖，就從舊衣箱裏拿給他一件夾克。第二天，他穿著夾克來上學。同學柯蒂斯與他打架，說夾克是他的，為此兩人都受到懲罰。課間休息時，弗朗西斯科坐在教室裏，發現小毛蟲已經結出繭。

學期結束時，弗朗西斯科的畫得了獎。柯蒂斯看著非常喜歡，弗朗西斯科把畫送給他。就在那天，蝴蝶破繭而出。弗朗西斯科沒有把蝴蝶捉起來，而是放它振翅高飛，全班同學都在一旁靜靜地看著弗朗西斯科。

## Từ Trong Ra Ngoài

Francisco từ Mễ Tây Cơ dọn đến Hoa Kỳ. Cậu bé không nói hoặc hiểu được tiếng Anh. Học hành là điều khó khăn.

Trong lớp học, Francisco ngồi gần một con sâu ở trong cái hủ. Francisco quan sát con sâu và mang lá đến cho sâu ăn. Trong giờ vẽ, Francisco vẽ chim và bướm. Thầy giáo để một trong những tranh vẽ của cậu lên bảng.

Francisco không có áo khoác ngoài. Ông Sims để ý thấy Francisco đang run rẩy. Thầy đưa cho Francisco một cái áo khoác từ một thùng đựng áo khoác cũ. Qua hôm sau, Francisco mặc áo này. Curtis gây sự với cậu bé và nói rằng chiếc áo khoác đó là của nó. Cả hai đứa bị phạt. Francisco ở lại lớp trong giờ ra chơi. Cậu bé để ý thấy con sâu đã làm một cái kén.

Cuối năm học, Francisco được giải thưởng cho tranh vẽ của mình. Curtis thích tranh vẽ này. Francisco cho nó bức tranh. Hôm đó, con bướm ra khỏi cái kén. Lớp học nhìn xem khi Francisco thả cho bướm bay đi.

# Multilingual Summaries

## 안에서 밖으로

프란시스코는 멕시코에서 미국으로 이주했다. 그는 영어를 말하지도 알아듣지도 못하고 학교 다니는 것을 힘들어 한다.

프란시스코는 교실에서 단지 안에 있는 애벌레 가까이에 앉아 애벌레를 지켜보다가 먹을 나뭇잎들을 가져다 준다. 미술 시간에 프란시스코는 새와 나비 그림을 그렸고 선생님은 그의 그림들 중 하나를 칠판에 걸어놓았다.

프란시스코에게는 재킷이 없다. 심스 선생님은 프란시스코가 추위에 떨고 있는 것을 알아채고 낡은 재킷들이 든 상자 속에서 재킷 하나를 준다. 다음 날 프란시스코가 그 재킷을 입고 오자 커티스가 싸움을 걸어오며 그 재킷이 자기 것이라고 말한다. 결국 두 소년은 모두 벌을 받는다. 프란시스코는 휴식 시간 중에 교실에 남아서 애벌레가 고치를 만든 것을 발견한다.

그 해 말 프란시스코는 그림을 잘 그려 상을 받았는데 커티스가 그 그림을 좋아하게 된다. 프란시스코는 그에게 그 그림을 준다. 그리고 그 날 고치에서 나비가 나왔고 반 아이들은 프란시스코가 나비가 날아가도록 하는 것을 지켜본다.

## Sab Hauv Sab Nrauv

Francisco tsiv Mexikaum teb tuaj rau Amiskas teb no. Nws tsis paub hais lus Miskas los to taub lus Miskas. Kev kawm ntawv nyuaj kawg.

Hauv nws hoob qhia ntawv, Francisco saum puab ib tug kab ntsig kaw rau hauv ib lub hub. Francisco ntsia tus kab ntsig ntawd thiab nqa nplooj ntoo tuaj rau nws noj. Thaum nyob hauv hoob teeb huj, Francisco teeb tau ib cov duab noog thiab duab npuj npaim. Tus nais khub muab nws ib daim duab dai rau saum daim txiag sau ntawv.

Francisco tsis muaj tsho loj. Mr. Sims pom tias nws tshee tshee. Nws muab tau ib lub tsho loj rau Francisco ntawm ib lub kav uas muaj ib co tsho loj qub. Hnub tom qab, Francisco hnav lub tsho loj. Curtis pib nrog nws sib ntaus thiab hais tias lub tsho loj ntawd yog nws lub. Ob tug tub ntawd tau raug txim. Francisco tau nyob sab hauv thaum txog caij mus ua si nraum zoov. Nws pom tias tus kab ntsig ntawd tau los kauv ua ib pob xov lawm.

Thaum xyoo tag, Francisco tau yeej ib yam khoom plig rau nws daim duab. Curtis nyiam daim duab. Francisco tau muab pub rau nws lawm. Hnub ntawd, tus npauj npaim tawm hauv lub pob xov tuaj. Cov neeg hauv hoob ntawd ntsia Francisco muab nws tso ya tawm mus.

# Passage to Freedom

| Week at a Glance | Customize instruction every day for your English Language Learners. | | | | |
|---|---|---|---|---|---|
| | **Day 1** | **Day 2** | **Day 3** | **Day 4** | **Day 5** |
| **Teacher's Edition** | Use the ELL Notes that appear throughout each day of the lesson to support instruction and reading. | | | | |
| **ELL Poster 7** | • Assess Prior Knowledge<br>• Develop Concepts and Vocabulary | • Preteach Tested Vocabulary | • Enact Consulate Scenes | • Refugee Needs | • Monitor Progress |
| **ELL Teaching Guide** | • Picture It! Lesson, pp. 43–44<br>• Multilingual Summaries, pp. 47–49 | • ELL Reader Lesson, pp. 224–225 | • Vocabulary Activities and Word Cards, pp. 45–46<br>• Multilingual Summaries, pp. 47–49 | | |
| **ELL Readers** | • Reread *Butterfly Garden* | • Teach *Making a Difference in Denmark* | • Reread *Making a Difference in Denmark* and other texts to build fluency | | |
| **ELL and Transition Handbook** | Use the following as needed to support this week's instruction and to conduct alternative assessments:<br>• Phonics Transition Lessons<br>• Grammar Transition Lessons<br>• Assessment | | | | |

**Picture It!** Comprehension Lesson
## Author's Purpose
Use this lesson to supplement or replace the skill lesson on pages 162–163 of the Teacher's Edition.

### Teach
Distribute copies of the Picture It! blackline master on page 44.
• Tell students that the picture shows a poster. Talk about the purpose of posters: to spread messages, post rules, give warnings, advertise things, and persuade people. Read the text on the poster aloud.
• Share the Skill Points (at right) with students.
• Ask: *What is the purpose of this poster?* (to encourage people to help refugees)

### Practice
Read aloud the directions on page 44. Have students answer the questions that appear below the poster. Tell them to select the answer choice that best completes each sentence. Have students keep their work for later reteaching.

**Answers for page 44: 1: C.** work for the Refugee Center;
**2: B.** do something; **3: A.** donations

> ### Skill Points
> ✓ Authors have a **purpose** for writing. The purpose is their reason for writing.
> ✓ To figure out the author's purpose, look closely at the words. Think about the message.
> ✓ Here are some common purposes for writing: to persuade, to inform, to entertain, to express thoughts or feelings.

Name _____

**Look** at the poster. **Answer** the questions that follow.

# HELP REFUGEES TODAY!

The Refugee Center needs your help. There are many refugees from all over the world at the center. They are trying to start a new life. Won't you please help?

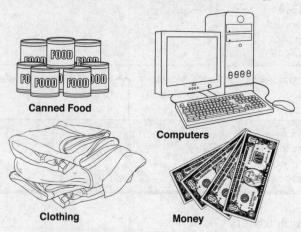

**Canned Food**

**Computers**

**Clothing**

**Money**

**Please make a donation today!**
**You will help make the world a better place.**

Circle the letter of the answer that correctly completes each sentence.

**1.** The people who wrote the poster _____.

    **A.** are refugees

    **B.** are from all over the world

    **C.** work for the Refugee Center

    **D.** live in a foreign country

**2.** The poster is trying to make people _____.

    **A.** feel better

    **B.** do something

    **C.** think about the world's problems

    **D.** change their way of life

**3.** The Refugee Center needs _____.

    **A.** donations

    **B.** volunteers

    **C.** computer specialists

    **D.** language teachers

# Vocabulary Activities and Word Cards

Copy the Word Cards on page 46 as needed for the following activities.
Use the blank cards for additional words that you want to teach.
Also see suggestions for teaching vocabulary in the ELL and Transition Handbook.

| Home Language Concentration | Cloze Paragraph | Newspaper Search |
|---|---|---|
| • Pair students who have writing fluency in the same home language. Give them a set of Word Cards and blank cards.<br><br>• Have pairs write a home language translation for each of the vocabulary words on a blank card. (See the Multilingual Lesson Vocabulary beginning on page 272 for suggested translations.)<br><br>• Students then mix both sets of cards together and lay them face down in a grid. They take turns choosing two cards. If the cards are a vocabulary word and its translation, they keep the pair. | • Write the following on the board. Replace the underscored words with lines: *When the war started, refugees arrived at the embassy. They wanted the diplomat to help them leave the country. He had to ask his superiors. They consulted representatives of the host country. Finally, they reached an agreement. They sent a cable saying that the diplomat could issue a visa to people in danger.*<br><br>• Have students tape Word Cards in the appropriate spaces. Ask a volunteer to read the completed paragraph aloud. | • Give one Word Card to each student or pair of students.<br><br>• Give each student or pair a newspaper, and have students search for their assigned word. Remind them to look in headlines as well as articles.<br><br>• Invite students to share their word and the context in which they found it. They can read aloud the headline or paragraph that included their word.<br><br>• Students who were not able to find their assigned word should instead create a sample sentence that might appear in a newspaper article. |

agreement

cable

diplomat

issue

refugees

representatives

superiors

visa

# Multilingual Summaries

## Passage to Freedom

Hiroki Sugihara's father was a Japanese diplomat in Lithuania in 1940. That June, Mr. Sugihara made a decision that saved many lives.

Many Polish Jews came to the Sugiharas' house. They left Poland to escape because Nazi soldiers had invaded their country. The Nazi soldiers were coming to Lithuania. The people in front of the house wanted Hiroki's father to give them visas to escape to Japan.

Mr. Sugihara asked the Japanese government for permission to give the people visas. He was not given permission.

But Hiroki's father would not turn the people away. He wrote 300 visas a day for a month. Hiroki's father had saved thousands of lives. Hiroki was very proud of what his father did.

**Spanish**

## Viaje a la libertad

El padre de Hiroki Sugihara era un diplomático japonés en Lituania en 1940. En junio de ese año, el señor Sugihara tomó una decisión salvó muchas vidas.

Muchos judíos polacos llegaron a la casa de Sugihara. Ellos escaparon de Polonia porque los soldados nazis habían invadido el país. Los soldados nazis estaban llegando a Lituania. La gente frente a la casa de Hiroki quería que su padre le diera visas para escapar a Japón.

El Sr. Sugihara le pidió permiso al gobierno japonés para darles visas a esas personas, pero no le dieron permiso.

Sin embargo, el padre de Hiroki no dejaría abandonada a esa gente. Todos los días, durante un mes, concedió 300 visas por día. El padre de Hiroki salvó miles de vidas. Hiroki estaba muy orgulloso de lo que hizo su padre.

# Multilingual Summaries

## 自由之門

　　1940年，杉原弘樹的爸爸在立陶宛做日本外交官。那年6月，杉原先生的勇敢決定挽救了很多人的生命。

　　由於納粹士兵入侵，許多波蘭猶太人逃離祖國，來到立陶宛。可是納粹士兵馬上又要進攻立陶宛，猶太人聚集在杉原家門口，希望杉原先生發給他們護照，可以讓他們去日本。

　　杉原先生向日本政府請示，請求發放護照，卻沒有得到允許。

　　但他沒有把這些猶太人拒之門外，整整一個月他每天都簽發300份護照。他的決定挽救了成千上萬的人，弘樹為他的爸爸感到非常自豪。

## Đường Đến Tự Do

Ba của Hiroki Sugihara là một nhà ngoại giao của Nhật ở Lithuania vào năm 1940. Vào tháng Sáu năm đó, Ông Sugihara có một quyết định mà đã cứu sống được nhiều người.

Nhiều người Do Thái gốc Ba Lan đến nhà của gia đình Sugihara. Họ rời Ba Lan để trốn tránh vì quân lính Đức Quốc Xã đã xâm lăng đất nước họ. Quân Đức Quốc Xã sắp đến Lithuania. Những người đến trước nhà muốn ba của Hiroki cấp giấy thị thực để họ được trốn thoát đến Nhật.

Ông Sugihara xin chính phủ Nhật cho phép ông cấp giấy thị thực cho những người này. Ông đã không được phép.

Nhưng ba của Hiroki không từ chối giúp đỡ những người này. Ông đã cấp 300 giấy thị thực mỗi ngày trong vòng một tháng. Ba của Hiroki đã cứu hàng ngàn mạng sống. Hiroki rất tự hào về ba của cậu.

# Multilingual Summaries

## 자유를 향한 통로

히로키 스기하라의 아버지는 1940년 당시 리투아니아의 일본 외교관이었다. 그 해 6월 스기하라씨는 많은 생명을 구한 결정을 내렸다.

많은 폴란드 계 유대인들이 스기하라씨의 집에 왔다. 나치군이 자신들의 조국을 침략했기 때문에 폴란드를 떠나 탈출한 것이었다. 이윽고 나치군이 리투아니아로 오고 있었다…… 집 앞에 있던 사람들은 히로키의 아버지가 그들이 일본으로 탈출할 수 있게끔 비자를 발급해 주기를 원했다.

스기하라씨는 그 사람들에게 비자를 내주는 허가를 일본 정부에게 요청했으나 허가가 떨어지지 않았다.

하지만 히로키의 아버지는 그 사람들을 내쫓지 않고 한 달 동안 하루에 300건의 비자를 써주었다. 히로키의 아버지는 수천 명의 생명을 구한 것이다. 히로키는 자신의 아버지가 한 일을 매우 자랑스러워했다.

## Zaj Rau Kev Ywj Pheej

Hiroki Sugihara txiv yog ib tug toj xeem rau cov neeg Nyij Pooj nyob rau hauv lub tebchaws Lithuania nyob rau xyoo 1940. Lub xyoo ntawd lub rau hlis ntuj, nws txiav txim siab mus cawm ntau leej neeg txojsia.

Muaj ntau leej uas yog cov neeg Yudais tuaj rau hauv tsevneeg Sugihara lub tsev. Lawv khiav tawm hauv lub tebchaws Poland vim rau qhov cov tub rog Nazi tuaj txeeb lawv lub tebchaws. Cov tub rog no hajtseem tuaj rau lub tebchaws Lithuania thiab. Cov tibneeg uas tuaj txog rau ntawm lawv lub tsev xav kom Hiroki txiv cia li ua cov ntaub ntawv rau lawv khiav mus rau Nyij Pooj tebchaws.

Leejtxiv Sugihara nug haivneeg Nyij Pooj cov lav thab npas seb lawv puas kam tso cai ua cov ntaub ntawv no rau cov neeg no. Lawv tsis kam tso cai.

Tiamsis Hiroki txiv yuav tsis cia cov neeg no tig rov qab. Ib hnub no nws thiaj li sau 300 daim ntawv tawm tebchaws tau muaj li ib lub hlis. Hiroki txiv cawm tau ntau leej tibneeg txojsia. Hiroki zoo siab qhuas nws txiv txog qhov uas nws txiv tau ua los no.

# The Ch'i-lin Purse

Student Edition pages 190–203

| Week at a Glance | Customize instruction every day for your English Language Learners. | | | | |
|---|---|---|---|---|---|
| | **Day 1** | **Day 2** | **Day 3** | **Day 4** | **Day 5** |
| **Teacher's Edition** | Use the ELL Notes that appear throughout each day of the lesson to support instruction and reading. | | | | |
| **ELL Poster 8** | • Assess Prior Knowledge<br>• Develop Concepts and Vocabulary | • Preteach Tested Vocabulary | • Holidays and Celebrations | • Proverbs | • Monitor Progress |
| **ELL Teaching Guide** | • Picture It! Lesson, pp. 50–51<br>• Multilingual Summaries, pp. 54–56 | • ELL Reader Lesson, pp. 226–227 | • Vocabulary Activities and Word Cards, pp. 52–53<br>• Multilingual Summaries, pp. 54–56 | | |
| **ELL Readers** | • Reread *Making a Difference in Denmark* | • Teach *Friends Across the Ocean* | • Reread *Friends Across the Ocean* and other texts to build fluency | | |
| **ELL and Transition Handbook** | Use the following as needed to support this week's instruction and to conduct alternative assessments:<br>• Phonics Transition Lessons<br>• Grammar Transition Lessons<br>• Assessment | | | | |

## Picture It! Comprehension Lesson
# Compare and Contrast

Use this lesson to supplement or replace the skill lesson on pages 186–187 of the Teacher's Edition.

## Teach

Distribute copies of the Picture It! blackline master on page 51.
• Tell students that the two passages are about New Year celebrations. Ask students to share what they know about these celebrations.
• Share the Skill Points (at right) with students.
• Read the passages aloud. Ask students to look at the pictures while you read.

## Practice

Read aloud the directions on page 51. Have students complete the chart, showing how these celebrations are similar and different. Tell students to write what else they know about these celebrations in the third column. Have students save their organizers for later reteaching.

**Answers for page 51:** *Similarities:* fireworks and parades; *Differences:* dragons, ball dropping in Times Square, date new year begins; *Compared with What I Know:* Answers will vary.

### Skill Points

✓ When writers **compare and contrast,** they show how things are similar and how they are different.

✓ You can use a chart or diagram to keep track of similarities and differences.

✓ You can compare information given to information you already know.

Name _____

**Read** the passages. **Then** complete the chart.

- **Write** the similarities and differences about New Year celebrations that are in the text.

- Then, **write** any additional similarities and differences you know about.

## New Year Celebrations

**The Chinese New Year** begins in late January or early February. During the celebration, people march in parades. They carry long, colorful dragon puppets and light fireworks. Many of the dragons are red because the color red is considered good luck.

In the United States and many other countries, **New Year's Eve** is on December 31. On that night, thousands of people go to Times Square in New York City. Just before midnight, a ball drops from the top of a tower. When the ball reaches the bottom, fireworks burst in the sky. Everybody sings and shouts. The next day, there is a big parade.

| Similarities in Text | Differences in Text | Compared with What I Know |
|---|---|---|
|  |  |  |

© Scott Foresman 5

# Vocabulary Activities and Word Cards

Copy the Word Cards on pages 52–53 as needed for the following activities.
Use the blank card for an additional word that you want to teach.
Also see suggestions for teaching vocabulary in the ELL and Transition Handbook.

| Synonyms | Charades | Cloze Sentences |
|---|---|---|
| • Write the following list of words on the board: *allocation, amazed, conduct, custom, donor, holy, parade, suggest, thankfulness.*<br><br>• Form pairs of students, and give each pair a set of Word Cards. Tell students to write a synonym from the board on the back of each card. Help students as necessary.<br><br>• Once all synonyms have been matched to vocabulary words, one student displays one side of a Word Card; the other student says the synonym. After going through the cards once, pairs switch roles. | • Divide the students into small groups. Assign each group a Word Card.<br><br>• Have each group discuss how best to act out the word.<br><br>• The group's first hint should be the number of syllables the word has. The students can indicate this however they choose (for example, clapping or holding up fingers).<br><br>• Groups take turns acting out scenes. Members of the other groups work together to try to guess the word. Award a point to the group that first guesses the word correctly. | • Form three groups of students. Give each group three Word Cards and paper strips. Tell groups to create a cloze sentence for each of the words they have.<br><br>• When they have finished, redistribute the cards so that groups have different words than the ones they were originally given.<br><br>• Invite each group to take turns displaying its cloze sentences. The group with the missing word must provide the correct Word Card to complete the sentence.<br><br>• Continue until all groups have presented their cloze sentences. |

## astonished

## behavior

© Scott Foresman 5

# benefactor

# distribution

# gratitude

# procession

# recommend

# sacred

# tradition

# Multilingual Summaries

## The Ch'i-lin Purse

Hsiang-ling was a spoiled child. She always got what she wanted. When she was sixteen, she married. Her mother gave her a Ch'i-lin purse and told her to open it later. But on her wedding day, Hsiang-ling gave her purse to another bride who was poor. She gave it away before she knew what was inside.

Hsiang-ling was happily married. She and her husband had a son. Six years later, the family was separated by a flood.

Hsiang-ling went to work for a man and his wife. She took care of their little son.

Hsiang-ling saw her old Ch'i-lin purse at her new house. The man's wife had been the poor bride! The purse had had valuable things in it. The poor bride and her husband had become wealthy. The wife was very happy to have found Hsiang-ling. She gave Hsiang-ling half of everything she owned. Hsiang-ling's family was found. The two families became friends.

## El bolso Ch'i-lin

Hsiang-ling era una niña malcriada. Siempre conseguía lo que quería. Cuando tenía dieciséis años se casó. Su madre le dio un bolso Ch'i-lin y le dijo que lo abriera después. Pero el día de su boda, ella le regaló el bolso a otra novia que era pobre. Se lo regaló antes de saber qué tenía adentro.

Hsiang-ling estaba felizmente casada. La pareja tuvo un niño. Seis años después, la familia fue separada por una inundación.

Hsiang-ling se fue a trabajar con un matrimonio. Ella se hizo cargo de su niño.

Hsiang-ling vio su bolso Ch'i-lin en su nuevo hogar. ¡La mujer era aquella novia pobre! El bolso tenía adentro cosas muy valiosas. La novia pobre y su esposo se habían vuelto ricos. La mujer estaba muy feliz de haber encontrado a Hsiang-ling. Ella le dio a Hsiang-ling la mitad de lo que poseía. Después, encontraron a la familia de Hsiang-ling. Las dos familias se hicieron amigas.

# Multilingual Summaries

**Chinese**

## 麒麟囊

香玲一直受到家人的嬌慣溺愛，總是能夠得到想要的一切。16歲出嫁時，母親交給她一個麒麟囊，囑咐她不要馬上打開。可是結婚那天，香玲隨便就把它送給另一個貧窮的新娘。她一點也不知道裏面到底裝了什麼。

結婚後，香玲生活得很快樂，不久就有了個兒子。六年時間一晃而過，一家人在意外的洪災中失散了。

香玲只好去別人家作傭人，幫忙照顧他們的小兒子。

有一天香玲在主人家看見自己的麒麟囊，女主人原來就是那個貧窮的新娘！麒麟囊裏藏有珍寶，令他們一家變得非常富有。女主人很高興找到香玲，把一半財產分給她。香玲也終於和家人團聚，兩家人成了好朋友。

**Vietnamese**

## Cái Ví Ch'i-lin

Hsiang-ling là một đứa trẻ được nuông chiều. Cô bé lúc nào cũng có được điều mình muốn. Khi cô lên mười sáu tuổi, cô lấy chồng. Mẹ của cô cho cô một cái ví Ch'i-lin và bảo cô chờ sau này hãy mở ví. Nhưng vào ngày cưới, Hsiang-ling tặng ví này cho một cô dâu nghèo. Cô cho ví này trước khi cô biết được có gì ở trong ví.

Hsiang-ling có chồng được hạnh phúc. Cô và chồng có được một đứa con trai. Sáu năm sau, gia đình phân ly vì một cơn lũ lụt.

Hsiang-ling đi làm mướn cho một người đàn ông và vợ của ông. Cô chăm sóc đứa con trai nhỏ của họ.

Hsiang-ling thấy cái ví Ch'i-lin của mình ở căn nhà mới này. Vợ của người đàn ông là cô dâu nghèo thuở trước! Cái ví có những vật quý báu trong đó. Cô dâu nghèo và chồng của cô trở nên giàu có. Người vợ rất vui mừng đã tìm gặp Hsiang-ling. Cô ấy cho Hsiang-ling phân nửa tài sản mà cô có. Gia đình của Hsiang-ling được tìm ra. Hai gia đình trở thành bạn.

# Multilingual Summaries

## 기린 지갑

샹링은 버릇없는 아이로 항상 원하는 것은 손에 넣었다. 16살이 되자 그녀는 결혼을 했다. 그녀의 어머니는 그녀에게 기린 지갑을 주며 나중에 열어보라고 말했다. 하지만 결혼식 날 샹링은 그녀의 지갑을 가난한 다른 신부에게 주었다. 그녀는 지갑 안에 무엇이 있는지도 알기 전에 남에게 줘버린 것이다.

샹링은 행복해하며 결혼식을 올렸고 남편과의 사이에 아들을 하나 두었다. 6년 뒤 샹링 가족은 홍수로 인해 흩어지게 되었다.

샹링은 한 부부 밑에서 그들의 어린 아들을 돌보게 되었다.

샹링은 그 새 집에서 자신의 지갑을 보았다. 남자의 아내가 바로 그 가난한 신부였던 것이다! 지갑 안에는 귀중한 물건들이 있었고 그 가난한 신부와 남편은 부자가 되어있었다. 그 아내는 샹링을 찾게 되어서 매우 기뻐했다. 그녀는 샹링에게 자신이 가진 것의 반을 주었고 샹링의 가족은 한자리에 모이게 되었다. 그 두 가족은 곧 친구가 되었다.

## Lub Hnab Ch'i-lin

Hsiang-ling yog ib tug menyuam uas tau txhua yam rau li nws lub siab ntsaw. Nws yeej ib txwm tau txhua yam uas nws xav yuav. Thaum nws muaj hnub nyoog kaum rau xyoo, nws mus yuav txiv. Nws niam muab ib lub hnab Ch'i-lin rau nws thiab hais rau nws kom tsis txhob rawm maj qheb. Tiamsis txog hnub uas yog nws rooj tshoob, Hsiang-ling tau muab lub hnab no rau ib tug nkauj nyab uas txom txomnyem. Nws cia li muab lub hnab no rau tus nkauj nyab ntawm ua ntej nws paub seb dab tsi nyob rau hauv.

Hsiang-ling tau ua lub neej nrog txoj kev zoo siab. Nws thiab nws tus txiv nkawd yug tau ib tug me tub. Rau xyoo tom ntej, dej los nyab ua rau lawv tsevneeg thiaj sib cais.

Hsiang-ling mus ua haujlwm rau ib tug pojniam thiab nws tus txiv. Nws tu nkawd tus tub.

Hsiang-ling pom lub hnab nyob rau hauv nkawd lub tsev. Tus pojniam ntawd txawm yog tus nkauj nyab uas txom txomnyem. Lub hnab no muaj ntau yam khoom uas muaj nuj nqes tshaj plaws nyob rau hauv. Tus nkauj nyab no thiab nws tus txiv nkawd thiaj li muaj nyiaj nplua nuj. Tus pojniam no zoo siab uas nws tseem nrhiav tau Hsiang-ling. Hsiang-ling los kuj mus nrhiav tau nws tsevneeg lawm. Nkawd ob tse neeg thiaj li los ua phooj ua ywg zoo.

# Jane Goodall's 10 Ways to Help Save Wildlife

Student Edition pages 212–223

| Week at a Glance | Customize instruction every day for your English Language Learners. | | | | |
|---|---|---|---|---|---|
| | **Day 1** | **Day 2** | **Day 3** | **Day 4** | **Day 5** |
| **Teacher's Edition** | Use the ELL Notes that appear throughout each day of the lesson to support instruction and reading. | | | | |
| **ELL Poster 9** | • Assess Prior Knowledge<br>• Develop Concepts and Vocabulary | • Preteach Tested Vocabulary | • Bird Watching | • Protecting Animals | • Monitor Progress |
| **ELL Teaching Guide** | • Picture It! Lesson, pp. 57–58<br>• Multilingual Summaries, pp. 61–63 | • ELL Reader Lesson, pp. 228–229 | • Vocabulary Activities and Word Cards, pp. 59–60<br>• Multilingual Summaries, pp. 61–63 | | |
| **ELL Readers** | • Reread *Friends Across the Ocean* | • Teach *Gorillas* | • Reread *Gorillas* and other texts to build fluency | | |
| **ELL and Transition Handbook** | Use the following as needed to support this week's instruction and to conduct alternative assessments:<br>• Phonics Transition Lessons<br>• Grammar Transition Lessons<br>• Assessment | | | | |

**Picture It!** Comprehension Lesson

# Fact and Opinion

Use this lesson to supplement or replace the skill lesson on pages 208–209 of the Teacher's Edition.

## Teach

Distribute copies of the Picture It! blackline master on page 58.

• Direct students' attention to the picture of the falcon. Ask the students to think of words that describe the falcon. List these words on the board.

• Share the Skill Points (at right) with students.

• Return to the word list. Ask: *Which words and phrases are facts? Which are opinion?* (*Sharp claws,* for example, is a fact, but *beautiful* is an opinion.)

• Read the paragraph aloud.

### Skill Points

✓ A **fact** is something that is true. It can be proved.

✓ An **opinion** is not true or false. It just describes how somebody thinks or feels.

✓ A single sentence can contain both a fact and an opinion.

## Practice

Read aloud the directions on page 58. Have students complete the chart. Have them keep their organizers for later reteaching.

**Answers for page 58:** Possible answers: *Facts:* have powerful eyesight, wild animals, can be seen in cities, nest on ledges, eat mice; *Opinions:* are fascinating, add beauty to the city, a good neighbor to have

Name _____

**Read** the paragraph. Then **complete** the chart.

- **Write** three facts you find in the paragraph.
- **Write** three opinions you find in the paragraph.

## Falcons in the City

Falcons are fascinating birds. They have very powerful eyesight. They are wild animals, but you can also see them in the city. They nest on the ledges of tall buildings. I think that they add beauty to the city. Falcons eat mice, so a falcon is a good neighbor to have.

| Facts | Opinions |
|-------|----------|
|       |          |

# Vocabulary Activities and Word Cards

Copy the Word Cards on page 60 as needed for the following activities.
Use the blank cards for additional words that you want to teach.
Also see suggestions for teaching vocabulary in the ELL and Transition Handbook.

| Free Association | Matching Game | Synonym or Antonym? |
|---|---|---|
| • Tape each Word Card to the board. Ask students to "free associate" other words and phrases that come to mind when they think of that word. For *environment,* for example, possible associations are *habitats, recycling, endangered animals, ecosystems,* etc. The word *contribute* may conjure up *charity, donation, and volunteer.* List students' ideas under each card, creating five lists of words that are related by meaning. | • On blank cards, write a definition for each of the vocabulary words. | • Give small groups of students sets of Word Cards and dictionaries. Allow groups enough time to study the meaning of each word. |
| | • Give a Word Card and its matching definition card to two students. (Distribute as many vocabulary and definition card pairs as you have pairs of students. You may not be able to use all the cards in one round.) Tell students to study their cards and memorize their words or definitions. | • Tape a set of Word Cards to the board in a column in alphabetical order. Next to the column, write the following words in another column, in the following order: *surroundings, subtract, preservation, uninterested, research.* You will have a list with five pairs of words. |
| • Form five groups of students, and assign one list to each group. Tell each group to create a one-paragraph story or essay using all the words on its list. | • Collect the cards and have the students circulate around the classroom saying their memorized word or definition aloud to each person until they find a "match." | • Go down the list, one pair at a time. Ask students whether each pair is a pair of synonyms or a pair of antonyms. If they are synonyms, draw an equal sign between them. If they are antonyms, draw a not equal sign. When finished, you should have the following list: *environment = surroundings contribute ≠ subtract conservation = preservation enthusiastic ≠ uninterested investigation = research* |
| • When the groups are finished, invite a member from each group to read his or her group's paragraph for the class. | • When all students have found their matching word or definition, you may play again with the remaining cards or with other students. | |

# environment

# contribute

# conservation

# enthusiastic

# investigation

# Multilingual Summaries

English

## Jane Goodall's 10 Ways to Help Save Wildlife

Jane Goodall has studied chimpanzees for many years. She now travels the world to teach about saving wildlife. She has ten suggestions for young people. They are:

1) Respect all living things. 2) Think of animals as individuals.
3) Remember that animals can think and feel. 4) Learn more about animals.
5) Learn from animals. 6) Speak up for what you believe. 7) Use less paper, gasoline, and red meat. 8) Learn what others do to help animals.
9) Join Jane Goodall's program called Roots and Shoots.
10) Believe that you can help make a difference in the world.

Spanish

## Diez maneras de Jane Goodall de proteger la vida silvestre

Jane Goodall ha estudiado a los chimpancés por muchos años. Ahora viaja alrededor del mundo para enseñar cómo proteger la vida silvestre. Ella tiene diez sugerencias para los jóvenes. Son las siguientes:

1) Respeta todas las cosas vivas. 2) Piensa en los animales como individuos.
3) Recuerda que los animales pueden pensar y sentir. 4) Aprende más sobre los animales. 5) Aprende de los animales. 6) Defiende lo que crees. 7) Consume menos papel, gasolina y carne roja. 8) Aprende lo que otros hacen para ayudar a los animales. 9) Únete al programa de Jane Goodall llamado *Roots and Shoots* (Raíces y retoños). 10) Cree en que tú puedes ayudar a cambiar el mundo.

# Multilingual Summaries

Chinese

## 珍古德拯救野生動物的十個建議

多年以來，珍古德一直在研究大猩猩。現在她在世界各地傳授拯救野生動物的方法。她給年青人提出的十個建議是：

1）尊重所有動物的生命；2）像對待朋友一樣對待動物；3）牢記動物也有思想與感情；4）學習更多關于動物的知識；5）要向動物學習；6）捍衛心中的信念；7）節約紙張與汽油，少吃紅肉；8）學習他人怎樣救助動物；9）加入珍古德的"根與芽"計劃；10）堅信自己的行動可以改變現狀。

Vietnamese

## 10 Cách Giúp Bảo Tồn Thú Rừng của Jane Goodall

Jane Goodall đã nghiên cứu những con tinh tinh qua hàng nhiều năm. Bà hiện đi khắp thế giới để giảng dạy về việc bảo tồn thú rừng. Bà có mười đề nghị cho giới trẻ. Mười điều này là:

1) Tôn trọng tất cả sinh vật. 2) Xem các thú vật như người. 3) Nên nhớ là thú vật có thể suy nghĩ và cảm nhận được. 4) Học hỏi thêm về thú vật. 5) Học từ thú vật. 6) Mạnh dạn nói lên những gì mình tin tưởng. 7) Giảm sử dụng giấy, xăng dầu, và thịt bò, cừu. 8) Học hỏi những gì người khác làm để giúp các thú vật. 9) Tham gia vào chương trình của Jane Goodall gọi là "Roots and Shoots" (Rễ và Chồi). 10) Tin tưởng là bạn có thể giúp thay đổi thế giới.

# Multilingual Summaries

## 제인 구달이 제안하는 야생 생물을 구하는 열 가지 방법

제인 구달은 여러 해 동안 침팬지를 연구해왔다. 그녀는 현재 세계 여행을 하며 야생 생물을 구하는 방법을 알리고 있다. 그녀는 젊은이들에게 열 가지 제안을 하는데 그것들은 다음과 같다.

1) 모든 생명을 존중하자. 2) 동물을 하나의 개체로 생각하자. 3) 동물들도 생각하고 느낄 수 있다는 것을 기억하자. 4) 동물에 관해 좀 더 배우자. 5) 동물로부터 배우자. 6) 우리의 믿음을 강하게 수호하자. 7) 종이와 휘발유, 붉은 육류를 덜 소비하자. 8) 남들이 동물을 돕기 위해 하는 일들을 배우자. 9) 제인 구달의 루츠 앤 슈츠 프로그램에 동참하자. 10) 당신이 이 세상에 변화를 가져올 수 있다는 것을 믿자.

## Jane Goodall 10 Nqe Uas Yuav Cawm Tau Cov Tsiaj Qus Txojsia

Jane Goodall kawm txog cov liab tau ntau xyoo. Ziag no nws mus ncig ntiajteb qhia txog tias yuav cawm cov tsiaj qus txojsia li cas. Nws tau qhia kaum nqe rau cov neeg hluas. Cov nqe no yog:

1) Saib taus txhua yam tsiaj uas muaj sia. 2) Xav tias tsiaj nws yog nws ib tug kheej. 3) Nco ntsoov tias tsiaj yeej txawj xav thiab yeeh mloog tau. 4) Kawm ntxiv txog tsiaj. 5) Kawm los ntawm tsiaj. 6) Tsa suab rau tej yam uas koj ntseeg. 7) Tsis txhob siv cov ntaub ntawv, cov roj, thiab cov nqaij liab ntau ntau. 8) Kawm txog seb lwm tus pab tsiaj li cas. 9) Mus koom Jane Goodall lub koom haum Roots thiab Shoots. 10) Ntseeg tias koj yuav pauv tau lub ntiajteb no.

# The Midnight Ride of Paul Revere

Student Edition pages 234–247

| Week at a Glance | Customize instruction every day for your English Language Learners. | | | | |
|---|---|---|---|---|---|
| | **Day 1** | **Day 2** | **Day 3** | **Day 4** | **Day 5** |
| **Teacher's Edition** | Use the ELL Notes that appear throughout each day of the lesson to support instruction and reading. | | | | |
| **ELL Poster 10** | • Assess Prior Knowledge<br>• Develop Concepts and Vocabulary | • Preteach Tested Vocabulary | • Time Line of the Revolutionary War | • Revolutionary Dialogues | • Monitor Progress |
| **ELL Teaching Guide** | • Picture It! Lesson, pp. 64–65<br>• Multilingual Summaries, pp. 68–70 | • ELL Reader Lesson, pp. 230–231 | • Vocabulary Activities and Word Cards, pp. 66–67<br>• Multilingual Summaries, pp. 68–70 | | |
| **ELL Readers** | • Reread *Gorillas* | • Teach *After the Midnight Ride* | • Reread *After the Midnight Ride* and other texts to build fluency | | |
| **ELL and Transition Handbook** | Use the following as needed to support this week's instruction and to conduct alternative assessments:<br>• Phonics Transition Lessons<br>• Grammar Transition Lessons<br>• Assessment | | | | |

**Picture It!** Comprehension Lesson

## Sequence

Use this lesson to supplement or replace the skill lesson on pages 230–231 of the Teacher's Edition.

### Teach

Distribute copies of the Picture It! blackline master on page 65.

• Tell students that the pictures tell a story from history. It is a true story. People call it the Boston Tea Party. Have students try to tell what happened, based on the pictures.

• Share the Skill Points (at right) with students.

• Explain that the written sentences below the pictures describe the events in the pictures. Students can think of them as four captions. However, they are currently out of order. Read the four captions aloud.

### Practice

Read aloud the directions on page 65. Have students number the sentences in order. Remind them to refer to the pictures to figure out the sequence of events. Have students keep their work for later reteaching.

**Answers for page 65:** 4, 2, 3, 1

> ### Skill Points
>
> ✓ The **sequence of events** is the order in which things happen.
>
> ✓ Dates and other clue words help readers to understand the sequence.
>
> ✓ You can take notes to keep track of the sequence.

**Look** at the pictures. They show four events in the order they happened.
- **Read** the sentences below. They are out of order.
- **Number** the sentences in the correct order, based on the pictures.

# The Boston Tea Party

___ The colonists threw all the tea into the harbor. This event is called the Boston Tea Party.

___ In 1773, ships from Great Britain came to Boston Harbor. The ships were loaded with tea.

___ On December 16, colonists climbed on the ships. They were dressed like Native Americans.

___ In 1768, British soldiers moved into Boston. They took control of the city.

# Vocabulary Activities and Word Cards

Copy the Word Cards on page 67 as needed for the following activities.
Use the blank card for an additional word that you want to teach.
Also see suggestions for teaching vocabulary in the ELL and Transition Handbook.

| Poster Clues | Yes or No? | Word Sort |
|---|---|---|
| • Distribute sets of Word Cards to students. Then, from your own set of Word Cards, have one student choose a card without letting the others see it.<br><br>• The student stands at the ELL Poster, points to the relevant area on it, and gives hints about the vocabulary word.<br><br>• Other students try to guess which vocabulary word the student has. The first person to guess correctly may choose the next Word Card and make up clues about it.<br><br>• Continue until all of the words have been used. | • Divide the students into two teams. Ask a student from Team A to come to the front of the class and take a Word Card without showing it to the others.<br><br>• The two teams will take turns asking the student yes-or-no questions about the hidden word. For example: *Is it a noun? Is it singular? Is it a person?*<br><br>• On a team's turn, if the students think they know what the word is, they ask, *Is it [word]?* If they identify the word, they receive a point. But if they are incorrect, they receive a negative point. Play continues until the word is guessed by either team. Then invite a student from the other team to present the next word.<br><br>• Continue switching between teams as you call on students to take a Word Card. When all words have been guessed, calculate the scores, subtracting any negative points, and declare the winning team. | • Give pairs of students sets of Word Cards. Ask them to sort their Word Cards into three categories: adjectives, nouns, and verbs.<br><br>• After five or ten minutes, create a chart on the board with the category headings given to students. Invite one pair of students to share the words that they have written under *Adjectives.* Ask another pair to share the words they have under *Nouns,* and a third pair to say what they have listed under *Verbs.* Complete the chart as dictated by students.<br><br>• Review the three lists. As you do so, check to make sure that students understand the meaning of each word. You may ask them to give a synonym, use the word in a sentence, act it out, or draw a picture. |

# fate

# fearless

# glimmer

# lingers

# magnified

# somber

# steed

# Multilingual Summaries

## The Midnight Ride of Paul Revere

On April 18, 1775, Paul Revere made a famous ride. British soldiers were coming to fight with Revolutionary soldiers. Paul Revere wanted to warn people.

The British troops had two ways to reach the towns. They could march by land. Or they could sail on the sea. That night, Revere told his friend to hang one lantern in the church tower if the British went by land. He asked the friend to hang two lanterns if they went by sea. If he knew how the British were coming, he could tell the people in the towns.

When it got dark, Revere saw two lanterns in the church tower. He rode his horse to tell the people to get ready to fight the British. He got to the first town at midnight. He rode through many towns on the way to Concord. The next morning was the first battle of the American Revolution.

## El viaje nocturno de Paul Revere

El 18 de abril de 1775, Paul Revere hizo un recorrido glorioso. Los soldados británicos llegarían a luchar contra los soldados revolucionarios. Paul Revere quería alertar a la gente.

Las tropas británicas tenían dos caminos para llegar a los pueblos. Podían marchar por tierra o podían llegar navegando. Esa noche, Revere le dijo a su amigo que pusiera un farol encendido en la torre de la iglesia si los británicos venían por tierra. Revere le dijo a su amigo que pusiera dos faroles si los británicos llegaban por mar. Si sabía cómo llegaban los británicos, él podía avisarle a la gente en los pueblos.

Cuando oscureció, Revere vio dos faroles en la torre de la iglesia. Montó en su caballo y se fue a decirle a la gente que estuviera preparada para luchar contra los británicos. Llegó al primer pueblo a la medianoche. Atravesó muchos pueblos en su camino a Concord. A la mañana siguiente, ocurrió la primera batalla de la Guerra de Independencia.

# Multilingual Summaries

## 保羅·瑞維爾午夜報信

保羅·瑞維爾騎馬報信的故事家喻戶曉。1775年4月18日那天，英軍要去鎮壓起義者，保羅想通知同胞們早做準備。

英軍有兩條路綫可選：或者從陸上進攻，或者從海上入侵。那天晚上，保羅對朋友說，如果英軍從陸上來，就在教堂鐘樓上挂一盞燈，如果從海上過，就挂兩盞燈。事先知道英軍的路綫，好給村民們報信。

天色漸漸黑了，保羅看見鐘樓上有兩盞燈。他騎馬飛奔去通知人們，做好迎擊英軍的準備。到達第一個村莊時，已經是午夜。他一路飛馳報信，穿過許多村莊，來到康科德城。第二天早上，打響了美國獨立革命的第一槍。

## Chuyến Cưỡi Ngựa Vào Lúc Nửa Đêm của Paul Revere

Vào ngày 18 tháng Tư, năm 1775, Paul Revere đã làm một chuyến đi lừng danh. Binh lính Anh sắp đến đánh với binh lính Cách Mạng. Paul Revere muốn báo trước cho mọi người biết.

Quân đội Anh có hai cách để đến các thành phố. Họ có thể hành quân bằng đường bộ. Hoặc họ có thể đến bằng thuyền buồm trên biển. Tối hôm đó, Revere dặn bạn của ông treo một ngọn đèn lồng trên tháp nhà thờ nếu quân Anh đến bằng đường bộ. Ông kêu người bạn này treo hai ngọn đèn lồng nếu họ đến bằng đường biển. Nếu ông biết cách quân Anh đến, ông có thể nói cho người trong các thành phố biết.

Khi trời tối, Paul thấy hai ngọn đèn lồng trên tháp ngôi nhà thờ. Ông cưỡi ngựa đi kêu mọi người chuẩn bị chiến đấu với quân Anh. Ông đến thành phố đầu tiên vào lúc nửa đêm. Ông cưỡi ngựa qua nhiều thành phố trên đường đến Concord. Sáng hôm sau là trận chiến đầu tiên của cuộc Cách Mạng Hoa Kỳ.

# Multilingual Summaries

## 한 밤중에 말을 탄 폴 리비어

1775년 4월 18일 폴 리비어는 말을 타고 유명해졌다. 그 당시 영국군은 독립군과 싸우기 위해 오고 있는 중이었다. 폴 리비어는 사람들에게 위험을 알리고 싶었다.

영국군이 마을에 도착할 수 있는 방법은 두 가지로 육지로 행군하거나 바다로 항해하는 것이었다. 그날 밤 리비어는 자신의 친구에게 만약 영국군이 육지로 가게 되면 교회 탑에 랜턴 하나를 걸어두고 바다로 가면 랜턴 두 개를 걸어달라고 부탁했다. 만약 영국군이 어떻게 오는지를 알게 된다면 마을 사람들에게 말을 해 줄 수 있을 것이었다.

어두워지자 폴은 교회 탑에 랜턴 두 개가 걸린 것을 보았다. 그는 영국군과 싸울 준비를 하도록 사람들에게 알려주기 위해 자신의 말을 몰았다. 그는 자정에 첫 번째 마을에 도착했고 콩코드까지 여러 마을들을 지나며 말을 달렸다. 그 다음날 아침이 바로 미국 독립전쟁의 첫 전투가 시작된 날이었다.

## Paul Revere Kev Caij Tshej Thaum Ib Tag Hmo

Hnub tim kaum yim lub plaub hlis ntuj xyoo ib txhiab xya pua xya caum tsib, Paul Revere tau caij ib kev tshej ua tau nto npe heev. Tub rog Askiv yuav tuaj tua cov tub rog Revolutionary. Paul Revere xav mus ceeb toom neeg sawvdaws.

Cov tub rog Askiv thaug tau ob txoj kev tuaj rau pem zos. Lawv tuaj tau kaw taw saum av tuaj. Lossis lawv kuj caij tau nkoj tuaj thiab. Hmo ntawd, Revere qhia nws tus phooj ywg kom nws dai ib lub teeb rau saum lub tshawj tus pejthuam yog cov tub rog Askiv tuaj kaw taw tuaj. Nws nug kom nws tus phooj ywg dai ob lub teeb yog lawv tuaj nkoj tuaj. Yog nws paub tias cov tub rog Askiv tuaj li cas tuaj ces nws thiaj li qhia tau zej zog sawvdaws.

Thaum tsaus ntuj lawm, Paul pom ob lub teeb dai rau saum lub tshawj tus pejthuam. Nws caij nws tus nees mus qhia neeg sawvdaws kom lawv npaj mus tuaj rog norg cov Askiv. Nws mus txog thawj lub zos thaum ib tag hmo. Nws caij nees dhau zos ntau kawg thiaj li mus txog Concord. Tag kis sawv ntxov tom qab ntawd yog thawj ntsug rog ntawm kev ua rog American Revolution.

# Wings for the King  Student Edition pages 266–279

| Week at a Glance | Customize instruction every day for your English Language Learners. | | | | |
|---|---|---|---|---|---|
| | **Day 1** | **Day 2** | **Day 3** | **Day 4** | **Day 5** |
| **Teacher's Edition** | Use the ELL Notes that appear throughout each day of the lesson to support instruction and reading. | | | | |
| **ELL Poster 11** | • Assess Prior Knowledge<br>• Develop Concepts and Vocabulary | • Preteach Tested Vocabulary | • Inventions and Innovations | • Invention Commercial | • Monitor Progress |
| **ELL Teaching Guide** | • Picture It! Lesson, pp. 71–72<br>• Multilingual Summaries, pp. 75–77 | • ELL Reader Lesson, pp. 232–233 | • Vocabulary Activities and Word Cards, pp. 73–74<br>• Multilingual Summaries, pp. 75–77 | | |
| **ELL Readers** | • Reread *After the Midnight Ride* | • Teach *Scientific Methods in Action* | • Reread *Scientific Methods in Action* and other texts to build fluency | | |
| **ELL and Transition Handbook** | Use the following as needed to support this week's instruction and to conduct alternative assessments:<br>• Phonics Transition Lessons<br>• Grammar Transition Lessons<br>• Assessment | | | | |

**Picture It!** Comprehension Lesson
## Author's Purpose

Use this lesson to supplement or replace the skill lesson on pages 262–263 of the Teacher's Edition.

### Teach

Distribute copies of the Picture It! blackline master on page 72.
• Share the Skill Points (at right) with students.
• Tell students they are going to read a story. Ask them to make a guess about the author's purpose. Ask: *Why do authors usually write stories?* Then read the story aloud.
• Ask: *What is the problem at the beginning of the story?* (The boy wants a puppy but has no money.) *How is it resolved?* (He decides to walk dogs for money.) *What do you think about the story's ending?*

### Practice

Read aloud the directions on page 72. Encourage students to write complete sentences in response to each question. Have students keep their work for later reteaching.

**Answers for page 72:** Possible answers: **1.** The author's purpose is to entertain. **2.** The author achieved his purpose using humor. The boy acts like he thought of the idea, but his sister did.

### Skill Points

✓ Authors have a **purpose** for writing. The purpose is their reason for writing.

✓ The author's words and the ideas in the writing will help you figure out the author's purpose.

✓ Here are some common purposes for writing: to persuade, to inform, to entertain, to express thoughts or feelings.

Name _____

**Read** the story. **Answer** the questions that follow.

## Walter's Great Idea

Walter wanted to buy a puppy, but he didn't have any money. He would have to get a job. But what kind of job?

Walter's sister saw him thinking. "Walter, what are you thinking about?"

"I'm thinking of a way to make money so I can buy a puppy."

"Why don't you start your own business walking dogs?"

"What a great idea," Walter said. "I'm glad I thought of it!"

**1.** What do you think was the author's purpose for writing this story?

_____

_____

_____

**2.** How did the author achieve his purpose? Explain.

_____

_____

_____

# Vocabulary Activities and Word Cards

Copy the Word Cards on page 74 as needed for the following activities.
Use the blank cards for additional words that you want to teach.
Also see suggestions for teaching vocabulary in the ELL and Transition Handbook.

| Group Story | Definitions | Synonym or Antonym? |
|---|---|---|
| • Form groups of students. Put a set of Word Cards into a paper bag for each group.<br><br>• Members of each group take turns drawing a card out of the bag. As they do so, they make a sentence with the word. Together, the sentences should tell a story. It is important that the first student create a good story starter, for example: *Once upon a time, a king called his favorite subject to the palace.*<br><br>• The next student then draws a card and creates the next sentence of the story, incorporating the new word. Groups continue in this way until all the words have been used.<br><br>• If possible, assign a member of the group to write the story down as the group dictates it. When the story is finished, invite one member from each group to read the story to the class. | • Form pairs of students, and give a set of Word Cards to each.<br><br>• Tell partners to work together, writing a definition for each word on the back of the card.<br><br>• Students can quiz each other by playing the following game: One student reads aloud a definition (making sure the word on the other side is not visible) and challenges his or her partner to guess what the word is, based on the definition. | • Give small groups sets of Word Cards. Provide each group with a dictionary and allow groups enough time to study the meaning of each word.<br><br>• Using an extra set of Word Cards, tape the words to the blackboard in a column in alphabetical order. Next to the column of Word Cards, write the following words in the order shown: *critically, forbid, rascal, king, priceless.*<br><br>• Go down the list, one pair at a time. Ask students whether each pair are synonyms or antonyms. If the words are synonyms, draw an equal sign between the two words. If they are antonyms, draw a not equal sign between them. When you are finished, your list will look like this:<br>*admiringly ≠ critically*<br>*permit ≠ forbid*<br>*scoundrel = rascal*<br>*subject ≠ king*<br>*worthless ≠ priceless*<br><br>• You may choose to include additional selection words for which you can write a synonym or antonym. |

admiringly

permit

scoundrel

subject

worthless

# Multilingual Summaries

English

## Wings for the King

The King is bored. He wants to travel to other lands. He wants someone to make wings for him. With wings he can fly to other lands. He will give a bag of gold to anyone who can make wings.

Tina brings wings that she made. The wings do not work. The King is angry. He sends Tina to the dungeon.

Geraldine brings a hat with propellers. The hat does not work. The King is angry. Geraldine is sent to the dungeon.

Isaac brings books. He says that the books are wings. With books, the King can travel to the lands of knowledge and fun. Isaac wins the bag of gold. The King and Queen read and travel to new lands.

Spanish

## Alas para el rey

Un rey estaba aburrido. Quería viajar a otras tierras. Quería que alguien le fabricara unas alas. Con alas, él podría volar a otras tierras. Prometió entregar una bolsa de oro a aquél que pudiera fabricar las alas.

Tina le llevó unas alas que ella armó. Las alas no funcionaron. El rey se puso furioso y envió a Tina al calabozo.

Geraldine le llevó un sombrero con hélices. El sombrero tampoco funcionó. El rey estaba furioso. Geraldine fue enviada al calabozo.

Isaac le llevó algunos libros. Le dijo que los libros eran las alas. Con los libros, el rey podría viajar a las tierras del conocimiento y de la diversión. Isaac se ganó la bolsa de oro. El rey y la reina leen y de esta manera viajan a nuevas tierras.

# Multilingual Summaries

## 國王的翅膀

國王最近老是無精打采。他很想走出王宮去遠方旅行，希望能有一對翅膀，這樣就可以四處自由飛翔。國王下令誰為他製作翅膀，就獎賞一袋金子。

蒂娜製作了鳥一樣的翅膀，卻飛不起來。國王非常生氣，把她關進了地牢。

杰拉爾丁送來帽子，上面裝著螺旋槳，可還是飛不起來。國王非常氣憤，把她也關進了地牢。

艾薩克給國王獻上書。他說書就是飛行的翅膀，有了它，國王可以在知識的世界裏自由飛翔。艾薩克得到了獎金。國王和王后一起讀書，在新世界裏快樂地旅行。

## Đôi Cánh cho Vua

Nhà Vua buồn chán. Ông muốn du lịch đến những xứ khác. Ông muốn có người làm đôi cánh cho mình. Với đôi cánh ông có thể bay đến những xứ khác. Ông sẽ trao một túi vàng cho bất cứ ai có thể làm cho ông đôi cánh.

Tina mang đến đôi cánh mà cô đã làm. Đôi cánh không bay được. Nhà Vua tức giận. Ông đày Tina vào ngục tối.

Geraldine mang đến một chiếc nón có các cánh quạt. Nón không bay được. Nhà Vua tức giận. Geraldine bị đày vào ngục tối.

Isaac mang các quyển sách đến. Cậu nói rằng sách là cánh. Với những quyển sách, Nhà Vua có thể du lịch đến những xứ sở đầy kiến thức và sự vui vẻ. Isaac thắng được túi vàng. Nhà Vua và Hoàng Hậu đọc sách và du lịch đến những xứ sở mới.

# Multilingual Summaries

## 왕을 위한 날개

왕은 지루하여 다른 지역으로 여행하고 싶어한다. 왕은 누군가가 자신에게 날개를 만들어주길 바란다. 날개가 있으면 다른 지역으로 날아갈 수 있기 때문이다. 왕은 날개를 만들어주는 사람 누구에게든지 금 한 자루를 줄 것이다.

티나는 자신이 직접 만든 날개를 가져오지만 날개가 움직이지 않는다. 왕은 화가 나서 티나를 지하 감옥으로 보내 버린다.

제랄딘은 프로펠러가 달린 모자를 가져오지만 모자가 움직이지 않는다. 왕은 화가 나서 제랄딘도 지하 감옥으로 보내 버린다.

아이작은 책을 가져와 책이 날개라며 책을 읽고 지식과 재미의 세계로 즐겁게 여행할 수 있다고 말한다. 결국 아이작은 금 한 자루를 받는다. 왕과 여왕은 함께 책을 읽으며 새로운 세계로 여행을 떠난다.

## Tis rau tus Vajntxwv

Tus Vajntxwv laj nyob kawg. Nws xav mus xyuas lwm lub teb chaws. Nws xav kom leej twg txua tis rau nws. Yog nws muaj tis ces nws ya ub rau lwm lub teb chaws. Nws yuav muab ib hnab kub rau tus uas txua tau tis.

Tina nqa cov tis uas nws ua tau tuaj. Cov tis tsis ua hauj lwm. Tus Vajntxwv chim heev. Nws xa Tina mus kaw rau hauv lub qhov tsaus ntuj.

Geraldine nqa tau ib lub kaus mom muaj tis tuaj. Lub kaus mom tsis ua hauj lwm. Tus Vajntxwv chim heev. Nws xa Geraldine mus kaw rau hauv lub qhov tsaus ntuj.

Isaac nqa ob peb phau ntawv tuaj. Nws hais tias cov ntawv ntawd muaj tis. Nrog ntawv, tus Vajntxwv mus tau teb chaws uas muaj laj lim tswvyim thiab uas lom zem. Isaac yeej lub hnab kub. Tus nom thiab tus Poj Vajntxwv nyeem thiab mus rau teb chaws tshiab.

| Week at a Glance | Customize instruction every day for your English Language Learners. | | | | |
|---|---|---|---|---|---|
| | **Day 1** | **Day 2** | **Day 3** | **Day 4** | **Day 5** |
| **Teacher's Edition** | Use the ELL Notes that appear throughout each day of the lesson to support instruction and reading. | | | | |
| **ELL Poster 12** | • Assess Prior Knowledge<br>• Develop Concepts and Vocabulary | • Preteach Tested Vocabulary | • Monuments of Washington D.C. | • Museum Tours | • Monitor Progress |
| **ELL Teaching Guide** | • Picture It! Lesson, pp. 78–79<br>• Multilingual Summaries, pp. 82–84 | • ELL Reader Lesson, pp. 234–235 | • Vocabulary Activities and Word Cards, pp. 80–81<br>• Multilingual Summaries, pp. 82–84 | | |
| **ELL Readers** | • Reread *Scientific Methods in Action* | • Teach *The Renaissance* | • Reread *The Renaissance* and other texts to build fluency | | |
| **ELL and Transition Handbook** | Use the following as needed to support this week's instruction and to conduct alternative assessments:<br>• Phonics Transition Lessons<br>• Grammar Transition Lessons<br>• Assessment | | | | |

**Picture It!** Comprehension Lesson

# Main Idea and Details

Use this lesson to supplement or replace the skill lesson on pages 288–289 of the Teacher's Edition.

## Teach

Distribute copies of the Picture It! blackline master on page 79.
- Tell students they are going to read a paragraph about metals. Point to the illustration that accompanies the text. Tell students that it will help them understand the text. Then read the paragraph aloud. Ask: *What was the paragraph about?* (how brass is created)
- Share the Skill Points (at right) with students.

## Practice

Read aloud the directions on page 79. Have students read the text and then complete the graphic organizer that follows it. Have students keep their organizers for later reteaching.

**Answers for page 79:** *Main Idea:* Brass is a mixture of metals; Possible answers: *Detail:* One of the metals is copper. *Detail:* The other metal is zinc.

### Skill Points

✓ The **main idea** is the most important idea in a paragraph. It usually comes at the beginning of the paragraph.

✓ **Details** are pieces of information that tell more about the main idea.

Name _____

**Look** at the picture. Read the paragraph.

- Which sentence tells the main idea of the paragraph? **Write** that sentence in the *Main Idea* box.

- Which sentences give details? **Write** them in the *Detail* boxes.

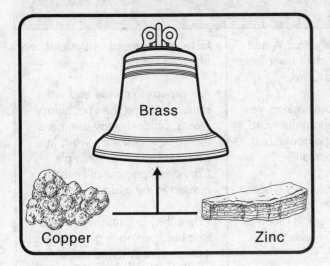

## Brass

Brass is not a metal that comes from nature. It is a mixture of two metals that uses the good qualities of both of them. One of the metals is copper; the other is zinc. To make brass, copper and zinc are melted. Then they are combined. Brass is used to make many things, including jewelry and musical instruments.

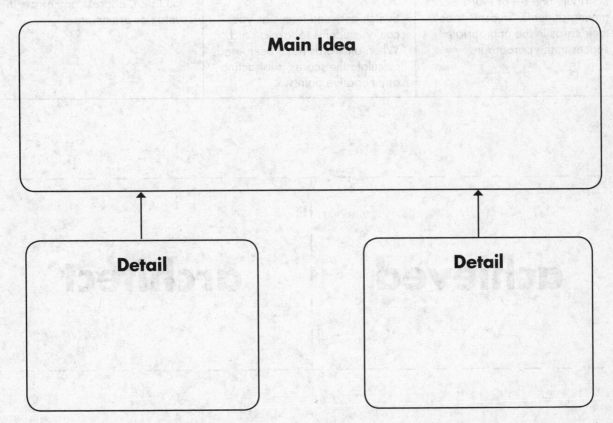

**Main Idea**

**Detail**

**Detail**

# Vocabulary Activities and Word Cards

Copy the Word Cards on pages 80–81 as needed for the following activities.
Use the blank card for an additional word that you want to teach.
Also see suggestions for teaching vocabulary in the ELL and Transition Handbook.

| Cloze Paragraph | Yes or No? | Sentence Builders |
|---|---|---|
| • Write the following paragraph on the board. Replace the underscored words with lines: *Da Vinci was a philosopher, artist, and architect. He fashioned instruments, bridges, cannon, chariots, and works of art. He once created a bronze horse while he was in the midst of making a painting. Despite everything he had achieved, da Vinci became depressed when his rival mocked him.*<br><br>• Distribute one set of Word Cards among students. Students tape their cards in the appropriate spaces in the paragraph. | • Create two teams, Team A and Team B. Ask a student from Team A to take a Word Card.<br><br>• The teams take turns asking yes-or-no questions about the word. For example: *Is it a noun? Is it singular? Is it a person?*<br><br>• If a team thinks it knows what the word is, it asks *Is it [word]?* If the team is correct, it receives a point. If not, it receives a negative point.<br><br>• Switch between teams as you call on students to take a card. When all words have been used, calculate the scores, subtracting any negative points. | • Give small groups of students sets of Word Cards.<br><br>• Ask groups to create and write sentences using the vocabulary words. Students may use more than one vocabulary word in each sentence. For example: *Cannons made out of bronze blasted in the midst of the battle.*<br><br>• When they are finished, invite a member from each group to read their sentences to the class. As you listen, address any errors in syntax or grammar. |

## achieved

## architect

**bronze**

**cannons**

**depressed**

**fashioned**

**midst**

**philosopher**

**rival**

# Multilingual Summaries

## Leonardo's Horse

As a boy, Leonardo da Vinci was curious about everything. As a teenager, he went to study art in Florence, Italy. He became a famous artist. He made a silver flute shaped like a horse's head. The ruler of Florence sent Leonardo to give the flute to the duke of Milan as a gift.

In Milan, the duke asked Leonardo to make a statue of a horse. It would be three times bigger than a real horse. Leonardo studied other statues and real horses. He made a clay model that was twenty-four feet tall.

France was threatening to invade Milan. The duke used the metal intended for the statue to make a cannon. The clay model became a pile of mud. Leonardo was sad about his horse. In the 1990s, two artists made a statue of a horse like Leonardo's. More than 450 years after Leonardo died, the horse was brought to Milan.

## El caballo de Leonardo

Cuando era niño, Leonardo da Vinci sentía curiosidad por todo. De adolescente, fue a estudiar arte a Florencia, Italia. Se convirtió en un artista famoso. Hizo una flauta de plata con la forma de una cabeza de caballo. El gobernador de Florencia envió a Leonardo con la flauta de regalo para el duque de Milán.

En Milán, el duque le pidió a Leonardo que hiciera la estatua de un caballo. Debería ser tres veces más grande que un caballo real. Leonardo estudió otras estatuas y caballos reales. Hizo un modelo de arcilla que tenía veinticuatro pies de alto.

Francia amenazaba con invadir Milán. El duque usó el metal de la estatua para hacer un cañón. El modelo de arcilla se convirtió en un montón de barro. Leonardo estaba muy triste por su caballo. Pero en la década de 1990, dos artistas hicieron una estatua de un caballo como el de Leonardo. Más de 450 años después de la muerte de Leonardo, el caballo fue llevado a Milán.

# Multilingual Summaries

## 達芬奇的馬

　　達芬奇小時候就對萬事萬物充滿好奇。青少年時，他前往意大利佛羅倫薩學習藝術，成為著名的藝術家。他創作了一隻銀笛，形狀就像馬頭。佛羅倫薩王公派他去米蘭，把銀笛送給公爵。

　　米蘭公爵請達芬奇做一個馬雕像，要求比真馬整整大三倍。達芬奇仔細研究了許多雕像與真馬，做了一個泥馬模型，足有24英尺高。

　　此時法國威脅入侵米蘭，公爵只好把做雕像的金屬造大炮。泥馬模型變成了一堆泥漿，達芬奇傷心極了。二十世紀90年代時，兩個藝術家特意仿製達芬奇的馬雕像。在紀念達芬奇逝世450多年時，送給了米蘭。

## Con Ngựa Của Leonardo

Khi còn là một đứa bé, Leonardo da Vinci tò mò về mọi thứ. Khi là một thanh thiếu niên, ông ấy đi học nghệ thuật ở Florence, nước Ý. Ông trở nên một họa sĩ nổi tiếng. Ông làm một ống sáo bằng bạc có hình dạng đầu ngựa. Nhà cai trị ở Florence sai Leonardo đi trao ống sáo này cho vị Công Tước ở Milan để làm quà.

Ở Milan, vị công tước yêu cầu Leonardo làm một bức tượng ngựa. Tượng này lớn hơn gấp ba lần một con ngựa thật. Leonardo nghiên cứu các bức tượng khác và những con ngựa thật. Ông làm một mô hình bằng đất sét cao hai mươi bốn bộ.

Pháp đang hăm he xâm lăng Milan. Vị công tước dùng kim loại làm bức tượng để làm ra súng đại bác. Mô hình đất sét trở thành một đống bùn. Leonardo buồn về con ngựa của mình. Vào thập niên 1990, có hai họa sĩ làm bức tượng ngựa giống như của Leonardo. Hơn 450 năm sau khi Leonardo qua đời, ngựa này được mang đến Milan.

# Multilingual Summaries

## 레오나르도의 말

　　레오나르도 다빈치는 소년 시절 호기심이 아주 많았다. 청소년 시절 그는 이탈리아 피렌체로 예술 공부를 하러 떠났고 유명한 예술가가 되었다. 그는 말의 머리처럼 생긴 은색 플루트를 만들었다. 피렌체의 군주는 레오나르도를 시켜 밀라노의 공작에게 그 플루트를 선물로 보냈다.

　　밀라노의 공작은 레오나르도에게 말 동상을 만들어달라고 요청했는데 그것은 실제 말보다 세 배나 더 큰 것이었다. 레오나르도는 다른 동상들과 실제 말에 대해 공부한 후 24피트 높이의 점토 모형을 만들었다.

　　프랑스가 밀라노를 침략하겠다고 위협하고 있었다. 공작은 말 동상에 쓸 금속으로 대포를 만들었다. 점토로 만든 말 모형은 진흙 더미가 되었고 레오나르도는 자기 작품이 그렇게 된 것에 슬퍼했다. 1990년대 들어 두 명의 예술가가 레오나르도의 것과 같은 말 동상을 만들었다. 레오나르도가 죽은 지 450년이 지나 그 말 동상은 밀라노로 돌려 보내졌다.

## Leonardo tus Nees

　　Thaum nws yog menyuam tub, Leonardo da Vinci xav paub txog txhua yam. Thaum ib yog ib tug tub hluas, nws mus kawm teeb duab nyob rau Florence, Italy. Nws los ua ib tug neeg teeb duab uas nto npe heev. Nws txua tau ib lub raj nyiaj zoo li ib tug nees lub taub hau. Tus tswv nyob Florence xa Leonardo mus muab lub raj ntawd ua ib qhov khoom plig rau tus tswv lub lav Milan.

　　Nyob Milan, tus tswv ntawd nug Leonardo kom nws puab ib tug nees kom loj tshaj ib tug nees tiag lawm li peb zaug. Leonardo kawm txog tej mlom uas tau puab lawm thiab kawm txog nees. Nws sim av nplaum puas tau ib tug qauv ua siab li nees nkaum plaub fiv (feet).

　　Fabkis phem tawm tsam tias lawv yuav tuaj tua Milan. Tus tswv ntawd siv cov hlau yuav los ua tus nees ntawd coj los ua phom. Cov av nplaum ua puas tau tus qauv ntawd cia li los ua ib phawg av nkos lawm xwb. Leonardo tu siab txog nws tus nees ntawd. Nyob rau lub caij ib txhiab cuaj puas cuaj caum ntawd, ob tug neeg teeb duab tau ua tau ib tug nees zoo li Leonardo tus. Tshaj plaub puas tsib caug xyoo tom qab Leonardo tuag lawm, luag coj tau tus nees ntawd tuaj rau Milan.

# The Dinosaurs of Waterhouse Hawkins

Student Edition pages 316–317

| Week at a Glance | Customize instruction every day for your English Language Learners. | | | | |
|---|---|---|---|---|---|
| | **Day 1** | **Day 2** | **Day 3** | **Day 4** | **Day 5** |
| **Teacher's Edition** | Use the ELL Notes that appear throughout each day of the lesson to support instruction and reading. | | | | |
| **ELL Poster 13** | • Assess Prior Knowledge<br>• Develop Concepts and Vocabulary | • Preteach Tested Vocabulary | • Museum Tour | • Directed Draw | • Monitor Progress |
| **ELL Teaching Guide** | • Picture It! Lesson, pp. 85–86<br>• Multilingual Summaries, pp. 89–91 | • ELL Reader Lesson, pp. 236–237 | • Vocabulary Activities and Word Cards, pp. 87–88<br>• Multilingual Summaries, pp. 89–91 | | |
| **ELL Readers** | • Reread *The Renaissance* | • Teach *Dinosaur Time Line* | • Reread *Dinosaur Time Line* and other texts to build fluency | | |
| **ELL and Transition Handbook** | Use the following as needed to support this week's instruction and to conduct alternative assessments:<br>• Phonics Transition Lessons<br>• Grammar Transition Lessons<br>• Assessment | | | | |

**Picture It!** Comprehension Lesson

## Fact and Opinion

Use this lesson to supplement or replace the skill lesson on pages 320–337 of the Teacher's Edition.

### Teach

Distribute copies of the Picture It! blackline master on page 86.
- Direct students' attention to the picture of Tyrannosaurus Rex. Tell them they are going to read a paragraph about this dinosaur.
- Ask: *Do you think you will be reading facts, opinions, or both?* Read the paragraph aloud, and then ask: *Was your prediction correct?*
- Share the Skill Points (at right) with students.

### Practice

Read aloud the directions on page 86. Have students read the paragraph and then complete the chart. Have students keep their organizers for later reteaching.

**Answers for page 86:** *Fact:* T. Rex was 18 feet tall and weighed 6 tons. Its teeth were sharp and pointed. They could cut through bone and meat.
*Opinion:* T. Rex was the "king" of dinosaurs. No other dinosaur can compare. People will always think of T. Rex as the biggest and scariest.

> ### Skill Points
> ✓ A **fact** is something that is true. It can be proved.
> ✓ An **opinion** is not true or false. It shows what somebody thinks or feels.
> ✓ A single sentence can contain both a fact and an opinion.

# Fact and Opinion

Name _____

**Read** the paragraph. Then **complete** the chart.

- **Find** information that can be proved. **Write** it in the *Facts* column.
- **Find** information that expresses the writer's thought or feelings. **Write** it in the *Opinions* column.

## The "King" of Dinosaurs

Tyrannosaurus Rex was the "king" of dinosaurs. It was 18 feet tall, and it weighed 6 tons or more. Its teeth were sharp and pointed. They could cut through bone and meat. No other dinosaur can compare to T. Rex. People will always think of T. Rex as the biggest and scariest dinosaur of all time.

| Facts | Opinions |
|-------|----------|
|       |          |

# Vocabulary Activities and Word Cards

Copy the Word Cards on page 88 as needed for the following activities.
Use the blank card for an additional word that you want to teach.
Also see suggestions for teaching vocabulary in the ELL and Transition Handbook.

| Synonym Concentration | Do or Draw | What Am I? |
|---|---|---|
| • Give pairs of students sets of Word Cards and blank cards. Ask the students to use a dictionary or thesaurus to find synonyms for each vocabulary word. Or, you can provide the synonyms for the students. Possible synonyms are: *built, bases, forms, event, ratio, neatened, studio.*<br><br>• Students write each synonym on a blank card and confirm which vocabulary word and synonym go together. They then shuffle the two sets of cards together and lay the cards face down in a grid pattern.<br><br>• Students take turns choosing two of the cards. If the two cards are synonyms, the student keeps the cards. If not, the cards are put back. Play continues until all of the cards have been matched. | • Give each student a set of Word Cards. Review what nouns and verbs are.<br><br>• Ask a student to come to the front of the class and choose a Word Card without showing it to anyone. Explain that the student will either act out or draw to demonstrate the word. If the word is a noun, the student will draw a picture of it. If it is a verb, the student will act it out. The rest of the class should try to guess the word.<br><br>• The first person to correctly guess the word is next to choose a word and either draw it or act it out. | • Write the vocabulary words on the board where everyone can see them. Then tape one Word Card to the back of each student. Not all students need to have cards to participate in the activity.<br><br>• Students circulate, asking each other yes-or-no questions to determine which word is on their backs. For example: *Am I a noun? Am I singular? Am I a place?*<br><br>• The student finally identifies his or her word by asking *Am I [word]?* The student who answers this question with *yes* should then remove the word from the other student's back. These students may continue in the game by answering other students' questions.<br><br>• Play continues until all students have identified their words. |

erected

foundations

molds

occasion

proportion

tidied

workshop

# Multilingual Summaries

## The Dinosaurs of Waterhouse Hawkins

Waterhouse Hawkins had a workshop. He created models of animals. His biggest project was to create life-sized models of dinosaurs. In 1853, people had discovered dinosaur bones. However, no one really knew what a dinosaur looked like. Hawkins asked a scientist to help. The scientist compared dinosaur bones with the bones of modern reptiles.

Hawkins saw that the bones were very much alike. He decided that dinosaurs must have looked like giant lizards. He used fossil bones to estimate how big the dinosaurs must have been. Then he made life-sized models of the dinosaurs.

Queen Victoria and Prince Albert admired Hawkins's models. Prince Albert wanted to display the dinosaurs in his new museum.

First, Hawkins wanted scientists to accept his work. He held a party on New Year's Eve. He had the dinner table inside one of his models. The guests loved Hawkins's creations.

Spanish

## Los dinosaurios de Waterhouse Hawkins

Waterhouse Hawkins tenía un taller. Él creaba modelos de animales. Su mayor proyecto fue crear modelos del tamaño real de los dinosaurios. En 1853, la gente había descubierto huesos de dinosaurios. Sin embargo, nadie sabía realmente cómo era un dinosaurio. Hawkins le pidió ayuda a un científico. El científico comparó los huesos de los dinosaurios con los huesos de los reptiles modernos.

Hawkins vio que los huesos eran muy parecidos. Él decidió que los dinosaurios parecían grandes lagartos. Usó huesos fósiles para estimar qué tan grandes eran los dinosaurios. Luego hizo modelos del tamaño real de los dinosaurios.

La reina Victoria y el príncipe Alberto admiraron los modelos de Hawkins. El príncipe Alberto quería exhibir los dinosaurios en su nuevo museo.

Primero, Hawkins quiso que los científicos aceptaran su trabajo. Hizo una fiesta la víspera del Año Nuevo. Tenía la mesa con la cena dentro de uno de sus modelos. Los invitados admiraron las creaciones de Hawkins.

# Multilingual Summaries

## 霍金斯的恐龍

霍金斯有一個工場，專門製做動物模型。他最遠大的計劃，就是做出與真恐龍大小一樣的恐龍模型。1853年，人們發現恐龍骨頭化石。然而，當時沒有人知道恐龍究竟長得什麼樣。霍金斯向科學家請教，將恐龍骨頭與現代爬行動物的骨頭進行對比。

霍金斯發現這些骨頭非常相像，心裏想恐龍肯定像現在的巨蜥。他用骨頭化石估算恐龍大小，然後製做出恐龍模型，與真的一般大小。

維多利亞女王與阿爾伯特王子很喜歡霍金斯的恐龍模型。王子想在新建的博物館裏，向公眾展示這些模型。

但是，霍金斯希望科學家們能夠首先接受他的作品，於是在新年前夕舉辦了一個晚會，請客人在他的恐龍模型裏就餐。大家都非常喜歡他的恐龍。

## Những Con Khủng Long của Waterhouse Hawkins

Waterhouse Hawkins có một xưởng nhỏ. Ông làm những mô hình thú vật. Dự án lớn nhất của ông là làm những mô hình khủng long to như thật. Vào năm 1853, người ta đã tìm ra xương khủng long. Tuy nhiên, không ai thật sự biết một con khủng long trông như thế nào. Hawkins nhờ một nhà khoa học giúp đỡ. Nhà khoa học này so sánh các xương của khủng long với các xương của loài bò sát cận đại.

Hawkins thấy là các xương đều rất giống nhau. Ông quyết định là những con khủng long chắc hẳn là trông giống như những con thần lằn khổng lồ. Ông ấy dùng những xương đã hóa thạch để phỏng đoán xem các con khủng long này đã to đến cỡ nào. Tiếp đó ông làm những mô hình khủng long to như thật.

Nữ Vương Victoria và Hoàng Tử Albert hâm mộ những mô hình của Hawkins. Hoàng Tử Albert muốn trưng bày những con khủng long này ở viện bảo tàng mới của ông.

Trước hết, Hawkins muốn các nhà khoa học chấp nhận công trình của mình. Ông tổ chức một buổi tiệc vào hôm Giao Thừa. Ông cho đặt bàn ăn bên trong một trong những mô hình của mình. Các quan khách đều yêu thích những sáng tác của Hawkins.

# Multilingual Summaries

## 워터하우스 호킨스의 공룡

워터하우스 호킨스는 작업장을 하나 갖고 있었다. 그는 동물 모형들을 만들었는데 그의 가장 큰 계획은 실제 크기의 공룡 모형을 만드는 것이었다. 1853년 사람들은 공룡의 뼈를 발견했지만 공룡의 모습을 알고 있는 사람은 아무도 없었다. 호킨스는 어느 과학자에게 도움을 요청했고 그 과학자는 공룡과 현대 파충류의 뼈를 비교해 주었다.

호킨스는 공룡과 파충류의 뼈가 아주 유사하다는 점을 발견하고 공룡이 거대한 도마뱀 같이 생겼을 것이라고 생각했다. 그는 화석 뼈를 이용해 공룡의 크기를 어림잡아 실제 크기의 공룡 모형을 만들었다.

빅토리아 여왕과 알버트 왕자는 호킨스의 모형을 보고 감탄했다. 알버트 왕자는 그 공룡 모형을 자신의 새 박물관에 전시하고 싶어했다.

먼저 호킨스는 과학자들이 자신의 업적을 인정해 주길 바랬다. 그는 새해 전날 밤 파티를 열었는데 자신이 만든 공룡 모형 중 한 개의 내부에 저녁 식탁을 차렸다. 손님들은 호킨스의 작품을 아주 좋아했다.

## Cov Tsiaj Daisnausxauj (dinosaurs) Ntawm Waterhouse Hawkins

Waterhouse Hawkins muaj ib lub lab ua hauj lwm. Nws txua ib cov tsiaj coj los ua qauv piv txwv. Nws txoj hauj lwm loj tshaj plaws yog txua kom tau ib cov qauv ua luaj li cov tsiaj uas muaj siab. Thaum xyoo ib txhiab yim puas tsib caug peb, neeg tau nrhiav pom ib cov pob txha daisnausxauj. Tiam sis, tsis muaj leej twg uas paub tias ib tug daisnausxauj zoo li cas tiag tiag. Hawkins tau nug ib tug xib hwb kawm txog cov tsiaj ntawd pab nws. Tus xibhwm ntawd muaj cov pob txha daisnausxauj coj los piv nrog cov pob txha ntawm tej tsiaj niaj hnub niam no.

Hawkins pom tau tias cov pob txha ntawd muaj tsis zoo ib yam. Nws tau txiav txim siab tias daisnausxauj yuav tsum muaj tsis zoo li ib cov dev nab qa uas loj kawg li. Nws siv cov pob txha qub uas qhuav rau hauv av lawm coj los kuaj xyuas seb cov daisnausxauj ntawd tau luaj li cas tiag. Ces nws tseem ua tau ib cov qauv daisnausxauj uas luaj li thaum tiag.

Tus pob huabtais Queen Victoria thiab tub nom Prince Albert nyiam Hawkins cov qauv ntawd kawg. Prince Albert xav muab cov daisnausxauj ntawd rau sawv daws saib nyob rau hauv nws tsev khaws khoom qub uas nws txua tshiab.

Hawkins xav kom sawv daws lees nws txoj hauj lwm ntawd. Nws thiaj tau ua ib pluag mov noj hmo ua ntej xyoo tshiab. Nws tau teeb lub rooj noj mov rau hauv ib tug qauv ntawd. Nws cov qhua tau suyiam nws tej khoom uas nws tau tsim kawg.

# Mahalia Jackson
Student Edition pages 350–357

| Week at a Glance | Customize instruction every day for your English Language Learners. | | | | |
|---|---|---|---|---|---|
| | **Day 1** | **Day 2** | **Day 3** | **Day 4** | **Day 5** |
| **Teacher's Edition** | Use the ELL Notes that appear throughout each day of the lesson to support instruction and reading. | | | | |
| **ELL Poster 14** | • Assess Prior Knowledge<br>• Develop Concepts and Vocabulary | • Preteach Tested Vocabulary | • Music-inspired Art | • Musical Inspiration | • Monitor Progress |
| **ELL Teaching Guide** | • Picture It! Lesson, pp. 92–93<br>• Multilingual Summaries, pp. 96–98 | • ELL Reader Lesson, pp. 238–239 | • Vocabulary Activities and Word Cards, pp. 94–95<br>• Multilingual Summaries, pp. 96–98 | | |
| **ELL Readers** | • Reread *Dinosaur Time Line* | • Teach *Willie Dixon's Blues* | • Reread *Willie Dixon's Blues* and other texts to build fluency | | |
| **ELL and Transition Handbook** | Use the following as needed to support this week's instruction and to conduct alternative assessments:<br>• Phonics Transition Lessons<br>• Grammar Transition Lessons<br>• Assessment | | | | |

**Picture It!** Comprehension Lesson
## Main Idea and Details
Use this lesson to supplement or replace the skill lesson on pages 346–347 of the Teacher's Edition.

### Teach
Distribute copies of the Picture It! blackline master on page 93.
• Tell students they are going to read a paragraph about soul music. Point to the illustration that accompanies the text. Tell students that it will help them understand the text. Then read the paragraph aloud.
• Share the Skill Points (at right) with students.
• Ask: *What is the main idea of this paragraph?*

### Practice
Read aloud the directions on page 93. Have students read the paragraph, and then complete the graphic organizer. Have students keep their organizers for later reteaching.

**Answers for page 93:** *Main Idea:* Rhythm is an important part of soul music. *Details:* Possible answers: The drumbeat starts the rhythm. The bass builds on the rhythm. Even the singer must have rhythm.

> ## Skill Points
> ✓ The **main idea** is the most important idea in a paragraph. It usually comes at the beginning of the paragraph.
> ✓ **Details** are pieces of information that tell more about the main idea.

**Read** the paragraph. Then **complete** the chart.
- **Write** the main idea of the paragraph in the top box.
- **Write** three details that support the main idea in the boxes below.

## The Rhythm of Soul

Rhythm is an important part of soul music. A good drumbeat starts the rhythm. The bass builds on that rhythm. Then the guitar player creates a melody to go with it. Even the singer must have a good sense of rhythm. When people listen to soul music, they feel like dancing.

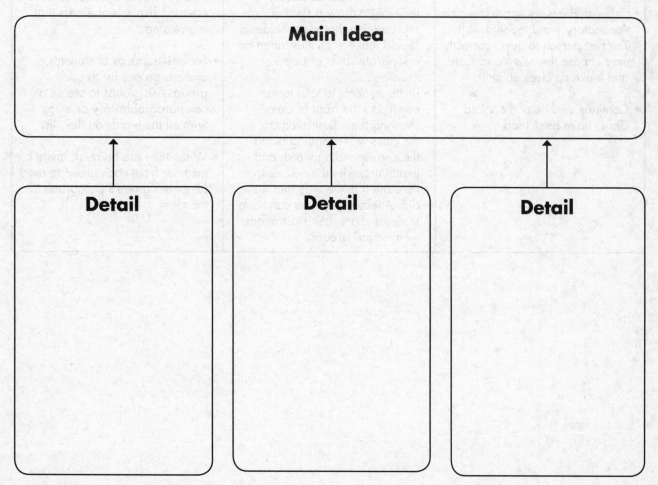

### Main Idea

### Detail

### Detail

### Detail

# Vocabulary Activities and Word Cards

Copy the Word Cards on page 95 as needed for the following activities.
Use the blank card for an additional word that you want to teach.
Also see suggestions for teaching vocabulary in the ELL and Transition Handbook.

| Poster Clues | Vocabulary Illustration | Word Association |
|---|---|---|
| • Distribute sets of Word Cards to students. Then, from your own set of Word Cards, have one student choose a card without letting the others see it.<br><br>• The student stands at the ELL Poster, points to the relevant area on it, and uses the information on the Poster to give hints about the vocabulary word.<br><br>• Other students try to guess which vocabulary word the student has. The first person to guess correctly may choose the next Word Card and make up clues about it.<br><br>• Continue until all of the Word Cards have been used. | • Create enough Word Cards so that you can give two or three cards to each student. Distribute the cards at random.<br><br>• Ask students to create a sketch, drawing, or symbol to illustrate their assigned words. For literal words such as *barber*, they can simply draw the person or thing named. For abstract ideas such as *released* or *slavery*, they might draw a symbol representing that idea. Students should make each illustration on a separate sheet of paper.<br><br>• Invite students to take turns coming to the front of class, showing their illustrations to the class while reading aloud the corresponding word, and explaining why they chose to illustrate it in the way that they did. Alternatively, you can have students share their illustrations within small groups. | • Tape a set of Word Cards to the board. Ask students to "free associate" words and phrases that come to mind when they think of each of the words. Under *barber*, for example, possible associations are *scissors, comb, haircut,* and so on. For *slavery,* students may be reminded of *the Civil War, Abraham Lincoln,* or *freedom.* List students' ideas under each card, creating five lists of words that are related.<br><br>• Form five groups of students, and assign one list to each group. Ask groups to create a one-paragraph story or essay with all the words on their list.<br><br>• When they are finished, invite a member from each group to read his or her group's paragraph to the class. |

**appreciate**

**barber**

**choir**

**released**

**religious**

**slavery**

**teenager**

# Multilingual Summaries

## English

## Mahalia Jackson

"Having the blues" is a way to describe feeling sad. Blues is also a kind of music. The blues started with slavery. Slaves sang about their sadness. Since then, there have been many great blues singers. Mahalia Jackson was a great blues singer.

Mahalia was born in New Orleans. When she was five years old, her mother died. Mahalia went to live with an aunt. She loved music. She wanted to sing like Bessie Smith, another great singer. Mahalia's aunt took her to church every Sunday. She heard gospel music there. Mahalia learned to love gospel music. It sounded like the blues.

Mahalia moved to Chicago. She joined a gospel group. Mahalia's singing became popular. She recorded albums. Martin Luther King, Jr., asked her to sing before he gave a famous speech. She had a powerful voice. Mahalia became the most famous gospel singer in the world.

## Spanish

## Mahalia Jackson

En inglés, "having the blues" es una manera de describir la tristeza. Los blues son también un tipo de música. Los blues comenzaron en la época de la esclavitud. Los esclavos cantaban sobre sus tristezas. Desde entonces, han habido muchos y grandes cantantes de blues. Mahalia Jackson fue una gran cantante de blues.

Mahalia nació en Nueva Orleáns. Cuando tenía cinco años, su madre murió. Mahalia se fue a vivir con una tía. Ella amaba la música. Quería cantar como Bessie Smith, otra gran cantante. La tía de Mahalia la llevaba a la iglesia todos los domingos. Ella escuchaba allí la música gospel. Mahalia aprendió a amar la música gospel. Esa música sonaba como los blues.

Mahalia se fue a vivir a Chicago. Se unió a un grupo de música gospel. Su manera de cantar se volvió popular. Grabó álbumes. Martin Luther King, Jr., le pidió que cantara antes de que él diera un discurso famoso. Ella tenía una voz potente. Mahalia se convirtió en la cantante de música gospel más famosa del mundo.

# Multilingual Summaries

## 瑪哈莉雅· 杰克森

英語裏"藍色"通常表示憂傷。有一種樂曲叫做藍調音樂，起源於黑人奴隸的歌唱，他們用音樂渲泄自己的悲傷。從那以後，出現過許多偉大的藍調歌唱家，瑪哈莉雅· 杰克森就是其中之一。

杰克森出生在新奧爾良，5歲時，媽媽就死了。她和姑姑住在一起。杰克森非常喜歡音樂，歌后貝西· 史密斯是她的偶像。每個星期天，姑姑都帶她去教堂。她在那聆聽福音音樂，漸漸地越來越喜歡，因為它聽起來和藍調音樂非常像。

杰克森後來到了芝加哥，成為福音團體的成員。她唱了許多有名的歌曲，錄了很多唱片。馬丁路德金發表著名演說前，還請她唱過歌。杰克森的嗓音很有穿透力，她是全世界最著名的福音歌唱家。

## Mahalia Jackson

Câu nói "Having the blues" là một cách diễn tả cảm giác buồn. "Blues" cũng là một loại nhạc. Nhạc blues bắt đầu từ thời nô lệ. Những người nô lệ hát về nỗi buồn của họ. Từ đó, có nhiều ca sĩ nhạc blues tài giỏi. Mahalia Jackson là một ca sĩ nhạc blues nổi bật.

Jackson sanh ở New Orleans. Khi cô lên năm, mẹ cô qua đời. Jackson đến ở với người cô. Cô bé yêu âm nhạc. Cô bé muốn hát như Bessie Smith, một ca sĩ xuất sắc khác. Cô của Mahalia dẫn cô đến nhà thờ vào mỗi Chủ Nhật. Cô bé nghe nhạc đạo ở đó. Mahalia bắt đầu yêu thích nhạc đạo. Nhạc này nghe giống như nhạc blues.

Mahalia dọn đến Chicago. Cô gia nhập một nhóm hát nhạc đạo. Tài ca hát của Mahalia được nhiều người ưa chuộng. Cô thu thanh vào đĩa hát. Martin Luther King, Jr. mời cô hát trước khi ông đọc bài diễn văn nổi tiếng. Cô có giọng hát ngân vang. Mahalia trở nên một ca sĩ nhạc đạo nổi tiếng nhất thế giới.

# Multilingual Summaries

## 마할리아 잭슨

'우울하다(blue)' 는 말은 마음이 울적한 것을 표현하는 한 가지 방법으로 블루스는 음악의 한 종류이기도 하다. 블루스는 노예 제도와 함께 시작되었다. 노예들은 자신들의 슬픈 처지를 노래로 불렀고 시간이 흘러 훌륭한 블루스 가수들이 많이 나왔다. 마할리아 잭슨도 그들 중 한 명이었다.

잭슨은 뉴올리언스에서 태어났다. 다섯 살 때 어머니가 돌아가시자 잭슨은 숙모와 함께 살았다. 그녀는 음악을 좋아해서 베시 스미스같은 훌륭한 가수처럼 노래를 하고 싶어했다. 마할리아의 숙모는 매주 일요일마다 그녀를 교회에 데려갔는데 그녀는 그곳에서 가스펠 뮤직을 듣고 가스펠을 무척 좋아하게 되었다. 그것은 블루스와 같은 느낌이었다.

마할리아는 시카고로 이사를 갔고 한 가스펠 단체에 가입했다. 그녀의 노래 솜씨가 유명해지자 음반 녹음을 했고 마틴 루터 킹 2세는 유명한 연설을 하기 전에 그녀에게 노래를 불러달라고 부탁하기도 했다. 그녀의 목소리에는 힘이 있었다. 곧 마할리아는 세계에서 가장 유명한 가스펠 가수가 되었다.

## Mahalia Jackson

Lus Miskas hais tias "having the blues" no txhais tau tias yus tsis zoo siab lossis ntxhov siab. Blues kuj yog ib yam nkauj thiab. Cov qhe pib hu cov nkauj blues ntawd. Txij thaum ntawd los, tau muaj coob tus neeg txawj hu nkauj blues zoo heev los. Mahalia Jackson yog ib tug uas txawj hu nkauj blues heev.

Jackson yug nyob rau New Orleans. Thaum nws muaj tsib xyoos, nws niam tau tuag lawm. Jackson tau mus nrog nws tu phauj nyob. Nws nyiam phee heev. Nws xav hu nkauj kom tau li Bessie Smith, ib tug ua hu nkauj zoo tshaj plaws thiab. Mahalia tus phauj coj nws mus tshawj (church) txhua hnub vas thiv. Nws tau mloog nkauj gospel ntawd. Mahalia tau los nyiam phee gospel heev. Yus hu cov nkauj ntawd muaj tsis zoo li cov nkauj blues.

Mahalia tsiv mus nyob rau Chicago. Nws tau mus hu nkauj nrog ib pab hu nkauj tshawj. Mahalia kev txawj hu nkauj pib nrov heev. Nws kaw tau ib co nkauj. Martin Luther King, Jr. nug nws kom nws pab tuaj hu nkauj ua ntej thaum nws yuav los hais lus rau sawvdaws. Nws lub suab muaj ceem heev. Mahalia tau los ua tus neeg hu nkauj gospel uas nto npe tshaj plaws thoob qab ntuj no.

# Special Effects in Film and Television

Student Edition pages 368–377

| Week at a Glance | Customize instruction every day for your English Language Learners. | | | | |
|---|---|---|---|---|---|
| | **Day 1** | **Day 2** | **Day 3** | **Day 4** | **Day 5** |
| **Teacher's Edition** | Use the ELL Notes that appear throughout each day of the lesson to support instruction and reading. | | | | |
| **ELL Poster 15** | • Assess Prior Knowledge<br>• Develop Concepts and Vocabulary | • Preteach Tested Vocabulary | • Storyboard Scenes | • Careers in Film and Television | • Monitor Progress |
| **ELL Teaching Guide** | • Picture It! Lesson, pp. 99–100<br>• Multilingual Summaries, pp. 103–105 | • ELL Reader Lesson, pp. 240–241 | • Vocabulary Activities and Word Cards, pp. 101–102<br>• Multilingual Summaries, pp. 103–105 | | |
| **ELL Readers** | • Reread *Willie Dixon's Blues* | • Teach *VActors: Virtual Actors on the Screen* | • Reread *VActors: Virtual Actors on the Screen* and other texts to build fluency | | |
| **ELL and Transition Handbook** | Use the following as needed to support this week's instruction and to conduct alternative assessments:<br>• Phonics Transition Lessons<br>• Grammar Transition Lessons<br>• Assessment | | | | |

**Picture It!** Comprehension Lesson
## Graphic Sources

Use this lesson to supplement or replace the skill lesson on pages 364–365 of the Teacher's Edition.

### Teach

Distribute copies of the Picture It! blackline master on page 100.
• Share the Skill Points (at right) with students.
• Point to the picture. Tell students that this is a graphic source.
• Ask students to make a guess about the topic of the reading, based on the picture.

### Practice

Read aloud the directions on page 100. Have students write their guess about the paragraph in the space provided. Then read the paragraph aloud. Discuss with students whether their predictions were correct. Then have them answer the questions that follow. Have students keep their work for later reteaching.

**Answers for page 100: 1.** Student responses will vary, but they should reflect what is shown in the picture. **2.** the use of makeup as a special effect **3.** mask, wig, makeup

> ### Skill Points
>
> ✓ **Graphic sources** are pictures, diagrams, maps, and time lines.
>
> ✓ A graphic source helps you to understand written text.
>
> ✓ Preview graphic sources before you read. Predict what the text is about, based on the graphic source.

**Look** at the picture. What do you think the paragraph is going to be about?
**1. Write** your guess.

_____

**Read** the paragraph. **Answer** the questions that follow.

# Making Faces

In film and television, makeup is a kind of special effect. It can totally change the way you look. It can even make a young man look old. Masks and wigs are part of the makeup department. These are the props that help actors "make faces."

**2.** What is this paragraph about?

_____

**3.** What items shown in the picture are also mentioned in the paragraph?

_____

# Vocabulary Activities and Word Cards

Copy the Word Cards on page 102 as needed for the following activities.
Use the blank cards for additional words that you want to teach.
Also see suggestions for teaching vocabulary in the ELL and Transition Handbook.

| Word Parts | Scrambled Sentences | Guess on Time |
|---|---|---|
| • Divide students into pairs. Create a set of Word Cards for each pair, omitting *miniature*. Cut the cards as follows: *back/ ground, land/scape, pre/historic, re/assembled*. Mix up the word parts and give a set to each pair. | • Form groups of students, and give each group one Word Card. | • Invite two players to the front of the class. Give one player a Word Card. Tell that player to look at the card carefully so that the other player can't see it. |
| • Explain to students that the vocabulary words have been divided to show two of their parts. Ask them to work with their partners to reassemble each Word Card. | • Tell groups to create sentences with their assigned words. Provide each group with index cards, and have the groups write each word of the sentence (except the word on the Word Card) on separate index cards. | • When you say *Go*, the player with the card gives clues to the other player about the word on the card. The clues can be single words, phrases, or whole sentences. They may not include any form of the word itself. |
| • After students have reassembled their words, lead the class in a discussion about them. Ask: *Which of these are compound words? (background, landscape) What are the two words in each compound word? Which of the words have prefixes? What are they? (pre-, re-) Can you think of other words that begin with these prefixes?* (Possible answers: *preschool, restate)* | • Invite a group to put all its cards in scrambled order. Challenge the class to arrange the cards in the correct order. The group that created the sentence can verify when it has been correctly reassembled. | • Time the students. When the player correctly guesses the word, write the time on the board along with the pair's names. You may set a time limit for guessing. |
| • Ask students to use one or more of the words in a sentence, until all of the words are used. | • Continue in this way until all groups have presented their scrambled sentences to the class. You can turn the activity into a game by giving a point to the team that correctly assembles each sentence. | • Invite other pairs of students to play additional rounds. Record each pair's time. The students who hint and guess the assigned word in the least amount of time are the winners. |

background

landscape

miniature

prehistoric

reassembled

# Multilingual Summaries

## Special Effects in Film and Television

Special effects help movies and television shows seem real. One special effect is to create imaginary landscapes. To do this, technicians make small models of landscapes.

First, the script or director describes a setting. Next, the special effects team decides how to build it. The team makes a small model of the scene. The team makes changes to the small model to make it more realistic. Then, the team makes a full-sized model.

This model is sprayed with foam to make the surface smooth. Then the model is cut into pieces and reassembled in the studio. Technicians use pictures of the small model as a guide. In the studio, little trees, rocks, and plants are added. The team makes the landscape look as real as possible. Everything is painted in detail. When the scene is filmed, the landscape will seem real to the audience.

## Efectos especiales en el cine y la televisión

Los efectos especiales permiten que las películas y los programas de televisión parezcan reales. Uno de los efectos especiales es hacer paisajes imaginarios. Para lograr esto, los técnicos hacen modelos pequeños de paisajes.

Primero, el guionista o director describe una escena. Después, el equipo de efectos especiales decide cómo construirla. El equipo hace un modelo pequeño de la escena. Hacen cambios al pequeño modelo para hacerlo más realista. Después, el equipo hace un modelo de tamaño natural.

El modelo es rociado con espuma para hacer la superficie más suave. Luego, se corta en pedazos y es reensamblada en el estudio. Los técnicos usan fotos del modelo pequeño como guía. En el estudio, se agregan árboles pequeños, rocas y plantas. El equipo hace que el paisaje parezca lo más real posible. Todo se pinta hasta en los más mínimos detalles. Cuando se filma la escena, el paisaje les parecerá real a los espectadores.

# Multilingual Summaries

## 電影電視的特效

特效讓電影和電視更加真實。做特效首先要有假想的場景。為此，技術人員要做許多縮小的場景模型。

首先，編劇或導演會描述場景，接著特效工作人員商談如何建造。他們先做一個縮小模型，然後做一些改動，讓它看上去更加真實。最後工作人員才會製做實物大小的模型。

模型表面要噴上泡沫，使它平滑。接著場景分成幾個部分，在攝影棚裏重新組裝。技術人員還要不時參照小模型照片。他們在攝影棚里加上小樹、小石頭和其它植物，讓場景儘量與真的一模一樣。每個地方都要仔細繪製。觀眾看到影片時，就會覺得和真的一樣。

## Các Kỹ Thuật Ấn Tượng Đặc Biệt Trong Phim Ảnh và Truyền Hình

Các kỹ thuật ấn tượng đặc biệt giúp cho phim và các chương trình truyền hình có vẻ như thật. Một kỹ thuật ấn tượng đặc biệt là tạo ra những phong cảnh tưởng tượng. Để làm điều này, các kỹ thuật viên làm những mô hình nhỏ của các phong cảnh này.

Đầu tiên, kịch bản hoặc nhà đạo diễn miêu tả một khung cảnh. Kế đến, đội chuyên trách về các kỹ thuật ấn tượng đặc biệt sẽ quyết định cách xây nên khung cảnh này. Đội này sẽ làm một mô hình nhỏ về cảnh này. Họ thay đổi mô hình nhỏ này để nó trông giống như thật hơn. Rồi đội này sẽ làm một mô hình với kích thước như thật.

Mô hình này được phủ bằng một chất bọt để làm cho bề mặt được trơn phẳng. Rồi cảnh này được cắt ra làm nhiều miếng và được ráp lại ở phim trường. Các kỹ thuật viên dùng những bức ảnh của mô hình nhỏ làm bản chỉ dẫn. Trong phim trường, các cây cối nhỏ, đá, và thảo mộc được thêm vào. Đội này làm phong cảnh trông càng giống như thật càng tốt. Mọi thứ được sơn phết thật chi tiết. Khi cảnh này lên phim, phong cảnh này sẽ trông giống như thật đối với khán giả.

# Multilingual Summaries

## Korean

## 영화와 텔레비전의 특수 효과

특수 효과는 영화와 텔레비전의 장면이 실제처럼 보일 수 있도록 해 준다. 특수 효과 중의 하나는 가상 풍경을 만드는 것으로 기술자들은 먼저 작은 풍경 모형을 만든다.

먼저 대본이나 감독이 배경을 결정한다. 그 다음으로 특수 효과팀이 그 배경을 어떻게 만들 지 결정하고 작은 장면 모형을 만든다. 이들은 좀더 현실감 있도록 모형에 변화를 준다. 그리고 나서 실제 크기의 모형을 만들게 된다.

이 모형에 거품을 뿌려 표면을 매끄럽게 만든 다음 장면을 조각조각으로 나누고 스튜디오에서 재조립한다. 이때 기술자들은 작은 모형 그림을 참고한다. 스튜디오에서는 작은 나무와 바위, 그리고 식물을 추가한다. 특수 효과팀은 풍경을 최대한 실제처럼 보이도록 만들며 모든 것에 세밀하게 색을 입힌다. 장면이 촬영되면 관객들은 실제 풍경인 것처럼 착각하게 될 것이다.

## Hmong

## Special Effects Nyob Hauv
## Moosvim thiab Tisvis

Special effects pab moosvim thiab tisvis kom tej yeeb yam ntawd ntxim muaj tiag. Ib qhov special effect yog kev tsim kom ntxim li muaj teb muaj chaws. Kom ua li ntawd, cov neeg technicians txua ib cov qauv teb chaws me me.

Ua ntej tshaj plaws, daim ntawv nyeem lossis tus coj piav kom tau se bib qhov chaws zoo li cas. Ces, pab neeg ua special effects txiav txim siab ua kom tau. Pab neeg ua hauj lwm uake los txua kom tau ib tug qauv ntawm qhov chaws ntawd. Lawm hloov tej yam me me kom ua ntxim li muaj tiag. Ces pab neeg ua hauj lwm uake mam li txua ib tug qauv loj zoo li teb chaws tiag.

Ces lawv mam li tsuag foam rau tus qauv ntawd kom tej nplaim khoom ntawd yaig heev. Ces lawv muab tus qauv loj ntawd txiav ua tej daim tej daim kom thiab li rov muab tso tau uake hauv hoom thaij duab. Cov neeg technician siv cov duab ntawm tus qauv me me los pab coj lawv kev. Hauv hoom thaij duab, lawv mam li ntxiv menyuam ntoo, pobzeb thiab pab ntoo rau. Pab neeg ua hauj lwm uake ua kom tus qauv ntawd txim li muaj tiag kom zoo li zoo tau. Lawv muab txhua yam tha kom zoo zoo. Thaum thaij duab, tus qauv ntawd thiaj li zoo li muaj tseeb tiag tiag.

# Weslandia
Student Edition pages 396–407

| **Week at a Glance** | Customize instruction every day for your English Language Learners. | | | | |
|---|---|---|---|---|---|
| | **Day 1** | **Day 2** | **Day 3** | **Day 4** | **Day 5** |
| **Teacher's Edition** | Use the ELL Notes that appear throughout each day of the lesson to support instruction and reading. | | | | |
| **ELL Poster 16** | • Assess Prior Knowledge<br>• Develop Concepts and Vocabulary | • Preteach Tested Vocabulary | • Design a Game | • Urban Planning | • Monitor Progress |
| **ELL Teaching Guide** | • Picture It! Lesson, pp. 106–107<br>• Multilingual Summaries, pp. 110–112 | • ELL Reader Lesson, pp. 242–243 | • Vocabulary Activities and Word Cards, pp. 108–109<br>• Multilingual Summaries, pp. 110–112 | | |
| **ELL Readers** | • Reread *VActors: Virtual Actors on the Screen* | • Teach *The Anasazi* | • Reread *The Anasazi* and other texts to build fluency | | |
| **ELL and Transition Handbook** | Use the following as needed to support this week's instruction and to conduct alternative assessments:<br>• Phonics Transition Lessons<br>• Grammar Transition Lessons<br>• Assessment | | | | |

## Picture It! Comprehension Lesson
# Draw Conclusions

Use this lesson to supplement or replace the skill lesson on pages 392–393 of the Teacher's Edition.

### Teach

Distribute copies of the Picture It! blackline master on page 107.
• Tell students to look at the picture and read the title. Have them guess what the story might be about.
• Share the Skill Points (at right) with students.
• Read the story aloud. Ask: *What is going on in this story? What makes you think so?*

### Practice

Read aloud the directions on page 107. Have students read the story and then complete the graphic organizer. Have students keep their organizers for later reteaching.

**Answers for page 107:** Answers may vary. Possible answers:
*Detail:* Veronique is at a starting line. *Detail:* Somebody says "Ready! Set! Go!" *What I Know:* That's what people say at a race. *Conclusion:* Veronique must be in a race.

### Skill Points

✓ When you **draw conclusions**, you combine what you know with details in the text.

✓ A **conclusion** is a decision you make after combining your knowledge with details from the text.

**Read** the story. Then fill in the four boxes that follow to show what the story is about.

- **Write** details from the text in the first two boxes.
- **Write** something from your own knowledge in the third box.
- **Write** a conclusion telling what the story is about in the fourth box.

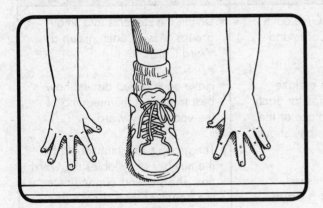

## The Moment of Truth

Veronique stood at the starting line.
She had prepared for this moment
all summer.

"Ready!" She knelt down.

"Set!" She straightened out her back leg.

"Go!" At the sound of the horn,
Veronique took off like a rocket.

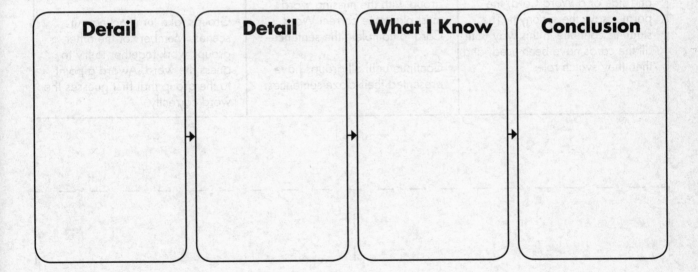

| Detail | Detail | What I Know | Conclusion |
|--------|--------|-------------|------------|

# Vocabulary Activities and Word Cards

Copy the Word Cards on page 109 as needed for the following activities.
Use the blank cards for additional words that you want to teach.
Also see suggestions for teaching vocabulary in the ELL and Transition Handbook.

| Synonyms | Cloze Sentences | Charades |
|---|---|---|
| • Write the following words on the board: *complicated, culture, encouraged, escaping, jealousy, mistakes, plan, fluttering.*<br><br>• Give pairs of students sets of Word Cards. Tell students to write a synonym from the board on the back of the appropriate Word Card.<br><br>• Have partners use the Word Cards to test their memories. A student shows his or her partner one side of a Word Card; the partner says the synonym. The students continue in this way until all the cards have been used, and then they switch roles. | • Form four groups. Give each group two Word Cards and paper strips.<br><br>• Tell groups to write a cloze sentence on the strips for each of their words. In place of the vocabulary words, they should leave blank lines.<br><br>• When they have finished, redistribute the Word Cards. Invite each group to take turns displaying the sentences. The group with the missing word must place the correct Word Card to complete the sentence.<br><br>• Continue until all groups have presented their cloze sentences. | • Divide the students into small groups. Assign each group a Word Card.<br><br>• Have each group discuss how best to act out the meaning of the vocabulary word.<br><br>• The group's first hint should be the number of syllables the word has. The students can indicate this however they choose (for example, clapping or holding up fingers).<br><br>• Groups take turns acting out scenes. Members of the other groups work together to try to guess the word. Award a point to the group that first guesses the word correctly. |

**blunders**

**civilization**

**complex**

**envy**

**fleeing**

**inspired**

**rustling**

**strategy**

# Multilingual Summaries

## Weslandia

Wesley was different. The other children did not like him. They did not like the same things. He did not have any friends. The other children chased Wesley.

One summer, Wesley decided to grow his own garden. He decided to found his own civilization. He would do everything his way. He called his civilization Weslandia. Soon his plants were taller than he was. Wesley ate their fruit and roots. He used their bark and fibers to make clothes.

After that, the neighborhood children who had teased Wesley wanted to be his friends. Wesley invented new games. The other children came to play with him. Wesley used the sun to tell time. He even made up his own language and alphabet. He went back to school with many friends.

## Weslandia

Wesley era diferente. A los otros niños no les gustaba Wesley. No les gustaban las mismas cosas. Él no tenía amigos. Los otros niños lo perseguían para burlarse.

Un verano, Wesley decidió plantar su propio jardín. Decidió fundar su propia civilización. Haría todo a su manera. Llamó a su civilización Weslandia. Muy pronto, sus plantas eran más altas que él. Wesley se comió sus frutos y raíces. También usó sus cortezas y fibras para hacer ropa.

Después de esto, los niños del barrio que se habían burlado de él querían ser sus amigos. Wesley inventó nuevos juegos. Los niños empezaron a jugar con él. Wesley usaba el Sol para saber qué hora era. Hasta inventó su propio lenguaje y alfabeto. Regresó a la escuela con muchos amigos.

# Multilingual Summaries

## 威斯利王國

　　威斯利是個異類，其他小孩都不喜歡他，他們不喜歡像威斯利那樣的怪人。威斯利沒有朋友，大家都排斥他。

　　某年夏天，威斯利決定開墾一個花園，他要創造一個屬於自己的文明，用自己喜歡的方式過日子，他管這個文明世界叫做「威斯利王國」。很快地，他在花園裡種的植物已經長得比他高了，威斯利吃這些植物的果實和根，還用樹皮和纖維來做衣服。

　　以前曾經嘲笑過威斯利的鄰居小孩看到他的花園後，都想要和他做朋友了。威斯利發明了新遊戲，其他小孩覺得很有趣也跑來跟他玩。威斯利很聰明會利用太陽來知道時間，他甚至創造了自己的語言和文字。後來，威斯利再回到學校的時候，身邊多了好多朋友。

## Weslandia

Wesley khác thường. Những đứa trẻ khác không thích cậu bé. Chúng không có cùng sở thích. Cậu không có bạn. Những đứa trẻ khác rượt đuổi Wesley.

Vào một mùa hè, Wesley quyết định làm một mảnh vườn riêng cho mình. Cậu quyết định thành lập một nền văn minh của riêng mình. Cậu sẽ làm mọi điều theo cách của mình. Cậu gọi nền văn minh của cậu là Weslandia. Không bao lâu các cây cối trong vườn cao hơn cậu. Wesley ăn trái cây và rễ của những cây đó. Cậu dùng vỏ cây và chất sợi trong cây để làm quần áo.

Sau đó, các đứa trẻ trong khu phố đã từng trêu ghẹo Wesley lại muốn làm bạn với cậu. Wesley phát minh những trò chơi mới. Các đứa trẻ khác đến chơi với cậu. Wesley dùng mặt trời để biết giờ giấc. Cậu bé thậm chí còn tạo ra mẫu tự và ngôn ngữ riêng. Cậu bé trở lại trường học có được nhiều bạn.

# Multilingual Summaries

## 웨슬랜디아

웨슬리는 특별하다. 그 점 때문에 다른 아이들은 그를 싫어한다. 그들은 서로 다른 것을 좋아한다. 아이들은 아무 친구도 없는 웨슬리를 뒤쫓아 다닌다.

어느 여름날 웨슬리는 자기만의 정원과 자기만의 세계를 만들기로 마음먹는다. 무엇이든 자기 마음대로 할 생각이었다. 그는 자기만의 세계를 웨슬랜디아라고 이름 붙인다. 정원에서 곧 웨슬리가 심은 식물들이 그보다 더 크게 자란다. 그는 정원에서 자란 과일과 식물 뿌리를 먹으며 나무껍질과 섬유로 옷을 만든다.

그러자 웨슬리를 괴롭혔던 주변의 아이들이 그와 친구가 되고 싶어한다. 웨슬리가 새로운 게임을 만들어내자 다른 아이들도 와서 함께 어울려 논다. 웨슬리는 시간을 알아보는데 해를 이용하고 자기만의 언어와 알파벳까지 만들어낸다. 결국 그는 많은 친구들과 함께 학교로 돌아간다.

## Wesley Thaj Av

Wesley yog ib tug txawv. Lwm cov menyuam tsis nyiam nws. Lawv tsis nyiam tej yam Wesley nyiam. Nws tsis muaj cov phoojywg. Luag lwm cov menyuam caum Wesley.

Muaj ib lub caij ntuj sov, Wesley txiav txim siab pib nws ib lub vaj. Nws txiav txim siab pib nws ib lub teb lub chaws. Txhua yam nws yuav ua yuav yog raws li nws lub siab nyiam. Nws tis ib lub npe rau nws lub teb lub chaws hu ua "Wesley Thaj Av". Tsis ntev tom qab, nws cov zaub siab tshaj nws. Wesley noj nws cov txiv ntoo thiab lawv cov cag. Nws siv cov tawv ntoo kom ua khaubncaws.

Tom qab ntawd cov menyuam uas tau thuam Wesley xav ua nws ib tug phoojywg. Wesley tau tsim tej kev ua si tshiab. Luag lwm cov menyuam twb tuaj nrog nws ua si. Wesley tau siv lub hnub kom paub saib pestsawg moo lawm. Nws twb tau tsim nws ib yam lus thiab cov tsiaj ntawv tshiab. Nws rov qab mus tom lub tsev kawm ntawv thiaj muaj cov phooj ywg coob.

# Stretching Ourselves  Student Edition pages 416–431

| Week at a Glance | Customize instruction every day for your English Language Learners. | | | | |
|---|---|---|---|---|---|
| | **Day 1** | **Day 2** | **Day 3** | **Day 4** | **Day 5** |
| **Teacher's Edition** | Use the ELL Notes that appear throughout each day of the lesson to support instruction and reading. | | | | |
| **ELL Poster 17** | • Assess Prior Knowledge<br>• Develop Concepts and Vocabulary | • Preteach Tested Vocabulary | • Who/What Is It? | • Interview | • Monitor Progress |
| **ELL Teaching Guide** | • Picture It! Lesson, pp. 113–114<br>• Multilingual Summaries, pp. 117–119 | • ELL Reader Lesson, pp. 244–245 | • Vocabulary Activities and Word Cards, pp. 115–116<br>• Multilingual Summaries, pp. 117–119 | | |
| **ELL Readers** | • Reread *The Anasazi* | • Teach *Strength of Spirit* | • Reread *Strength of Spirit* and other texts to build fluency | | |
| **ELL and Transition Handbook** | Use the following as needed to support this week's instruction and to conduct alternative assessments:<br>• Phonics Transition Lessons<br>• Grammar Transition Lessons<br>• Assessment | | | | |

**Picture It!** Comprehension Lesson

# Generalize

Use this lesson to supplement or replace the skill lesson on pages 412–413 of the Teacher's Edition.

## Teach

Distribute copies of the Picture It! blackline master on page 114.
• Share the Skill Points (at right) with students.
• Tell students they are going to read about physical therapy. Explain that physical therapists help people regain their strength and mobility after injuries or illnesses. Then read the paragraph aloud.
• Ask: *Who needs the help of a physical therapist?* (aging people, people recovering from injury or illness, people with physical problems)

## Practice

Read aloud the directions on page 114. Have students read the paragraph and then fill in the graphic organizer with a generalization about why physical therapy is a growing field.

**Answers for page 114:** Possible answers: *Generalization:* Medicine is improving, so more people can benefit from physical therapy. *Details:* People are living longer. People are surviving serious illnesses and injuries. People are more careful about their health.

> ### Skill Points
> ✓ A **generalization** may not be true all of the time, but it is true most of the time.
> ✓ A good generalization uses details and examples for support.

**Read** the paragraph. Then **complete** the graphic organizer with a general statement about why physical therapy is a growing field.

- **Write** one detail from the paragraph in each of the small boxes.
- **Write** a generalization that these details support in the top box.

## Physical Therapy: A Growing Medical Field

More and more people are visiting physical therapists today. Why? There are several reasons. First, people are living longer. People need more help staying healthy as they age. Second, doctors keep getting better at saving lives. The people they save need help recovering from their injuries or illnesses. Finally, people in general are more careful about their health. Instead of ignoring problems, people get help. All of these changes are good, and all of them mean more jobs for physical therapists.

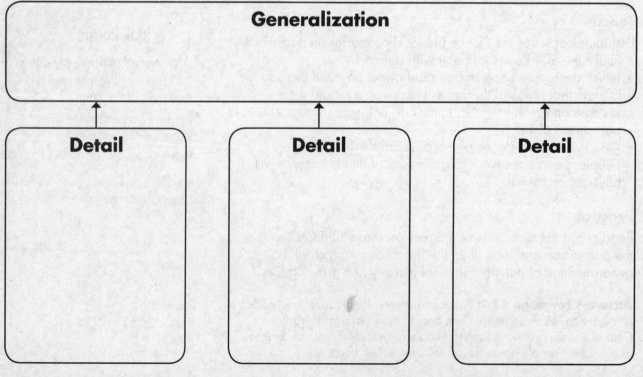

## Generalization

| Detail | Detail | Detail |

# Vocabulary Activities and Word Cards

Copy the Word Cards on page 116 as needed for the following activities.
Use the blank cards for additional words that you want to teach.
Also see suggestions for teaching vocabulary in the ELL and Transition Handbook.

| Fishing Game | Parts of Speech | Poster Clues |
|---|---|---|
| • Use one or more sets of Word Cards. Attach a metal paper clip to each card. Put the words in a bucket. Then tie a string to a short stick and a magnet at the end of the string to make a "fishing pole." <br><br>• Have students take turns "fishing" for words. When they "catch" a word, students should make a sentence using that word. If they use the word correctly in a sentence, they keep the "fish." If they cannot, they must return the word to the bucket. The student who has the most "fish" at the end of the game wins. | • Form groups of students. Give each group a set of Word Cards. <br><br>• Ask groups to sort their Word Cards into two categories: nouns and adjectives. Give students access to dictionaries for help. <br><br>• On the board, write the headings *Nouns* and *Adjectives*. Invite members from each group to tape cards to the board under the correct heading. As they do so, encourage the students to supply sentences showing how the words are used. | • Distribute sets of Word Cards to students. Then, from your own set of Word Cards, have one student choose a card without letting the others see it. <br><br>• The student stands at the ELL Poster, points to the relevant area on it, and uses the information on the Poster to give hints about the vocabulary word. <br><br>• Other students try to guess which vocabulary word the student has. The first person to guess correctly may choose the next Word Card and make up clues about it. <br><br>• Continue until all of the words have been used. |

# abdomen

# artificial

# gait

# handicapped

# therapist

# wheelchair

# Multilingual Summaries

English

## Stretching Ourselves

Emily has cerebral palsy (CP). She needs help stretching her muscles. Her leg muscles are tight, so she doesn't move easily. She goes to a physical therapist for exercises.

At school, Emily is in a special class with Nic. He has CP too. He uses a wheelchair, and he cannot speak well. Nic uses a special computer that talks. Nic goes to swimming class.

Tanner wants to be a football player. He has mild CP. Many people do not notice that he walks with a limp. His left arm is weak, so he exercises it.

Children with CP work hard. They like to do the same things that other children do.

Spanish

## Estirarnos

Emily tiene parálisis cerebral. Necesita ayuda para estirar sus músculos. Los músculos de sus piernas están muy tensos y no los puede mover fácilmente. Ella va a ver a un fisioterapeuta para hacer ejercicios.

En la escuela, Emily está con Nic en una clase especial. Él también tiene parálisis cerebral. Él usa una silla de ruedas, y no puede hablar bien. Nic usa una computadora especial que habla. Nic va a clases de natación.

Tanner quiere ser jugador de fútbol americano. Él tiene una parálisis moderada. Mucha gente no se da cuenta de que él cojea. Su brazo izquierdo es débil, por eso él lo ejercita.

Los niños con parálisis cerebral se esfuerzan mucho. A ellos les gusta hacer las mismas cosas que los otros niños hacen.

# Multilingual Summaries

## 活出自己

艾蜜莉得了腦性麻痺，需要別人幫她伸展肌肉。她的腿部肌肉緊繃，行動不便。她需要去物理治療師那裡做運動。

在學校裡，艾蜜莉和尼克是特別班的同學，尼克也有腦性麻痺，他坐輪椅，講話也不清楚，他用一台會說話的電腦和別人溝通，尼克還會去上游泳課。

坦納想當足球選手，不過他有輕微的腦性麻痺，走路有點跛，但大部分的人都不會注意到這個。他的左臂沒什麼力氣，所以必須時常鍛鍊。

有腦性麻痺的小朋友都很認真地生活著，其他小朋友能做的事，他們希望自己也能做到。

## Vươn Duỗi Thân Mình

Emily bị bệnh tê liệt não (CP). Cô bé cần được giúp để vươn duỗi các cơ bắp của mình. Các cơ bắp chân của cô bị sơ cứng, vì vậy cô không cử động được dễ dàng. Cô ấy đi đến một chuyên viên vật lý trị liệu để tập thể dục.

Ở trường, Emily ở trong một lớp đặc biệt với Nic. Cậu bé cũng bị CP. Cậu phải dùng xe lăn, và không nói chuyện được rõ ràng. Nic dùng một máy vi tính đặc biệt biết nói. Nic đi học bơi.

Tanner muốn là một cầu thủ chơi bóng bầu dục. Cậu bé bị CP nhẹ. Nhiều người không thấy là cậu đi hơi khập khiễng. Cánh tay trái của cậu bị yếu, vì vậy cậu phải tập thể dục cho cánh tay này.

Các trẻ em bị CP cố gắng nhiều hơn. Các em thích làm những công việc giống như những đứa trẻ khác.

# Multilingual Summaries

## 팔다리 뻗기

에밀리에게는 뇌성마비 증세가 있다. 그녀는 다리를 뻗을 때 다른 사람의 도움이 필요하다. 다리 근육이 굳어 있어 쉽게 움직이지 못하기 때문이다. 그래서 물리치료사와 함께 운동을 한다.

학교에서 에밀리는 닉과 함께 특수반에 속해 있다. 닉에게도 뇌성마비 증세가 있다. 그는 휠체어를 타고 다니는데 말을 잘 하지 못해 말하는 특수 컴퓨터를 사용하며 수영 수업을 듣는다.

축구 선수가 되고 싶어하는 태너에게는 가벼운 뇌성마비 증세가 있는데 대부분의 사람들은 그가 발을 저는 것을 눈치채지 못한다. 태너는 왼쪽 팔이 약해서 왼쪽 팔 운동을 한다.

뇌성마비 증세가 있는 아이들은 운동을 열심히 하며 다른 아이들이 하는 것과 같은 것들을 하고 싶어한다.

## Ncab Peb Tus Kheej

Emily mob caws tes taw. Nws toob kas(n) kev pab ncab nws thooj nqaij leeg. Nws cov nqaij leeg ceev ceev thiaj tsis yoojyim ua zog. Nws mus tom ib tug thaj maum, tus thaj maum pab nws cov nqaij leeg kom muaj zog.

Thaum Emily thiab Nic mus kawm ntawv, nkawd nyob hauv ib hoob kawm ua ke. Nic kuj muaj mob caws tes taw. Nic siv ib lub rooj zaum uas muaj cov lub log, Nic kij hais lus tsis tau zoo. Nic mus kawm ua luam dej.

Tanner xav ua ib tug kws ua si football. Nws mob caws tes taw tsis tshua ntau. Neeg feem coob tsis pom nws mus kev ib dhees rau ib dhees. Nws sab caj npab laug tsis muaj zog ntau, nws thiaj siv caj npab ntawd kom tau zog ntxiv.

Cov menyuam uas mob caws tes taw ua haujlwm nquag. Lawv kuj nyiam mus ua si zoo li lwm cov.

# Exploding Ants
Student Edition pages 440–451

| Week at a Glance | Customize instruction every day for your English Language Learners. | | | | |
|---|---|---|---|---|---|
| | **Day 1** | **Day 2** | **Day 3** | **Day 4** | **Day 5** |
| **Teacher's Edition** | Use the ELL Notes that appear throughout each day of the lesson to support instruction and reading. | | | | |
| **ELL Poster 18** | • Assess Prior Knowledge<br>• Develop Concepts and Vocabulary | • Preteach Tested Vocabulary | • Animal Guessing Game | • Food Chains | • Monitor Progress |
| **ELL Teaching Guide** | • Picture It! Lesson, pp. 120–121<br>• Multilingual Summaries, pp. 124–126 | • ELL Reader Lesson, pp. 246–247 | • Vocabulary Activities and Word Cards, pp. 122–123<br>• Multilingual Summaries, pp. 124–126 | | |
| **ELL Readers** | • Reread *Strength of Spirit* | • Teach *Surprising Insects Magazine* | • Reread *Surprising Insects Magazine* and other texts to build fluency | | |
| **ELL and Transition Handbook** | Use the following as needed to support this week's instruction and to conduct alternative assessments:<br>• Phonics Transition Lessons<br>• Grammar Transition Lessons<br>• Assessment | | | | |

**Picture It!** Comprehension Lesson
## Graphic Sources

Use this lesson to supplement or replace the skill lesson on pages 436–437 of the Teacher's Edition.

### Teach

Distribute copies of the Picture It! blackline master on page 121.
• Share the Skill Points (at right) with students.
• Point to the graphic. Ask students what they think the paragraph is going to be about, based on the diagram.
• Tell students they are going to label the diagram with words from the paragraph. Then read the paragraph aloud.

### Practice

Read aloud the directions on page 121. Remind students to look at the diagram as they read. Have them look for words in the passage that they can use to complete the diagram. Then have them label the diagram. Have students keep their diagrams for later reteaching.

**Answers for page 121:** Students should label the diagram with these words, starting at the top and going in a clockwise direction: *eggs, caterpillar, pupa, butterfly.*

### Skill Points

✓ **Graphic sources** include pictures, diagrams, maps, and time lines.

✓ A graphic source helps you to understand written text.

✓ Preview graphic sources before you read. Predict what the text is about, based on the graphic source.

Name _____

**Read** the paragraph and **study** the diagram. **Label** the diagram using information from the paragraph.

# Metamorphosis

The life cycle of a butterfly starts with an egg. A caterpillar hatches from the egg. The caterpillar turns into a pupa. When the pupa becomes an adult butterfly, it emerges transformed from its protective cocoon. This stage of the life cycle is known as *metamorphosis*. Later, the female butterfly will lay eggs, and the whole cycle starts again.

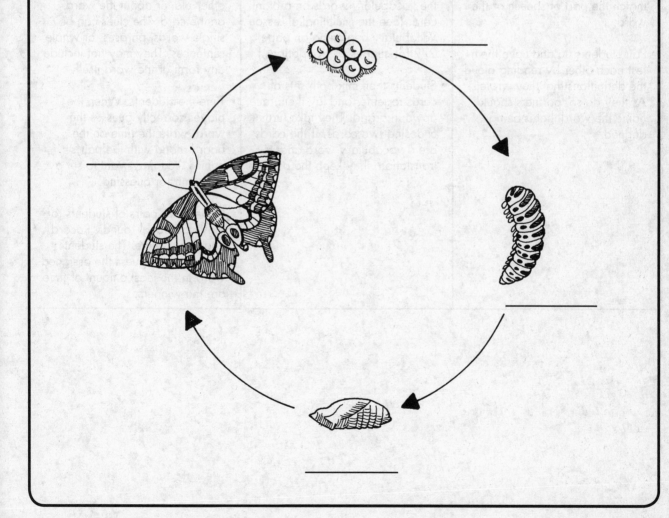

# Vocabulary Activities and Word Cards

Copy the Word Cards on page 123 as needed for the following activities.
Use the blank cards for additional words that you want to teach.
Also see suggestions for teaching vocabulary in the ELL and Transition Handbook.

| Definitions | Home Language Concentration | Guess on Time |
|---|---|---|
| • Distribute a set of Word Cards to each student, and provide dictionaries for classroom use.<br><br>• Tell students to write definitions for the vocabulary words on the back of the cards. Remind students that the definition must match the part of speech of the word.<br><br>• Pair students up and have them test each other by reading aloud the definitions that they wrote. As they do so, partners should name the word that is being defined. | • Pair students who have writing fluency in the same home language. Give them a set of Word Cards and an equal number of blank cards.<br><br>• Have pairs write a home language translation for each of the vocabulary words on a blank card. (See the Multilingual Lesson Vocabulary beginning on page 272 for suggested translations.)<br><br>• Students then mix both sets of cards together and lay them face down in a grid. They take turns choosing two cards. If the cards are a vocabulary word and its translation, they keep the pair. | • Invite two players to the front of the class. Give one player a Word Card. Tell that player to look at the card carefully so that the other player can't see it.<br><br>• When you say *Go,* the player with the card gives clues to the other player about the word on the card. The clues can be single words, phrases, or whole sentences. They may not include any form of the word itself.<br><br>• Time the students. When the player correctly guesses the word, write the time on the board along with the pair's names. You may want to set a time limit for guessing.<br><br>• Invite other pairs of students to play additional rounds. Record each pair's time. The students who hint and guess the assigned word in the least amount of time are the winners. |

**critical**

**enables**

**mucus**

**scarce**

**specialize**

**sterile**

# Multilingual Summaries

## Exploding Ants

Animals do things that seem gross. They eat things that people would not eat. They live in all kinds of places, even inside other animals. They use their bodies in strange ways.

Honey ants swell up and keep honey in their bodies. They feed other ants with it. Some soldier ants explode if they are attacked. They spray chemicals that kill the attacker.

Owls eat small animals whole. Later, they spit out pellets of bones and fur. Snakes also eat their food whole. Their mouths can expand. A snake can eat something bigger than its own head.

**Spanish**

## Hormigas que explotan

Algunos animales hacen cosas que parecen repugnantes. Comen cosas que las personas no comerían. Viven en todo tipo de lugares, hasta dentro de otros animales. Otros usan sus cuerpos de maneras muy extrañas.

Las hormigas de miel se hinchan y mantienen miel en sus cuerpos. Con esta miel alimentan a otras hormigas. Algunas hormigas soldado explotan si son atacadas. Ellas lanzan químicos que matan al atacante.

Los búhos se comen enteros a los pequeños animales. Después arrojan bolas con los huesos y la piel. Las serpientes también se comen los animales enteros. Su boca se puede expandir. Una serpiente puede comerse algo más grande que su propia cabeza.

# Multilingual Summaries

## 會爆炸的螞蟻

動物會做一些看起來很噁心的事情，他們吃人類不吃的東西，住在各式各樣的地方，包括其他動物的身體裡。他們會用很奇怪的方式對待自己的身體。

蜜蟻會膨脹身體好將蜂蜜存放在裡面，然後再將身體裡的蜂蜜提供給其他同伴吃。有些兵蟻如果遭遇到攻擊，身體會爆炸，噴出有毒的化學物質殺死入侵者。

貓頭鷹會把小動物整個吃下去，然後再吐出骨頭和毛皮混雜而成的小球。蛇也能把食物整個吞下去，牠們的嘴巴可以張很大很大，吞下比自己的頭還要大的食物。

## Kiến Nổ

Thú vật làm những chuyện có vẻ kinh tởm. Chúng ăn những thứ mà con người không ăn. Chúng sống trong đủ loại chỗ, thậm chí ở trong những con thú khác. Chúng dùng thân thể của mình trong nhiều cách lạ thường.

Các kiến mật căng người ra và giữ mật trong cơ thể chúng. Chúng nuôi những con kiến khác từ mật này. Có loại kiến lính bùng nổ nếu chúng bị tấn công. Chúng phun chất hóa học để giết kẻ tấn công mình.

Những con chim cú nuốt trửng các con thú nhỏ. Sau đó chúng nhổ ra những viên xương và lông. Rắn cũng nuốt trửng thức ăn của chúng. Miệng rắn có thể giãn nở. Một con rắn có thể ăn một vật to hơn cả cái đầu của chính nó.

# Multilingual Summaries

## 스스로 몸을 터뜨리는 개미

동물들은 지독해 보이는 일들을 한다. 사람들이 먹지 않는 것들도 먹고 다른 동물의 몸 속을 포함한 모든 종류의 장소에서 살기도 한다. 동물들은 이상한 방법으로 자신의 몸을 사용한다.

꿀개미는 몸을 부풀려 몸 안에 꿀을 보관하고 그 꿀을 다른 개미들에게 먹인다. 어떤 병정개미들은 공격을 받으면 몸을 터뜨리는데 이때 화학 성분을 뿌려 공격자를 죽인다.

올빼미는 작은 동물들을 통째로 먹고 나중에 뼈와 털로 된 작은 덩어리를 뱉어낸다. 뱀도 먹이를 통째로 먹는데 뱀의 입은 늘어나기 때문에 자기 머리보다 더 큰 것도 먹을 수 있다.

## Cov Ntsaum Raug Tawg

Cov tsiaj txhu ua tej yam txawv. Lawv noj tej yam cov neeg yuav tsis noj. Lawv nyob txhua txhia qhov chaw, twb nyob rau hauv lwm cov tsiaj txhu. Nyias siv nyias lub cev txawv.

Cov ntsaum zib lub cev su, kom ceev zib tseg. Lawv pub zib rau lwm cov ntsaum noj. Thaum ib txhia cov ntsaum tub rog ntsib txoj kev tawm tsam, ces lawv lub cev tawg. Lawv tsuag tshuaj rau tus tawm tsam kom tuag.

Cov plas noj cov menyuam tsiaj txhu kom tas. Ib mentsis tom qab, lawv nti cov plaub thiab pob txha. Cov nab kuj noj lawv cov mov keev hlo. Lawv cov ncauj muaj peevxwm nthuav ntxiv kom dav. Ib lub nab noj tau ib qhov loj tshaj tus nab ntawd lub taub hau.

# The Stormi Giovanni Club   Student Edition pages 462–477

| Week at a Glance | Customize instruction every day for your English Language Learners. | | | | |
|---|---|---|---|---|---|
| | **Day 1** | **Day 2** | **Day 3** | **Day 4** | **Day 5** |
| **Teacher's Edition** | Use the ELL Notes that appear throughout each day of the lesson to support instruction and reading. | | | | |
| **ELL Poster 19** | • Assess Prior Knowledge<br>• Develop Concepts and Vocabulary | • Preteach Tested Vocabulary | • Review Generalize | • School Clubs and Activities | • Monitor Progress |
| **ELL Teaching Guide** | • Picture It! Lesson, pp. 127–128<br>• Multilingual Summaries, pp. 131–133 | • ELL Reader Lesson, pp. 248–249 | • Vocabulary Activities and Word Cards, pp. 129–130<br>• Multilingual Summaries, pp. 131–133 | | |
| **ELL Readers** | • Reread *Surprising Insects Magazine* | • Teach *In This New Place* | • Reread *In This New Place* and other texts to build fluency | | |
| **ELL and Transition Handbook** | Use the following as needed to support this week's instruction and to conduct alternative assessments:<br>• Phonics Transition Lessons<br>• Grammar Transition Lessons<br>• Assessment | | | | |

**Picture It!** Comprehension Lesson

# Generalize

Use this lesson to supplement or replace the skill lesson on pages 458–459 of the Teacher's Edition.

## Teach

Distribute copies of the Picture It! blackline master on page 128.
• Tell students they will read a story about a boy's first day at a new school.
• Share the Skill Points (at right) with students.
• Read the story aloud. Ask: *What do you think about the people at Hugo's new school?*

## Practice

Read aloud the directions on page 128. Have students complete the graphic organizer at the bottom of the page. Remind them that the generalization may not be specifically stated in the text. Have students keep their organizers for later reteaching.

**Answers for page 128:** *Generalization:* The students at Hugo's school are nice. *Support from Text:* One student showed him the way to the office. Another student took him to all his classes. At lunch, a girl offered to share her sandwich.

> ### Skill Points
> ✓ A **generalization** may not be true all the time, but it is true most of the time.
> ✓ A good generalization uses details and examples for support.

**Read** the story. Then **complete** the graphic organizer.
- **Write** a generalization about the students at Hugo's school.
- **Write** the information from the text that supports that generalization.

## New Boy at School

Today was Hugo's first day at school. He was nervous. "Will the other students be nice or mean?" he wondered.

When he got to school, somebody showed Hugo to the office. Another student took him to all his classes.
At lunch, a girl offered to share her sandwich with him.

"This isn't going to be too bad," Hugo thought.

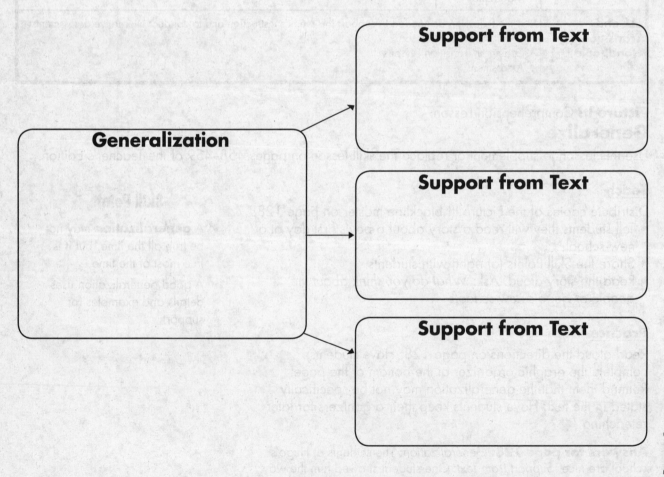

**Support from Text**

**Generalization**

**Support from Text**

**Support from Text**

# Vocabulary Activities and Word Cards

Copy the Word Cards on page 130 as needed for the following activities.
Use the blank cards for additional words that you want to teach.
Also see suggestions for teaching vocabulary in the ELL and Transition Handbook.

| Synonym Concentration | Scrambled Sentences | Matching Game |
| --- | --- | --- |
| • Give pairs of students sets of Word Cards and blank cards. Ask the students to use a dictionary or thesaurus to find synonyms for each vocabulary word. Or you can provide the synonyms for the students. Possible synonyms are: *hollow, mixture, shows, incident, outline, stern.*<br><br>• Students write each synonym on a blank card and confirm which word and synonym go together. They then shuffle the two sets of cards together and lay the cards face down in a grid pattern.<br><br>• Students take turns choosing two of the cards. If the two cards are synonyms, the student keeps the cards. If not, the cards are put back. Play continues until all of the cards have been matched. | • Form groups of students, and give each group a Word Card.<br><br>• Tell each group to create a sentence with their word. Provide the group with index cards, and have the students write each word of the sentence (except the word on the Word Card) on separate index cards.<br><br>• Invite a group to put its index cards and assigned Word Card on the chalk tray in scrambled order. Challenge the rest of the students to arrange the cards in the correct order. The group that created the sentence can verify when it has been correctly reassembled.<br><br>• Continue in this way until all groups have presented their scrambled sentences to the class. You can turn the activity into a game by giving a point to the team that correctly assembles each sentence. | • On blank cards, write a definition for each of the vocabulary words.<br><br>• Give a Word Card and its matching definition card to two different students. (Distribute as many vocabulary and definition card pairs as you have pairs of students. You may not be able to use all the cards in one round.) Tell students to study their cards and memorize the words or definitions on them.<br><br>• Collect the cards and have the students circulate around the classroom saying their memorized word or definition aloud to each person until they find a match.<br><br>• When all students have found their matching word or definition, you may play again with the remaining cards or with other students. |

cavity

combination

demonstrates

episode

profile

strict

# Multilingual Summaries

## The Stormi Giovanni Club

Stormi Giovanni Green has just moved to a new city. She misses her friends back in Chicago. She decides that she will be happier if she does not make new friends. She says that she will start the Stormi Giovanni Club, and she will be the only member.

Stormi meets a girl named Hannah at school. Hannah invites Stormi to sit with her and her friends at lunch. Stormi wants to sit alone.

The next day, the cafeteria is full. Stormi sits with Hannah and her friends. The new people remind Stormi of her friends in Chicago. Stormi decides that she will be happier now that she has made some new friends.

**Spanish**

## El club Stormi Giovanni

Stormi Giovanni Green se acaba de mudar a una nueva ciudad. Extraña a sus amigos de Chicago. Ella decide que será más feliz si no hace nuevos amigos. Dice que va a crear el club Stormi Giovanni y ella será su única socia.

En la escuela, Stormi conoce a una niña llamada Hannah. Hannah invita a Stormi a sentarse con ella y con sus amigos a la hora del almuerzo. Stormi quiere sentarse sola.

Al día siguiente, la cafetería está llena. Stormi se sienta con Hannah y sus amigos. Ellos le recuerdan a sus amigos de Chicago. Stormi decide que será más feliz ahora que ha hecho algunos nuevos amigos.

# Multilingual Summaries

Chinese

## 史托蜜俱樂部

　　史托蜜・喬凡妮格林剛剛搬到一個新城市，她很想念以前在芝加哥的朋友，希望他們能回到她身邊。她覺得不交新朋友的話自己會比較快樂，所以她就決定不交新朋友了。她說她要成立史托蜜俱樂部，裡面唯一的會員就是她自己。

　　史托蜜在學校遇到一個名叫漢娜的女孩，漢娜邀請史托蜜和她們一起吃午餐，史托蜜拒絕了，她想自己吃。

　　隔天午餐時，餐廳竟然客滿，史托蜜只好跟漢娜還有她的朋友一起吃飯。結果，這群新同學讓史托蜜想起她在芝加哥的朋友。史托蜜覺得如果交些新朋友自己會比較快樂，所以她決定敞開心門去交新朋友了。

Vietnamese

## Câu Lạc Bộ Stormi Giovanni

　　Stormi Giovanni Green vừa mới dọn đến một thành phố mới. Cô bé nhớ các bạn của mình ở Chicago. Cô quyết định mình sẽ vui hơn nếu không có bạn mới. Cô nói là sẽ lập ra Câu Lạc Bộ Stormi Giovanni, và cô sẽ là thành viên duy nhất.

　　Stormi gặp một cô gái tên Hannah ở trường. Hannah rủ Stormi đến ngồi với mình và các bạn của cô ở buổi ăn trưa. Stormi lại muốn ngồi một mình.

　　Hôm sau, phòng ăn ở trường có đông người. Stormi ngồi chung với Hannah và các bạn của cô. Các người mới làm Stormi nhớ đến các bạn của mình ở Chicago. Stormi quyết định là mình sẽ vui hơn vì bây giờ cô đã có vài bạn mới.

# Multilingual Summaries

## 스토미의 지오반니 클럽

이제 막 새 도시로 이사온 스토미 지오반니 그린은 시카고에 있는 친구들을 그리워한다. 그녀는 새 친구를 만들지 않으면 더 행복해 질 것이라고 마음먹는다. 그녀는 스토미 지오반니 클럽을 만들고 자신만이 유일한 회원이 될 것이라고 말한다.

스토미는 학교에서 한나라는 친구를 만난다. 한나는 점심시간에 자기와 자기 친구들과 함께 앉자고 스토미를 초대하지만 스토미는 혼자 앉고 싶어한다.

다음 날 학교 식당은 사람들로 가득하다. 한나와 한나 친구들과 함께 앉아 있는 스토미는 새 친구들을 보자 시카고에 있는 친구들이 생각난다. 스토미는 이제 새 친구가 있어서 더 행복해질 것이라고 생각한다.

---

**Hmong**

## Stormi Giovanni lub Pawg Ua Si

Stormi Giovanni Green nyuam qhuav tsiv rau lub zog tshiab. Nws nco nco nws cov phoojywg uas tseem nyob hauv lub zog Chicago. Nws txiav txim siab tias nws yuav zoo siab dua yog nws tsis ntsib cov phoojywg tshiab. Nws qhia tias nws yuav pib Stormi Giovanni lub Pawg Ua Si, thiab nws yuav yog tib tug mej zeej xwb.

Stormi ntsib Hannah, ib tug mentxhais, tom lub tsev kawm ntawv. Hannah caw Stormi los tuaj noj su nrog nws thiab nws cov phoojywg. Stormi xav zaum nws ib leeg xwb.

Hnub tom qab ntawd, hoob noj mov muaj cov neeg puv npo. Stormi zaum nrog Hannah thiab Hannah cov phoojywg. Cov neeg tshiab kom Stormi nco txog nws cov phoojywg nyob hauv Chicago. Stormi txiav txim siab tias nws yuav zoo siab dua rau qhov nws ntsib cov phoojywg tshiab.

# The Gymnast   Student Edition pages 488–497

| Week at a Glance | Customize instruction every day for your English Language Learners. | | | | |
|---|---|---|---|---|---|
| | **Day 1** | **Day 2** | **Day 3** | **Day 4** | **Day 5** |
| **Teacher's Edition** | Use the ELL Notes that appear throughout each day of the lesson to support instruction and reading. | | | | |
| **ELL Poster 20** | • Assess Prior Knowledge<br>• Develop Concepts and Vocabulary | • Preteach Tested Vocabulary | • Developing Strength | • Review Draw Conclusions | • Monitor Progress |
| **ELL Teaching Guide** | • Picture It! Lesson, pp. 134–135<br>• Multilingual Summaries, pp. 138–140 | • ELL Reader Lesson, pp. 250–251 | • Vocabulary Activities and Word Cards, pp. 136–137<br>• Multilingual Summaries, pp. 138–140 | | |
| **ELL Readers** | • Reread *In This New Place* | • Teach *Fast as Lightning* | • Reread *Fast as Lightning* and other texts to build fluency | | |
| **ELL and Transition Handbook** | Use the following as needed to support this week's instruction and to conduct alternative assessments:<br>• Phonics Transition Lessons<br>• Grammar Transition Lessons<br>• Assessment | | | | |

**Picture It!** Comprehension Lesson

# Draw Conclusions

Use this lesson to supplement or replace the skill lesson on pages 484–485 of the Teacher's Edition.

## Teach

Distribute copies of the Picture It! blackline master on page 135.
• Tell students to look at the picture and read the title of the paragraph.
• Share the Skill Points (at right) with students.
• Read the paragraph aloud. Say: *This paragraph tells about the qualities of a good gymnast. What conclusion can you draw about gymnasts, based on the details in this paragraph?* Discuss students' ideas.

## Practice

Read aloud the directions on page 135. Have students read the paragraph and then complete the graphic organizer. Have students keep their organizers for later reteaching.

**Answers for page 135:** *Details:* Gymnasts can bend over backward and can touch the floor. Gymnasts can hang from bars and lift their own weight. *Conclusion:* Possible answer: Gymnasts must be flexible and strong.

### Skill Points

✓ When you **draw conclusions**, you combine details in the text. Together, the details tell you something that might not be actually said in the text.

✓ A **conclusion** is a decision you make after combining details and your personal knowledge.

Name _____

**Read** the paragraph, and then complete the graphic organizer.

- In the *Detail* boxes, **write** information from the paragraph.
- In the *Conclusion* box, **write** a conclusion you have made about gymnasts.

## Gymnastics

Gymnastics is a difficult sport. To be a gymnast, you must be flexible. You must be able to bend over backward. You have to be able to touch the floor. But that's not all. You have to be able to hang from bars and lift your own weight. Good gymnasts have all these skills.

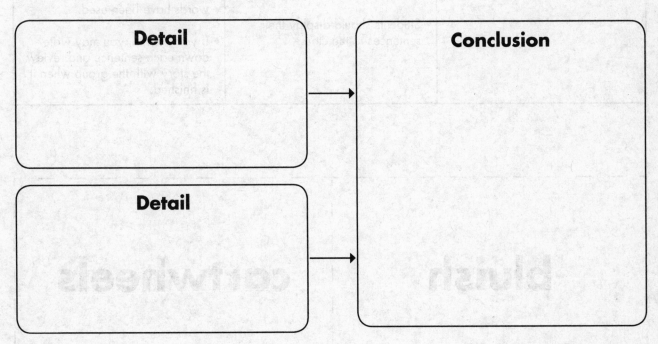

**Detail**

**Detail**

**Conclusion**

© Scott Foresman 5

# Vocabulary Activities and Word Cards

Copy the Word Cards on pages 136–137 as needed for the following activities.
Use the blank card for an additional word that you want to teach.
Also see suggestions for teaching vocabulary in the ELL and Transition Handbook.

| Sorting Activity | Sports Headlines | Group Story |
|---|---|---|
| • Form groups of students, and give each group a set of Word Cards.<br><br>• Ask groups to sort their cards into different categories. Tell them that they are free to decide what the categories are but that they will be asked to explain their categories to the other groups.<br><br>• When groups are finished, invite them to take turns presenting their word sorts to the class. Remind students to explain the rationale behind their categories. | • Show students the sports section of a newspaper, and read aloud some of the headlines.<br><br>• Form groups of students and give each group a set of Word Cards and several sentence strips. Tell groups to create headlines using all the cards. (There can be more than one vocabulary word per headline.) Have students write their headlines on sentence strips, gluing the Word Cards on the strips at the appropriate places in the sentences.<br><br>• Students should display their sentences to the class. | • Put a set of Word Cards into a paper bag. Sit in a circle with the students.<br><br>• Draw a card out of the bag and make up a story starter using that word, for example: *Last week I went to a gymnastics competition.*<br><br>• Invite the student next to you to draw a card and create the next sentence of the story, incorporating the new word. Continue in this way until all the words have been used.<br><br>• If you wish to, you may write down each sentence and review the story with the group when it is finished. |

## bluish

## cartwheels

gymnastics

hesitation

limelight

skidded

somersault

throbbing

wincing

# Multilingual Summaries

## The Gymnast

Gary's cousin, Issac, was a gymnast. Gary was jealous of his cousin. He liked his cousin's special shoes. Gary also liked the tape around his cousin's wrists. Gary wanted to do cartwheels and back flips like his cousin.

Gary's cousin let him try on the special shoes and the tape. The shoes came off when Gary tried to do a cartwheel. Gary went home. The next day he found old slippers and put them on. He practiced doing cartwheels.

Gary got hurt when he tried to do a back flip. He landed on his head. His feet were sore and his neck hurt. Later, Gary tried to do a back flip again. He landed on his neck. Gary rested and thought about his cousin the gymnast.

## El gimnasta

Isaac, el primo de Gary, era gimnasta. Gary estaba celoso de su primo. Le gustaban las zapatillas especiales que él usaba. También le gustaba la cinta que se ponía en sus muñecas. Gary quería dar volteretas laterales y saltos mortales como su primo.

El primo de Gary lo dejó probarse las zapatillas especiales y la cinta. Las zapatillas se le salieron cuando trató de dar una voltereta lateral. Gary se fue a su casa. Al día siguiente se encontró unas zapatillas viejas y se las puso. Practicó las volteretas laterales.

Gary se lastimó cuando trató de hacer un salto mortal. Cayó de cabeza. Tenía los pies adoloridos y le dolía el cuello. Más tarde, Gary trató nuevamente de dar un salto mortal. Cayó y se torció el cuello. Gary descansó y pensó en su primo gimnasta.

# Multilingual Summaries

## 體操選手

蓋瑞的表哥－伊薩克是個體操選手。蓋瑞嫉妒他的表哥，因為他喜歡表哥那雙特別的鞋子，也喜歡表哥手腕上的包紮貼布。蓋瑞想學表哥做側手翻和後空翻。

蓋瑞的表哥讓他試穿鞋子、試綁包紮貼布，可是當蓋瑞試著做側手翻時，鞋子卻飛出去了。蓋瑞回家後第二天發現一雙舊拖鞋，於是穿上他們練習做側手翻。

蓋瑞在做後空翻的時候不小心頭先著地受傷了，他覺得腳和脖子都很痛。蓋瑞休息一下之後又想再試一次，結果這次是他的脖子先著地。蓋瑞只得躺在床上好好養傷，他覺得表哥真是個厲害的體操選手。

## Vận Động Viên Thể Dục

Anh họ của Gary, Issac, là một vận động viên thể dục. Gary ghen tỵ với anh họ của mình. Gary thích đôi giày đặc biệt của anh họ. Gary cũng thích miếng băng vải quấn ở cổ tay của người anh họ. Gary muốn lộn nhào và lộn ngược như anh họ của mình.

Người anh họ cho Gary thử đôi giày đặc biệt và miếng băng quấn của mình. Đôi giày tuột ra khi Gary thử lộn nhào. Gary về nhà. Ngày hôm sau cậu tìm được đôi dép cũ và mang vào. Cậu tập lộn nhào.

Gary bị đau khi cậu thử lộn ngược. Cậu ngã đập đầu xuống. Chân cậu ê ẩm và cổ bị đau. Sau đó Gary thử lộn ngược lần nữa. Cậu ngã đập vào cổ. Gary nghỉ ngơi và suy nghĩ về người anh họ, nhà vận động viên thể dục của mình.

# Multilingual Summaries

## 체조 선수

게리의 사촌인 아이작은 체조 선수이다. 게리는 사촌을 부러워해서 사촌이 체조할 때 신는 특수 신발이나 손목 주변에 감는 테이프를 좋아한다. 게리는 사촌처럼 옆으로 재주넘기나 뒤로 재주넘기를 하고 싶어 한다.

게리의 사촌은 게리에게 특수 신발과 테이프를 빌려준다. 게리가 옆으로 재주넘기를 하려고 하는데 신발이 벗겨지고 게리는 집으로 돌아간다. 다음 날 게리는 낡은 슬리퍼를 찾아서 신고는 옆으로 재주넘는 연습을 한다.

게리가 뒤로 재주넘기를 하려다 머리로 착지해 다친다. 발이 따끔거리고 목도 아프다. 게리는 나중에 뒤로 재주넘기를 다시 해보지만 이번에는 목으로 착지한다. 게리는 쉬면서 체조선수인 사촌을 생각해 본다.

## Tus Gymnast

Gary ib tug kwvtij Isaac, yog ib tug gymnast. Gary khib siab ntawm nws tus kwvtij. Nws nyiam nws tus kwvtij nkawm khau. Gary kuj nyiam cov ntawv nplaum nyob ib ncig nws tus kwvtij cov dab teg. Gary twb xav ua gymnastics zoo li nws tus kwvtij.

Gary tus kwvtij los pub nws siv nkawm khau, thiab cov ntawv nplaum. Thaum Gary sim ua gymnastics ces nkawm khau hle mus ub mus no. Gary tau mus tsev. Hnub tom qab ntawd nws tau nrhiav lwm nkawm khau, thiab muab lawv siv. Nws xyaum ua gymnastics.

Gary raug mob thaum nws sim ua gymnastics. Nws taubhau tsaws ua ntej nws cov kotaw. Nws cov kotaw thiab caj dab mob mob li. Ib chim Gary tau sim ua gymnastics ib zaug ntxiv. Nws caj dab raug av ua ntej nws cov kotaw. Gary zaum los so thiab xav txog nws ib tug kwvtij txawj ua gymnastics.

# The Three-Century Woman
Student Edition pages 516–529

| Week at a Glance | Customize instruction every day for your English Language Learners. | | | | |
|---|---|---|---|---|---|
| | **Day 1** | **Day 2** | **Day 3** | **Day 4** | **Day 5** |
| **Teacher's Edition** | Use the ELL Notes that appear throughout each day of the lesson to support instruction and reading. | | | | |
| **ELL Poster 21** | • Assess Prior Knowledge<br>• Develop Concepts and Vocabulary | • Preteach Tested Vocabulary | • Review Character and Plot | • In Other Words | • Monitor Progress |
| **ELL Teaching Guide** | • Picture It! Lesson, pp. 141–142<br>• Multilingual Summaries, pp. 145–147 | • ELL Reader Lesson, pp. 252–253 | • Vocabulary Activities and Word Cards, pp. 143–144<br>• Multilingual Summaries, pp. 145–147 | | |
| **ELL Readers** | • Reread *Fast as Lightning* | • Teach *My Great-Grandpa Collins* | • Reread *My Great-Grandpa Collins* and other texts to build fluency | | |
| **ELL and Transition Handbook** | Use the following as needed to support this week's instruction and to conduct alternative assessments:<br>• Phonics Transition Lessons<br>• Grammar Transition Lessons<br>• Assessment | | | | |

## Picture It! Comprehension Lesson
## Character and Plot

Use this lesson to supplement or replace the skill lesson on pages 512–513 of the Teacher's Edition.

### Teach

Distribute copies of the Picture It! blackline master on page 142.
• Tell students they are going to read a story. Have them guess what the story is about, based on the picture.
• Share the Skill Points (at right) with students.
• Tell students to pay attention to Sonja's character. Read the story aloud. Ask: *What words would you use to describe Sonja?*

### Practice

Read aloud the directions on page 142. Have students read the story and then complete the character map at the bottom of the page. Have students keep their organizers for later reteaching.

**Answers for page 142:** Possible *Traits:* determined, focused, smart, strong, healthy

### Skill Points

✓ A story is usually made up of a problem and a solution to that problem.

✓ The people in a story are called **characters**.

✓ A character has **traits**. The traits show what kind of person that character is.

Name _____

**Read** the story. Then complete the character map. **Write** words that show what Sonja is like.

## Sonja Makes It to the Top

At last! Sonja was climbing Mount Washington. All the members of her group were excited too. But after two hours, three people quit. They were too tired. After two more hours, another person quit. Sonja was the last person. She was tired too. But she had an idea. She took off her backpack. The only thing she kept was her water bottle. Now it was easier. She had new energy. Sonja reached the top, just as she knew she would.

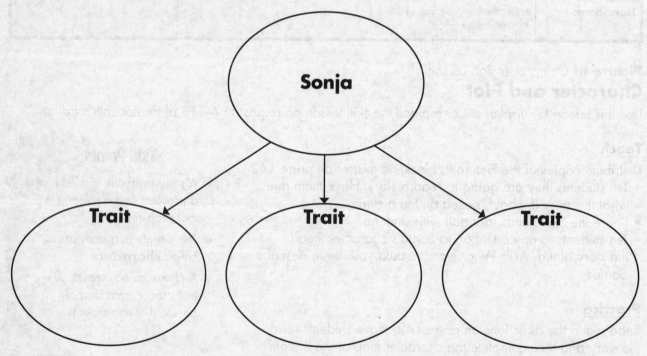

**142** *The Three-Century Woman*  Unit 5, Week 1

ELL Teaching Guide

© Scott Foresman 5

# Vocabulary Activities and Word Cards

Copy the Word Cards on page 144 as needed for the following activities.
Use the blank cards for additional words that you want to teach.
Also see suggestions for teaching vocabulary in the ELL and Transition Handbook.

| Parts of Speech | Sentence Building | Team Concentration |
|---|---|---|
| • Form groups of students, and give each group one set of Word Cards.<br><br>• Ask groups to sort their Word Cards into three categories: nouns, verbs, and adjectives. Give students access to dictionaries for help.<br><br>• On the board, write the headings *Nouns, Verbs,* and *Adjectives.* Invite members from each group to tape a card to the board under the correct heading. As they do so, encourage students to supply a sentence showing how the word is used. Provide feedback as necessary. You may want to talk about how *withered,* an adjective in this story, can also be a verb. | • Form small groups of students, and give each group a set of Word Cards.<br><br>• Tell groups to create sentences with the words on the cards. Students may include more than one vocabulary word in each sentence if it makes sense for them to do so.<br><br>• When groups are finished, invite a member from each group to read their sentences to the class. As you listen and look at students' sentences, address any errors in syntax or grammar. Write corrected sentences on the board. | • Create a set of Word Cards. On blank cards, write a synonym for each of the vocabulary words; for example: *strange, crossing, thought, harsh, glasses, shriveled.* Teach students these synonym pairs using the cards.<br><br>• Shuffle all of the cards together and write a numeral on the back of each card. Then arrange the cards, number side up, in a grid pattern on a corkboard or magnet board.<br><br>• Form two teams, and ask Team A to name a pair of cards by their numbers (e.g., *four* and *sixteen*).<br><br>• Turn the cards up; if they are a pair of synonyms, the team gets to keep the pair and scores a point. Otherwise, turn the cards face down once again. Then Team B gets a turn.<br><br>• Teams continue to take turns calling out pairs of cards until all the synonyms have been matched. The team with the most points wins. |

eerie

intersection

pondered

severe

spectacles

withered

# Multilingual Summaries

## The Three-Century Woman

Megan's Great-Grandmother Breckenridge has lived in three centuries. She was born in 1899, and now it is 2001. She lived in the 1800s, 1900s, and the 2000s. On the first day of 2001 Great-Grandma begins her third century. Megan and her mom go to visit her. Camera crews and reporters are already there. They want to interview the Three-Century Woman.

Megan and her mother find an anchorman in Great-Grandma's room. He asks her questions about the amazing times she has lived through. Great-Grandma tells him a story about living through the 1906 San Francisco earthquake. She also tells him a story about being on the *Hindenburg* when it crashed in 1937. The earthquake and the crash did happen, but Megan knows that Great-Grandma wasn't there.

Great-Grandma tells these stories because she knows the anchorman only cares about the story. He does not care about her.

## La mujer de los tres siglos

La bisabuela de Megan, la señora Breckenridge, ha vivido en tres siglos. Nació en 1899 y estamos en 2001. Vivió en los siglos XIX, XX y XXI. El primer día del año 2001, la bisabuela ha empezado su tercer siglo. Megan y su mamá la visitan. Las cámaras y los reporteros ya están allí. Ellos quieren entrevistar a la mujer de los tres siglos.

Megan y su mamá encuentran a un presentador en la habitación de la bisabuela. Él le hace preguntas sobre los acontecimientos asombrosos en los que ella ha vivido. La bisabuela le cuenta una historia sobre su experiencia en el terremoto de San Francisco de 1906. También le cuenta del accidente, en 1937, cuando estaba en el *Hindenburg.* El terremoto y el accidente sí sucedieron, pero Megan sabe que la bisabuela no estaba allí.

La bisabuela cuenta estas historias porque sabe que al presentador sólo le interesa la historia. A él no le interesa ella.

© Scott Foresman 5

# Multilingual Summaries

## 三世紀老太太

邁格的老奶奶布瑞金利吉，生命歷程跨越了三個世紀。她生於1899年，而現在已經踏入了2001年，經歷了十九、二十和二十一一共三個世紀。從2001年第一天起，老奶奶跨入了第三個世紀。邁格和媽媽去看她，發現許多攝影師與記者早就來了，他們都想採訪這位"三世紀老太太"。

邁格和媽媽看見一個主持人在老奶奶家裏，問奶奶一生中有哪些最難忘的時光。老奶奶說，有1906年的舊金山大地震，以及1937年興登堡號飛艇的爆炸。邁格知道地震和爆炸都真的發生過，但奶奶當時沒在場。

老奶奶之所以對主持人說這些故事，因為她知道主持人只對大事感興趣，並不會關心她的個人生活。

## Người Phụ Nữ của Ba Thế Kỷ

Bà cố tên Breckenridge của Megan đã sống qua ba thế kỷ. Bà sanh vào năm 1899 và bây giờ là năm 2001. Bà đã sống trong những thập niên của 1800, 1900, và 2000. Vào ngày đầu của năm 2001 Bà Cố bắt đầu thế kỷ thứ ba của bà. Megan và mẹ đến thăm bà. Các phóng viên và các toán quay phim đã có mặt ở đó. Họ muốn được phỏng vấn Người Phụ Nữ của Ba Thế Kỷ.

Megan và mẹ thấy có một người phóng viên chính trong phòng của Bà Cố. Ông ta hỏi bà về những thời kỳ lạ lùng mà bà đã trải qua. Bà Cố kể cho ông ấy nghe về lần trải qua cuộc động đất vào năm 1906. Bà cũng kể cho ông ấy nghe về lần ở trên chiếc khinh khí cầu Hindenburg khi chiếc này bị rớt vào năm 1937. Kỳ động đất và việc chiếc khinh khí cầu rơi có xảy ra, nhưng Megan biết là Bà Cố không có ở đó.

Bà Cố kể những câu chuyện này vì bà biết người phóng viên chính này chỉ quan tâm đến chuyện. Ông ta chẳng quan tâm gì đến bà.

# Multilingual Summaries

## 3 세기째 살고 계신 브레켄리지 할머니

메건의 증조할머니인 브레켄리지 할머니는 3세기 동안 살아왔다. 1899년에 태어난 할머니는 지금이 2001년이니 1800년대와 1900년대, 그리고 2000년대를 사신 것이다. 2001년의 첫 날은 증조할머니가 세 번째 세기를 맞이한 날로 메건은 어머니와 함께 할머니 댁을 방문한다. 이미 카메라맨들과 기자들이 할머니 집에 와 있었고 이들은 3세기 동안 산 여인을 취재하고 싶어한다.

메건과 어머니는 증조할머니 방에서 앵커 한 명을 만난다. 그는 증조할머니가 그간 살아온 놀라운 시간들에 대해 묻고 증조할머니는 1906년에 있었던 샌프란시스코 지진을 이겨낸 이야기와 1937년 추락한 힌덴부르크 여객선에 탑승했던 이야기를 해 준다. 그 당시의 지진과 추락 사건은 실제 일어난 일이긴 하지만 메건은 증조할머니가 그 일을 겪지 않았다는 것을 알고 있다.

증조할머니는 앵커가 증조할머니의 이야기에만 신경을 쓴다는 것을 알고 있기 때문에 이런 이야기를 들려준다. 그는 증조할머니에 대해서는 신경을 쓰지 않는다.

## Tus Poj niam Nyob Peb Tiam Neeg

Megan tus pog koob Breckenridge tau nyob dhau peb tiam neeg. Nws yug los thaum ib txhiab yim pua cuaj caum cuaj es tam sim no twb yog ob txhiab ib lawm. Nws tau nyob hauv lub caij ib txhiab yim puas, dhau lub caij ib txhiab cuaj puas thiab los rau lub caij ob txhiab no lawm. Hnub xyoo tshiab nyob rau xyoo ob txhiab ib, nws pog koob tau pib tiam thib peb lawm. Megan thiab nws niam tau mus xyuas nws. Neeg thaij duab thiab neeg tshaj xov xwm twb mus txog tag lawm. Lawv xav nrog tus poj niam uas tau nyob dhau peb tiam neeg tham.

Megan thiab nws niam pom ib tug neeg tshaj xov xwm nyob hauv lawv pog koob lub hoob. Nws nug nws ob peb qhov txog tej sij hawm uas nws tau nyob dhau ntawd. Pog koob piav rau nws ib zaj dab neeg hais txog thaum av qeeg nyob rau San Francisco xyoo ib txhiab cuaj pua rau. Nws qhia txog ib thaum nws tau caij lub Hindenburg thaum nws tau poob xyoo ib txhiab cuaj pua peb caug xya thiab. Av yeej qeeg thiab lub Hindenburg yeej poob lawm thiab, tiam sis Megan paub tias nws pog koob tsis nyob ntawd thiab tsis tau ua li ntawd.

Pog koob tsuas lam piav tej zaj no vim tias nws paub tias tus neeg tshaj xov xwm tsuas quav ntsej txog tej zag dab neeg no xwb. Nws tsis quav ntsej txog nws.

# Wreck of the *Titanic*   Student Edition pages 540–551

| Week at a Glance | Customize instruction every day for your English Language Learners. | | | | |
|---|---|---|---|---|---|
| | **Day 1** | **Day 2** | **Day 3** | **Day 4** | **Day 5** |
| **Teacher's Edition** | Use the ELL Notes that appear throughout each day of the lesson to support instruction and reading. | | | | |
| **ELL Poster 22** | • Assess Prior Knowledge<br>• Develop Concepts and Vocabulary | • Preteach Tested Vocabulary | • Future Transportation | • Scientist Skills | • Monitor Progress |
| **ELL Teaching Guide** | • Picture It! Lesson, pp. 148–149<br>• Multilingual Summaries, pp. 152–154 | • ELL Reader Lesson, pp. 254–255 | • Vocabulary Activities and Word Cards, pp. 150–151<br>• Multilingual Summaries, pp. 152–154 | | |
| **ELL Readers** | • Reread *My Great-Grandpa Collins* | • Teach *Exploring the Oceans with Alvin* | • Reread *Exploring the Oceans with Alvin* and other texts to build fluency | | |
| **ELL and Transition Handbook** | Use the following as needed to support this week's instruction and to conduct alternative assessments:<br>• Phonics Transition Lessons<br>• Grammar Transition Lessons<br>• Assessment | | | | |

**Picture It!** Comprehension Lesson
## Graphic Sources

Use this lesson to supplement or replace the skill lesson on pages 536–537 of the Teacher's Edition.

### Teach

Distribute copies of the Picture It! blackline master on page 149.
• Share the Skill Points (at right) with students.
• Point to the map. Ask students what they can tell from looking at the map.
• Tell students they are going read about a shipwreck. Read the paragraph aloud.

### Practice

Read aloud the directions on page 149. Have students read the passage. When they are finished, tell them to write the important things that happened to the *Atocha* on the appropriate lines on the map. Tell them to look back at the passage for help. Have students keep their maps for later reteaching.

**Answers for page 149:** *Cadiz:* The *Atocha* leaves on March 23, 1622. *Off La Habana:* The *Atocha* sinks on September 5, 1622, and is discovered in 1985.

### Skill Points

✓ Pictures, diagrams, maps, and time lines are **graphic sources**.

✓ A graphic source helps you to understand written text.

✓ Preview graphic sources before you read. Predict what the text is about, based on the graphic source.

**Read** the paragraph.

- **Study** the map. **Look** at the blank lines.
- **Write** what happens in those places on the lines. **Remember** to include the dates!

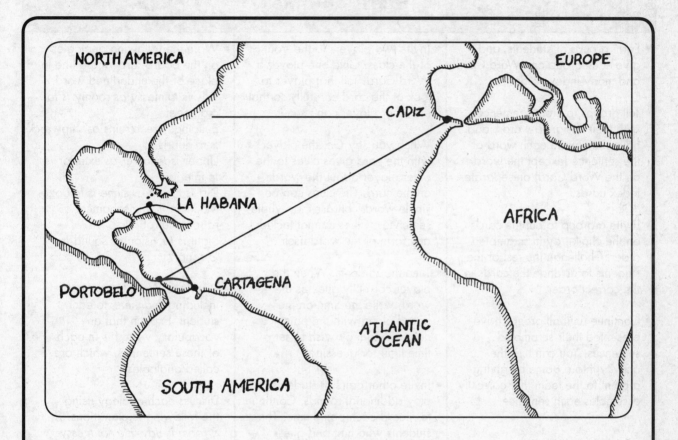

# The *Atocha*

The *Atocha* was a Spanish treasure ship. On March 23, 1622, it left Cadiz, Spain. It went to South America to pick up gold, silver, and other treasures. Then it stopped in La Habana, Cuba. On September 5, the *Atocha* started on its trip back to Spain. But a hurricane sank the ship. The shipwreck was finally discovered in 1985. A fortune in gold and silver had been found after more than 300 years!

# Vocabulary Activities and Word Cards

Copy the Word Cards on page 151 as needed for the following activities.
Use the blank card for an additional word that you want to teach.
Also see suggestions for teaching vocabulary in the ELL and Transition Handbook.

| Scrambled Sentences | Guess on Time | Analogies |
|---|---|---|
| • Form groups of students, and give each group one Word Card and many index cards.<br><br>• Tell groups to create sentences with their assigned words, and have them write each word of the sentence (except the word on the Word Card) on separate index cards.<br><br>• Invite a group to put the cards on the chalk tray in scrambled order. Challenge the rest of the students to arrange the cards in the correct order.<br><br>• Continue until all groups have presented their scrambled sentences. You can turn the activity into a game by giving a point to the team that correctly assembles each sentence. | • Invite two players to the front of the class. Give one player a Word Card. Tell that player to look at the card carefully so that the other player can't see it.<br><br>• When you say *Go,* the player with the card gives clues to the other player about the word on the card. The clues can be single words, phrases, or whole sentences. Clues cannot include any form of the word itself.<br><br>• Time the students. When the player correctly guesses the word, write the time on the board along with the pair's names. You may wish to set a time limit for guessing.<br><br>• Invite other pairs of students to play additional rounds. Continue to record each pair's time. The students who hint and guess the assigned word in the least amount of time are the winners. | • Write the following analogies on the board, drawing a line in place of the underlined word.<br>Tidy *is to* messy *as* roomy *is to* <u>cramped</u>.<br>Buildings *are to* ruins *as* shipwreck *is to* <u>debris</u>.<br>Upper *is to* lower *as* exterior *is to* <u>interior</u>.<br>Dirt *is to* soil *as* slime *is to* <u>ooze</u>.<br>Machine *is to* mechanical *as* robot *is to* <u>robotic</u>.<br>Sight *is to* vision *as* sound *is to* <u>sonar</u>.<br><br>• Distribute Word Cards, not including *sediment,* to each student. Explain that one vocabulary word fits in each of these sentences, which are called analogies.<br><br>• Discuss each analogy using the following explanations: *If a room is tidy, it's not messy; After a disaster, buildings are in ruins; Upper and lower are opposites; Dirt and soil are synonyms; A machine moves in a mechanical way; Vision is the use of sight.*<br><br>• After each explanation, ask students to hold up the Word Card that completes the analogy. Provide help as needed. |

**cramped**

**debris**

**interior**

**ooze**

**robotic**

**sediment**

**sonar**

# Multilingual Summaries

## The Unsinkable Wreck of the R.M.S. *Titanic*

Scientists went underwater to study the wreck of the *Titanic*. They traveled in a submarine called *Alvin*. The *Titanic* was the largest, finest ship ever built. On its first trip to sea in 1912, it hit an iceberg and sank. There were not enough lifeboats. There were 2,200 people on the ship. 1,500 of them drowned.

The scientists in *Alvin* were the first to see the *Titanic* in more than seventy years. *Alvin* moved past the front part of the ship. One of the crew remembered the story of two little boys who survived the sinking.

The crew saw debris on the ocean floor. The ship broke into two parts when it sank. Objects fell everywhere when it split. The crew returned to the surface after only two hours. They will go back again to study the wreck.

## Los restos del *Titanic* que nunca se hunden

Los científicos fueron debajo del agua para estudiar los restos del *Titanic*. Viajaron en un submarino llamado *Alvin*. El *Titanic* es el barco más grande y elegante que se ha construido. En su primer viaje por mar, en 1912, chocó contra un iceberg y se hundió. No había suficientes botes salvavidas. Había 2,200 personas en el barco. Se ahogaron 1,500 de ellas.

Los científicos en el *Alvin* fueron los primeros en ver el *Titanic* después de más de setenta años. Uno de los tripulantes recordó la historia de dos niños que sobrevivieron el hundimiento.

Los tripulantes vieron escombros en el fondo del océano. El barco se partió en dos partes cuando se hundió. Los objetos cayeron en todas direcciones cuando éstas se separaron. Los tripulantes volvieron a la superficie después de sólo dos horas. Ellos regresarán de nuevo para estudiar los restos.

# Multilingual Summaries

## 泰坦尼克號的殘骸

　　科學家乘坐阿爾文號潛艇，到達深海研究泰坦尼克號的殘骸。泰坦尼克號是歷史上最大、最豪華的輪船。可是在1912年第一次出海時，就撞上了冰山永遠沈入海底。由於沒有足夠的救生艇，船上2,200乘客中有1,500人不幸溺斃了。

　　科學家乘坐阿爾文號，七十多年來首次看到泰坦尼克。潛艇駛過沈船前端時，一名考察隊隊員清楚地記得，當年兩個小男孩逃生的故事。

　　他們還看見海底有許多碎片。泰坦尼克沈沒時斷成了兩段，因此在裂開時有許多東西散落到外面。科學家結束了兩小時的考察，回到海面，將來還會再回來仔細研究。

## Xác Chiếc Tàu Không Chìm R.M.S *Titanic*

Các nhà khoa học đã lặn xuống nước để nghiên cứu xác chiếc tàu Titanic. Họ du hành trong một chiếc tàu ngầm tên Alvin. Tàu Titanic là chiếc tàu lớn nhất, đẹp nhất được xây từ trước đến nay. Trong chuyến khởi hành ra biển đầu tiên vào năm 1912, tàu đụng một tảng băng và bị chìm. Không có đủ thuyền cứu đắm trên tàu. Có 2,200 người ở trên tàu. 1,500 người trong số họ bị chết đuối.

Các nhà khoa học trên chiếc Alvin là những người đầu tiên được thấy chiếc Titanic trong hơn bảy mươi năm. Alvin đi qua phần phía trước của chiếc tàu. Một người trong đoàn nhớ lại câu chuyện về hai cậu bé sống sót qua kỳ đắm tàu.

Những người này thấy các mảnh vụn dưới đáy đại dương. Chiếc tàu gẫy ra làm đôi khi bị chìm. Các đồ vật rơi rớt khắp nơi khi chiếc tàu vỡ. Chỉ sau hai giờ đồng hồ những người này trở lên mặt nước. Họ sẽ trở xuống lần nữa để nghiên cứu xác tàu.

# Multilingual Summaries

## 침몰하지 않는 R.M.S. 타이타닉 호의 잔해

과학자들은 타이타닉 호의 잔해를 연구하기 위해 앨빈이라는 잠수정을 타고 해저로 들어갔다. 타이타닉 호는 사상 최대 크기의 가장 훌륭한 선박이었는데 1912년 첫 항해 때 빙산에 부딪혀 가라앉게 되었다. 배에는 구명보트가 충분하지 않았고 배에 탄 2,200명 중 1,500명이 익사했다.

사고 후 70년도 더 지나서 잠수정 앨빈 호를 탄 과학자들이 최초로 타이타닉 호를 조사했다. 앨빈 호는 타이타닉 호의 앞부분을 지나 이동했다. 선원 중 한 명이 침몰에서 살아남은 어린 두 남자아이에 대한 이야기를 기억해냈다.

선원들은 바다 밑바닥에서 파편들을 발견했다. 타이타닉 호가 가라앉을 때 두 부분으로 부러졌고 그 때 배에 있는 물건들이 사방으로 떨어진 것이었다. 선원들은 두 시간 동안만 탐색 한 후 수면 위로 돌아왔다. 그들은 잔해를 연구하기 위해 바다 밑으로 되돌아갈 것이다.

## Kev Puas Tsuaj ntawm lub RMS Titanic uas Tsis Txawj Tog

Cov tub kawm txog dej tau mus hauv qab nruab deg mus kawm txog kev puas tsuaj ntawm lub nkoj Titanic. Lawv tau caij ib lub nkoj submarine hu uas Alvin uas yog ib lub mus rau hauv qab nrug dej. Lub Titanic thaum ub yog lub nkoj loj tshaj plaws thiab zoo tshaj plaws uas tau txua los. Thawj zaug luag tau caij lub nkoj ntawd nyob rau xyoo ib txhiab cuaj pua kaum ob, nws tau mus tsoo raug ib thooj nas kuab loj thiab tau tog lawm. Tsis muaj cov nkoj me cawm neeg txaus. Ob phav ob puas leej neeg caij nkoj. Ib txhiab tsib puas leej tau poob dej tuag lawm.

Cov tub kawm txog dej uas tau caij Alvin yog thawj cov uas tau pom lub Titanic tau muaj li xya caum xyoo no. Alvin mus dhau thawj feem ua ntej ntawm lub nkoj. Lawv ib tug nco qab txog zaj dab neeg piav txog ob tug menyuam tub uas nyob dhau lub nkoj tog.

Pab tub kawm ntawd pom khib nyiab nyob puas hauv qab thus dej. Lub nkoj tau tu nrho ua ob ya thaum nws tog ntawd. Khoom ub khoom no poob qhov txhia qhov chaws thaum lub nkoj tu nrho. Pab tub kawm rov qab mus rau saum nplaim dej tom qab ob xuab moo. Lawv yuav rov qab mus kawm txog kev puas tsuaj ntawd ntxiv.

# Talk with an Astronaut
Student Edition pages 564–575

| Week at a Glance | Customize instruction every day for your English Language Learners. | | | | |
|---|---|---|---|---|---|
| | **Day 1** | **Day 2** | **Day 3** | **Day 4** | **Day 5** |
| **Teacher's Edition** | Use the ELL Notes that appear throughout each day of the lesson to support instruction and reading. | | | | |
| **ELL Poster 23** | • Assess Prior Knowledge<br>• Develop Concepts and Vocabulary | • Preteach Tested Vocabulary | • E-mail from Space | • Training Schedule | • Monitor Progress |
| **ELL Teaching Guide** | • Picture It! Lesson, pp. 155–156<br>• Multilingual Summaries, pp. 159–161 | • ELL Reader Lesson, pp. 256–257 | • Vocabulary Activities and Word Cards, pp. 157–158<br>• Multilingual Summaries, pp. 159–161 | | |
| **ELL Readers** | • Reread *Exploring the Oceans with Alvin* | • Teach *Fixing Hubble's Troubles* | • Reread *Fixing Hubble's Troubles* and other texts to build fluency | | |
| **ELL and Transition Handbook** | Use the following as needed to support this week's instruction and to conduct alternative assessments:<br>• Phonics Transition Lessons<br>• Grammar Transition Lessons<br>• Assessment | | | | |

**Picture It!** Comprehension Lesson
## Author's Purpose
Use this lesson to supplement or replace the skill lesson on pages 560–561 of the Teacher's Edition.

### Teach
Distribute copies of the Picture It! blackline master on page 156.
• Review the Skill Points (at right) with students.
• Point to the chart at the top left of the page. Ask students to predict what the paragraph is about, based on the chart.
• Ask students what they think the author's purpose was for writing this paragraph. Then read the paragraph aloud.

### Practice
Read aloud the directions on page 156. Have students read the paragraph. Ask students if their predictions about the purpose were correct. Then have them write answers to the questions. Have students keep their work for later reteaching.

**Answers for page 156: 1.** The purpose is to give information. **2.** Possible answers: It contains a lot of facts. It does not tell a story or express personal feelings. **3.** It is about the history of space exploration.

### Skill Points
✓ The **author's purpose** is the reason an author writes a selection.

✓ An author may write to entertain, inform, or express feelings or ideas.

✓ Entertaining passages are fun to read. Informative passages contain many facts. Personal expression tells about the author.

© Scott Foresman 5

ELL Teaching Guide

Unit 5, Week 3 *Talk with an Astronaut* **155**

**Read** the paragraph. **Study** the chart. Then **write** answers to the questions that follow.

| Mission | Years of Mission |
|---------|------------------|
| Sputnik 1 | 1957–1958 |
| Apollo 11 | 1968–1972 |
| Pathfinder | 1996–1997 |
| Spirit | 2003–2004 |
| Cassini-Huygens | 1997–2005 |

### Space Exploration

Space exploration began in 1957. That was the year Russia put *Sputnik 1* into orbit. In 1969, the United States put the first man on the moon. Since then, *Pathfinder* and *Spirit* have brought rocks back to Earth from Mars. Those missions showed that water probably existed on Mars at one time. More recently, the *Cassini-Huygens* mission took photos of Titan, Saturn's largest moon. Titan may also have frozen ice. Many more discoveries await us. Who knows what we will learn from future missions?

**1.** What is the purpose of this paragraph?

_____

_____

**2.** How can you tell?

_____

_____

**3.** What is the paragraph mainly about?

_____

_____

# Vocabulary Activities and Word Cards

Copy the Word Cards on page 158 as needed for the following activities.
Use the blank cards for additional words that you want to teach.
Also see suggestions for teaching vocabulary in the ELL and Transition Handbook.

| Cloze Paragraph | Synonyms or Antonyms? | Home Language |
|---|---|---|
| • Write the following paragraph on the board. Replace the underscored words with blank lines: *On a space mission, each astronaut has a different role. Each has very specific tasks. One astronaut studies the monitors, and another operates equipment. It's important for an astronaut to keep his or her focus while operating this equipment. And it isn't easy. There's no gravity in space, and the tasks are very complex. A successful mission is a major accomplishment.*<br><br>• Distribute Word Cards to six students or pairs.<br><br>• Provide tape, and ask each student or pair to tape the card in the appropriate space. When finished, ask a volunteer to read the paragraph aloud. | • Form small groups of students. Give each group a set of Word Cards and a dictionary, and allow groups enough time to study the meaning of each word.<br><br>• Tape a set of Word Cards to the blackboard in a column in alphabetical order. Next to the column, write the following words in another column, in the following order: *failures, concentration, flotation, screens, position, general.*<br><br>• Go down the list, one pair at a time. Ask students whether each pair is synonyms or antonyms. If they are synonyms, draw an equal sign between them. If they are antonyms, draw a not equal sign. When finished, you should have the following list: *acccomplishments ≠ failures focus = concentration gravity ≠ buoyancy monitors = screens role = position specific ≠ general*<br><br>• You may choose to include additional selection words and their synonyms or antonyms. | • Give each student a set of Word Cards, and provide access to bilingual dictionaries in students' home languages.<br><br>• Have students write translations of the vocabulary words in their home language on the backs of the cards.<br><br>• When they are finished, invite volunteers to take turns teaching the rest of the students how to say each vocabulary word in their home language.<br><br>• You can even encourage students to make up sentences in their home language with the targeted word. They should then state the sentence for the other students to listen to and, if possible, learn. |

© Scott Foresman 5

# accomplishments

# focus

# gravity

# monitors

# role

# specific

# Multilingual Summaries

## Talk with an Astronaut

Fifth-grade students interviewed Ellen Ochoa. She decided to become an astronaut during graduate school and after the first six women astronauts were chosen.

Ellen is thankful for her hard training. It helps prevent problems during missions. Ellen thinks that floating in zero gravity is fun! The astronauts sleep in floating beds attached to hooks in the wall. Most of their food is freeze-dried, and they just add water.

Ellen misses her family while she is in space. She is able to e-mail them daily. Sometimes they can have a video conference. Ellen thinks space travel is exciting, not scary. Ellen suggests that if students want to be astronauts, they should study math and science. Students should also get involved in team activities. This is helpful because the astronauts work closely in teams.

**Spanish**

## Conversación con un astronauta

Los estudiantes de quinto grado entrevistaron a Ellen Ochoa. Ella les contó que decidió hacerse astronauta durante su postgrado y después que ya habían sido elegidas las primeras seis mujeres astronautas.

Ellen está agradecida por el fuerte entrenamiento que se recibe. Esto ayuda a prevenir problemas durante las misiones. ¡Ellen piensa que flotar cuando no hay gravedad es muy divertido! Los astronautas duermen en camas flotantes amarradas con ganchos a las paredes. La mayor parte de la comida es congelada y seca, y ellos sólo le agregan agua.

Ellen extraña a su familia cuando está en el espacio. Ella puede enviarles un correo electrónico todos los días. Algunas veces, ellos tienen videoconferencias. Ellen piensa que los viajes en el espacio son emocionantes, no aterradores. Ellen sugiere que si los estudiantes quieren ser astronautas deben estudiar matemáticas y ciencias. Los estudiantes también deben participar en trabajos de equipo. Esto ayuda mucho porque los astronautas con frecuencia trabajan en equipos.

# Multilingual Summaries

## 訪問宇航員

　　五年級學生一起去拜訪埃倫·奧喬亞。她在研究院時，就立志當一名宇航員。第一批女宇航員挑選了六人，她就是其中一個。

　　埃倫說艱苦訓練非常重要，它可以防止執行任務時出現差錯。她還說體驗零重力漂浮很有趣！宇航員睡在漂浮的床裏，兩邊繫在墙壁的勾子上。許多食物是乾凍的，吃的時候要加水。

　　在太空時，埃倫很想念家人，因此每天給他們發電子郵件，有時還通過電視交談。埃倫認為太空旅行很有意思，一點也不可怕。她告訴同學們，如果要當宇航員，必須學好數學與科學，還要積極參加團隊活動，這非常必要，因為宇航員需要密切的合作。

## Nói Chuyện Với Một Phi Hành Gia Vũ Trụ

　　Các học sinh lớp năm phỏng vấn Ellen Ochoa. Cô quyết định làm phi hành gia vũ trụ khi học ở trường cao học và sau khi sáu nữ phi hành gia vũ trụ đầu tiên được chọn.

　　Ellen mừng là đã được khổ công huấn luyện. Việc này giúp ngăn ngừa những vấn đề xảy ra trong các lần bay. Ellen nghĩ là lơ lửng vì không có trọng lực là điều vui! Các phi hành gia vũ trụ ngủ trong những cái giường treo lơ lửng gắn vào những cái móc trên tường. Hầu hết những thức ăn của họ đã được đông khô, và họ chỉ cần để nước vào.

　　Ellen nhớ gia đình khi bay trong không gian. Cô có thể "email" cho họ mỗi ngày. Thỉnh thoảng họ có thể có buổi hội đàm bằng "video". Ellen nghĩ là du hành vũ trụ là hứng thú, chứ không đáng sợ. Ellen đề nghị là nếu học sinh muốn trở thành những phi hành gia vũ trụ, thì các em nên học toán và khoa học. Học sinh cũng nên tham gia vào những sinh hoạt đồng đội. Điều này hữu ích vì các phi hành gia vũ trụ làm việc chặt chẽ với nhau trong đội.

# Multilingual Summaries

## 우주 비행사와의 대화

　5학년 학생들이 엘렌 오코어와 인터뷰를 했다. 그녀는 대학원을 다니는 동안 여섯 명의 최초 여성 우주 비행사가 선출되자 우주 비행사가 되기로 마음먹었다.

　엘렌은 힘든 훈련 기간에 대해 감사해한다. 그 덕분에 임무를 수행하는 동안 문제들을 예방할 수 있었기 때문이다. 엘렌은 무중력 상태에서 떠 다니는 것을 재미있어 한다! 우주 비행사들은 벽의 고리에 연결되어 있는 떠다니는 침대에서 잠을 잔다. 그들이 먹는 음식의 대부분은 동결 건조되어 있어 물만 부어 먹는다.

　엘렌은 우주에 있는 동안 가족을 그리워하며 매일 이메일을 보낸다. 그들은 가끔 비디오 회의도 한다. 엘렌은 우주 여행은 무서운 것이 아니라 아주 신나는 것이라고 생각한다. 엘렌은 학생들에게 우주 비행사가 되고 싶으면 수학과 과학 공부를 해야 한다고 얘기해준다. 우주 비행사들은 그룹으로 긴밀히 활동하기 때문에 학생들은 그룹 활동에도 참여해야 한다.

## Nrog ib tug Astronaut Tham

　Cov tub kawm ntawv nyob qib tsib tau nrog Ellen Ochoa tham. Nws tau txiav txim siab kawm los ua ib tug astronaut, ib tug ua ya ub rau saum nruab ntug, thaum nws kawm ntawv qib siab thiab tom qab rau leej poj niam astronaut tau nruag xaiv los lawm.

　Ellen txaus siab rau nws txoj kev kawm uas nyuaj heev. Kev kawm ntawd pab lawm tiv thaiv teeb meem thaum lawv ua hauj lwm. Ellen xav tias thaum yus ya thaum tsis muaj kev nqus mas lom zem kawg nkaus li. Cov astronauts pw saum ib co txaj uas nta saum ib ya thiab uas luag siv nqe lauj muab pav rau tim phab ntsa. Feem ntau ntawm lawm cov zoo mov khov qhuav qhuav lawm ces lawv tsuas ntxiv ntej rau xwb.

　Ellen nco nws tsev neeg thaum nws nyob saum ntuab nrug. Nws sau tau ntawv hauv kosputawj (computer) tuaj rau lawv txhua txhua hnub. Muaj tej zaum uas lawv sib koob thaij duab los sib tham (video conference) tau thiab. Ellen xav tias kev tau nchim ntuab nrug lom zem heev, tsis muaj kev ntshai li. Ellen xav tias yog cov tub kawm ntawv leej twg xav mus ua ib tug astronaut, kom lawv yuav tsum kawm leeb thiab tswvyim txawj ntse (science). Cov tub kawm ntawv yuav tsum koom tes nrog tej pab neeg ua ub ua no uake thiab. Qhov ntawd yuav pab lawv heev vim tias cov astronaut sawvdaws ua hauj lwm uake heev.

# Journey to the Center of the Earth

| Week at a Glance | Customize instruction every day for your English Language Learners. | | | | |
|---|---|---|---|---|---|
| | **Day 1** | **Day 2** | **Day 3** | **Day 4** | **Day 5** |
| **Teacher's Edition** | Use the ELL Notes that appear throughout each day of the lesson to support instruction and reading. | | | | |
| **ELL Poster 24** | • Assess Prior Knowledge<br>• Develop Concepts and Vocabulary | • Preteach Tested Vocabulary | • Minerals and Metals | • Core Picture | • Monitor Progress |
| **ELL Teaching Guide** | • Picture It! Lesson, pp. 162–163<br>• Multilingual Summaries, pp. 166–168 | • ELL Reader Lesson, pp. 258–259 | • Vocabulary Activities and Word Cards, pp. 164–165<br>• Multilingual Summaries, pp. 166–168 | | |
| **ELL Readers** | • Reread *Fixing Hubble's Troubles* | • Teach *Jules Verne's Imagination* | • Reread *Jules Verne's Imagination* and other texts to build fluency | | |
| **ELL and Transition Handbook** | Use the following as needed to support this week's instruction and to conduct alternative assessments:<br>• Phonics Transition Lessons<br>• Grammar Transition Lessons<br>• Assessment | | | | |

Picture It! Comprehension Lesson
## Cause and Effect

Use this lesson to supplement or replace the skill lesson on pages 582–583 of the Teacher's Edition.

### Teach

Distribute copies of the Picture It! blackline master on page 163.
• Point out the picture at the top of the page. Ask students if they know what it shows. (a volcano)
• Share the Skill Points (at right) with students.
• Tell students they are going to learn about Mount St. Helens, a volcano in Washington. Read the paragraph aloud.

### Practice

Read aloud the directions on page 163. Have students read the passage and then complete the charts at the bottom of the page. Remind students that they may need to reread to find the information they need. Have students keep their organizers for later reteaching.

**Answers for page 163:** *Effects:* An avalanche tore open the side of the mountain. Steam blasted from the volcano. *Causes:* Steam blasted sideways from the volcano. Mud started to flow down.

### Skill Points

✓ A **cause** makes something happen. An **effect** is what happens.

✓ A cause may have several effects. An effect may have several causes.

Name _____

**Read** the paragraph. Then complete the graphic organizers.

- **Write** two effects of the cause in the first organizer.
- **Write** two causes for the effect in the second organizer.

## When Mount St. Helens Erupted

Mount St. Helens is an active volcano in Washington. On May 18, 1980, an earthquake started an avalanche. The avalanche tore open the side of the mountain. Steam blasted sideways from the volcano in a violent wind. The steam melted ice and snow at the top of the mountain, which caused mud to flow down the mountain. Together, the steam blast and mudflow flattened the forest at the bottom of the mountain. It took many years for the forest to grow back.

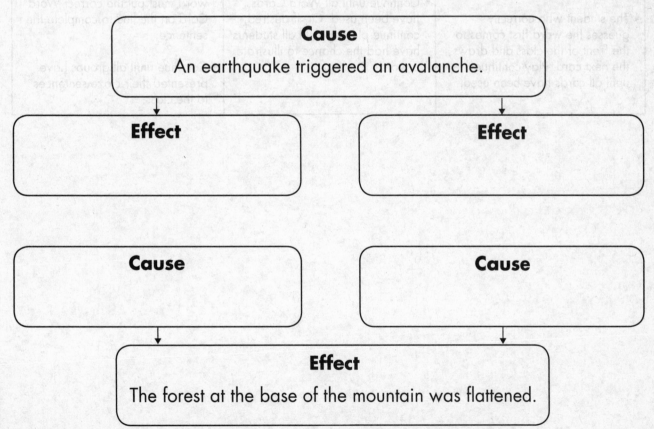

**Cause**
An earthquake triggered an avalanche.

**Effect**

**Effect**

**Cause**

**Cause**

**Effect**
The forest at the base of the mountain was flattened.

# Vocabulary Activities and Word Cards

Copy the Word Cards on page 165 as needed for the following activities.
Use the blank cards for additional words that you want to teach.
Also see suggestions for teaching vocabulary in the ELL and Transition Handbook.

| Riddle Games | Picture It! | Cloze Sentences |
| --- | --- | --- |
| • Give sets of Word Cards to pairs of students. Have students study the meaning of each word using a dictionary. Then take the cards away. Shuffle and keep one set.<br><br>• Invite a student to the front of the class. Have the student draw a card from the top of your stack. The student should hold the card so that his or her classmates can't see the word. Then the student gives clues to the card in the following pattern: *This word starts with the letter ____. This word ends with the letter ____. This word means ____.*<br><br>• The student who correctly guesses the word first comes to the front of the class and draws the next card. Play continues until all cards have been used. | • Ask one student to come to the front of the class while the remaining students look on. Ask the student to choose a Word Card. Explain that the student will illustrate the word on the board. Allow the student to consult a dictionary for ideas.<br><br>• As the student draws, the remaining students try to guess which vocabulary word is represented. The first student to guess correctly gets to come to the front of the class, choose the next Word Card, and illustrate it.<br><br>• Continue until all Word Cards have been used. Or, if desired, continue playing until all students have had the chance to illustrate a word. | • Form three groups. Give each group two Word Cards and paper strips.<br><br>• Tell groups to create a cloze sentence on the paper strips for each of their words.<br><br>• When the students have finished, redistribute the Word Cards so that groups have different words than the ones they were originally given.<br><br>• Invite each group to take turns displaying their cloze sentences. The group with the missing word must put the correct Word Card on the line to complete the sentence.<br><br>• Continue until all groups have presented their cloze sentences to the class. |

**armor**

**encases**

**extinct**

**hideous**

**plunged**

**serpent**

# Multilingual Summaries

## Journey to the Center of the Earth

In this story, three men take a trip to explore the center of the Earth. They are floating on a raft on an underground sea. The travelers see many huge animals. They look like monsters. The animals are fighting each other in the sea. The men fear that their raft will turn over from the crashing waves. They feel tiny compared to the monsters.

Then the animals disappear. After a short time, one animal rises to the surface and slowly dies. The men realize that the monsters are really dinosaurs. The men hope the other dinosaur has gone to hide. They worry that it will come back.

## Viaje al centro de la Tierra

En esta historia, tres hombres hacen un viaje al centro de la Tierra. Ellos están flotando en una balsa en un mar debajo de la superficie. Los viajeros ven muchos animales enormes. Estos animales parecen monstruos. Los animales están luchando unos contra otros en el mar. Los hombres temen que las olas al estrellarse le den vuelta a su balsa. Ellos se sienten pequeños comparados con los monstruos.

Luego, los animales desaparecen. Después de poco tiempo, uno de los animales emerge en la superficie y muere lentamente. Los hombres se dan cuenta de que los monstruos son realmente dinosaurios. Los hombres tienen la esperanza de que el otro dinosaurio se haya ido a esconderse. Ellos se preocupan de que él regrese.

# Multilingual Summaries

## 地心曆險記

　　故事要說的是，三個朋友出發去地心探險，乘著皮筏，漂浮在地下海洋。他們看見許多巨獸，像是可怕的怪物，在海裏互相搏鬥。三個人害怕洶涌的海浪會把皮筏打翻。與巨獸相比，人簡直像小小的螞蟻。

　　這時所有巨獸突然消失了。過了不久，有一頭巨獸浮出水面，掙扎著慢慢死了。三個人這才發現，巨獸原來是恐龍。他們希望另一隻恐龍已經離開，擔心它隨時會回來。

## Đi Vào Tâm Điểm Địa Cầu

Trong câu chuyện này, có ba ông đi thám hiểm tâm điểm Địa Cầu. Họ đi trên một chiếc thuyền bè trên biển ở dưới lòng đất. Những người du hành thấy có nhiều thú vật đồ sộ. Chúng trông giống như quái vật. Các con thú này đang đánh nhau dưới biển. Ba ông này sợ là chiếc thuyền bè của họ sẽ bị lật vì những cơn sóng đập mạnh. Họ cảm thấy mình bé nhỏ so với những con quái vật.

Rồi cả hai quái vật biến mất. Sau chốc lát, một con nổi lên mặt nước, và từ từ chết. Ba ông nhận ra rằng những con quái vật thật ra là những con khủng long. Ba ông này hy vọng là con khủng long kia đã đi trốn. Họ lo sợ là nó sẽ quay lại.

# Multilingual Summaries

## 지구 중심으로의 여행

세 남자가 지구의 중심부를 탐사하기 위해 여행을 떠난다. 그들은 지하의 바다에서 뗏목을 타고 떠다니고 있다. 그들은 괴물같이 생긴 큰 동물들을 많이 만나게 된다. 동물들이 바다에서 서로 싸우는 바람에 뗏목이 파도에 부딪혀 뒤집힐까봐 세 남자는 두려워한다. 이들은 자신이 괴물에 비해 아주 작다고 느낀다.

그때 동물들이 사라진다. 잠시 후 동물 한 마리가 표면으로 떠올라 천천히 죽는다. 세 남자는 괴물이 진짜 공룡이라는 것을 알게 되고 다른 공룡이 숨어버렸기를 바라며 공룡이 다시 돌아올까봐 걱정한다.

## Nchim mus txog hauv Plawv Ntiaj Teb

Zaj dab neeg no piav txog peb tug txiv neej uas mus ncig txog hauv plaws ntiaj teb no. Lawv ntab sau ib phuaj ntoo nyob hauv ib lub hiavtxwv nyob sab hauv av. Cov neeg ncig ntawd pom ib cov tsiaj loj loj kawg. Lawv ntxim zoo li dab. Cov tsiaj ntawd sib ntaus hauv dej. Cov txiv neej ntshai tsam lawv lub phuaj ntoo ntxeev vim dej txaws ntxhee. Lawv txim li lawv me heev thaum muaj lawv piv nrog rau cov dab ntawd.

Ces ob tug tsiaj ntawd cia li ploj lawm. Ib me ntsis tom qab, ib tug tsiaj maj mam tshwm los saum nplaim dej ces cia li maj mam tuag lawm. Cov txiv neej ntawd pom tau tias cov dab ntawd yog daisnausxauj (dinosaurs) tiag xwb. Cov txiv neej ntawd cia siab tias lwm cov daisnausxauj ib mus nkaum lawm. Cov neeg ncig ntawd ntshai tsam nws yuav rov qab los.

# Ghost Towns of the American West

Student Edition pages 608–619

| Week at a Glance | Customize instruction every day for your English Language Learners. | | | | |
|---|---|---|---|---|---|
| | **Day 1** | **Day 2** | **Day 3** | **Day 4** | **Day 5** |
| **Teacher's Edition** | Use the ELL Notes that appear throughout each day of the lesson to support instruction and reading. | | | | |
| **ELL Poster 25** | • Assess Prior Knowledge<br>• Develop Concepts and Vocabulary | • Preteach Tested Vocabulary | • Review Generalize | • Greetings from California | • Monitor Progress |
| **ELL Teaching Guide** | • Picture It! Lesson, pp. 169–170<br>• Multilingual Summaries, pp. 173–175 | • ELL Reader Lesson, pp. 260–261 | • Vocabulary Activities and Word Cards, pp. 171–172<br>• Multilingual Summaries, pp. 173–175 | | |
| **ELL Readers** | • Reread *Jules Verne's Imagination* | • Teach *Gold in the American River* | • Reread *Gold in the American River* and other texts to build fluency | | |
| **ELL and Transition Handbook** | Use the following as needed to support this week's instruction and to conduct alternative assessments:<br>• Phonics Transition Lessons<br>• Grammar Transition Lessons<br>• Assessment | | | | |

**Picture It!** Comprehension Lesson
# Generalize

Use this lesson to supplement or replace the skill lesson on pages 604–605 of the Teacher's Edition.

## Teach

Distribute copies of the Picture It! blackline master on page 170.
• Point to the map at the top of the page. Tell students it shows the route of a railroad.
• Share the Skill Points (at right) with students.
• Read the paragraph aloud. Ask: *How did this railroad change the western United States?*

## Practice

Read aloud the directions on page 170. Have students read the paragraph and then complete the graphic organizer. Have students keep their organizers for later reteaching.

**Answers for page 170:** *Generalization:* Possible answer: The Transcontinental Railroad made settling the western United States easier; *Examples:* Before 1869, it was difficult to cross the country. After the railroad was finished, people could travel from Nebraska to California. Many farmers traveled west to start farms.

### Skill Points

✓ To **generalize** means to make a broad statement. It is a way of summarizing several details or examples.

✓ Words such as *always, never, forever, all, many,* and *most* signal a generalization.

**Look** at the map, then **read** the paragraph. **Complete** the graphic organizer at the bottom of the page.

- In the first box, **write** a generalization about the Transcontinental Railroad.
- In the three smaller boxes, **write** examples from the text that support your generalization.

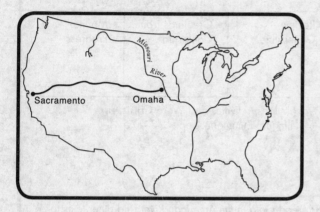

## The Transcontinental Railroad

The Transcontinental Railroad changed the United States forever. It was built in 1869. Before that time, it was difficult to cross the country. People had to use horses or walk. The Transcontinental Railroad went all the way from Nebraska to California. When the railroad was finished, it was possible to travel from the Missouri River to Sacramento. Soon after that, many people traveled west to establish farms and raise cattle. These farmers started towns throughout the west.

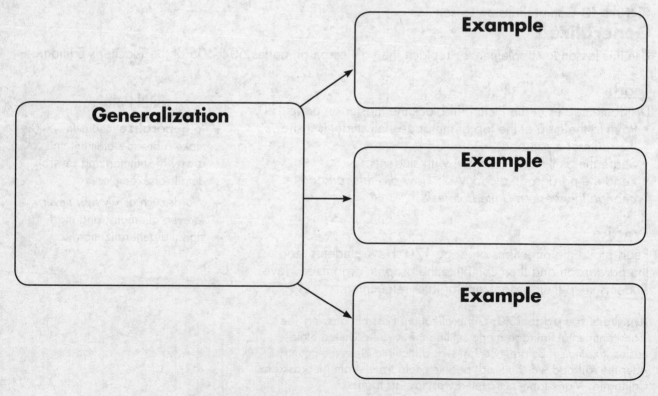

# Vocabulary Activities and Word Cards

Copy the Word Cards on page 172 as needed for the following activities.
Use the blank cards for additional words that you want to teach.
Also see suggestions for teaching vocabulary in the ELL and Transition Handbook.

| Newspaper Search | Another Way to Say It | Definition Game |
| --- | --- | --- |
| • Create a set of Word Cards, and distribute cards evenly to students or groups of students.<br><br>• Give each group a newspaper, and have the students search the newspaper for their assigned word or words. Remind students to look in the headlines as well as the articles.<br><br>• Invite students to share their words and the context in which they found them with the class. Students can read aloud the headlines or paragraphs that included their assigned words. If students are not able to find an assigned word, allow them to create a sample sentence that might appear in a newspaper article or headline. | • Write the following sentences on the board.<br>*Once, the town had been <u>infested</u> with people. (overrun)*<br>*The names of all the residents were <u>scribbled</u> in an old record book. (scrawled)*<br>*The people were looking for <u>freedom</u>. (independence)*<br>*They were also looking for <u>financial</u> rewards. (economic)*<br>*Now the streets of the town were <u>empty</u>. (vacant)*<br><br>• Give students sets of Word Cards. As you read each sentence aloud, ask the students to hold up the vocabulary word that could be substituted for the word that is underlined.<br><br>• Ask volunteers to restate the sentence using the vocabulary word in place of the word that is underlined. | • Form pairs of students, and give each pair a set of Word Cards.<br><br>• Tell partners to work together, writing the definition for each word on the back of the card.<br><br>• Students can quiz each other by playing a game. Have one student read aloud a definition (making sure the word on the other side isn't visible). His or her partner tries to guess what the word is, based on the definition. |

economic

independence

overrun

scrawled

vacant

# Multilingual Summaries

## Ghost Towns of the American West

Ghost towns were once busy mining camps or cowboy towns. Thousands of people moved to the West when gold was discovered there in 1848.

Towns were built where gold, silver, and copper were discovered. Towns were also built near the railroad and railroad stations. Most of these towns' people were men. Some towns put ads in the newspapers. The ads asked for women to come and live there.

Some towns became big cities. Other towns failed because the mines closed. Some failed because they were too far from the railroad when it came. People moved away to be nearer to more gold and closer to the railroad. They left empty towns behind. The towns that were once full of people are now the ghost towns of today.

## Los pueblos fantasmas del Oeste estadounidense

Los pueblos fantasmas fueron alguna vez activos campamentos mineros o pueblos de vaqueros. Miles de personas se mudaron al Oeste cuando oro fue descubierto allí en 1848.

Los pueblos se construyeron donde se había encontrado oro, plata y cobre. Además se construyeron cerca de los ferrocarriles y de las estaciones ferroviarias. La mayoría de la gente que vivía en esos pueblos eran hombres. Algunos pueblos ponían avisos en los periódicos. Los avisos les pedían a las mujeres que fueran a vivir allí.

Unos pueblos se convirtieron en grandes ciudades. Otros fracasaron porque las minas cerraron. Algunos fracasaron porque estaban muy lejos de los ferrocarriles cuando estos se construyueron. La gente se fue para estar más cerca del oro y de los ferrocarriles. Los pueblos que antes estaban llenos de personas, ahora son pueblos fantasmas.

# Multilingual Summaries

**Chinese**

## 美國西部無人鎮

　　無人鎮曾經住著繁忙的礦工和嘈雜的牛仔。1848年西部發現金礦後，許多人來到這裏。

　　哪里發現金礦、銀礦或銅礦，哪里就有村莊。哪里靠近鐵路與車站，哪里就有城鎮。來這裏的大都是男人。有些村鎮就在報紙做廣告，吸引女人搬到這些地方。

　　有些村鎮後來變成大城市，有些卻因為礦場關閉、離通車的鐵路太遠而衰落。人們都搬到金礦和鐵路附近，只留下一些空城。原來這裏有許多居民，現在卻成了荒涼的無人鎮。

**Vietnamese**

## Những Thị Trấn Bỏ Hoang ở Miền Tây Hoa Kỳ

　　Các thị trấn bỏ hoang đã từng là những trại khai thác hầm mỏ nhộn nhịp hoặc là những phố thị của các tay chăn bò. Hàng ngàn người đã dọn đến miền Tây khi vàng được tìm thấy ở đó vào năm 1848.

　　Các thị trấn được dựng lên ở nơi nào vàng, bạc, và đồng được tìm thấy. Thị trấn cũng được dựng lên gần đường rày xe lửa và trạm xe lửa. Đa số dân sinh sống ở những thị trấn này là đàn ông. Một vài thị trấn đăng quảng cáo trên báo. Các quảng cáo này mời gọi phụ nữ đến và sinh sống ở đó.

　　Một vài thị trấn trở thành những thành phố lớn. Vài thị trấn khác bị bỏ vì các hầm mỏ đóng cửa. Vài thị trấn bị bỏ vì cách đường rày xe lửa quá xa khi đường rày được xây. Người ta dọn đến ở gần nơi nào có nhiều vàng hơn và gần với đường rày xe lửa hơn. Họ bỏ lại sau lưng những thị trấn không người. Những thị trấn đã có một thời đông đúc thì ngày nay là những thị trấn bỏ hoang.

# Multilingual Summaries

## 미국 서부의 유령 도시

유령 도시는 한때 금광 캠프 또는 카우보이 마을로 분주한 곳이었다. 1848년 서부에서 금이 발견되자 수천 명의 사람들이 서부로 몰려 왔다.

도시는 금, 은 또는 구리가 발견된 곳이나 기찻길 근처와 기차역 주변에 만들어졌다. 이런 도시에 사는 사람들은 대부분 남자여서 어떤 도시에서는 여자들에게 와서 살라는 광고를 신문에 내기도 했다.

몇몇 도시는 대도시가 되었고 몇몇 도시는 금광이 문을 닫거나 처음부터 기찻길에서 너무 멀리 떨어진 곳에 있어서 쇠퇴했다. 사람들은 금이 더 많이 나는 곳이나 기찻길에서 더 가까운 곳으로 가기 위해 빈 도시를 남겨두고 떠나갔다. 한때 사람들로 가득했던 도시는 이제 유령 도시가 되었다.

## Zos Dab nyob rau Amiskas Teb Sab Hnub Poob

Puag thaum ub mas cov zos dab niaj hnub niam no yog ib co zos ua neeg khawb nyiaj khawb kub los khawb tooj khawb hlau tau nyob lossis lawv yog zos cowboy. Tshej phav leej neeg tau tsiv mus nyob rau sab hnub poob thaum luag nrhiav tau nyiaj kub ntawd nyob rau xyoo ib txhiab yim puas plaub caug yim.

Qhov twg luag nrhiav tau nyiaj tau kub los tau tooj liab ces qhov ntawd luag tau ua zos nyob. Luag kuj tau ua zos nyob ze kev tshe ciav hlau thiab ntawm tej chaws nres tshe ciav hlau. Feem coob ntawm cov neeg nyob tej zos ntawd yog txiv neej. Ib txhia zos kuj khu xab nas hauv ntawv xov xwm thiab. Cov ntawv khu xas nas ntawd thov kom poj niam tuaj nyob ntawd.

Ib txhia zos kuj loj tuaj ua zos loj kawg li. Ib txhia kuj poob lawm vim cov qhov khawb nyiaj kub thiab tooj ntawd tau raug kaw lawm. Ib txhia ho poob lawm vim lawv nyob deb kev tsheb ciav hlau dhau lawm thaum lawv tuaj. Tib neeg tsiv mus nyob kom ze nyiaj kub thiab ze kev tsheb ciav hlau tshaj. Lawv cia li tseg tej zos ntawd tseg xwb. Cov zos uas thaum ub muaj neeg nyob coob coob niaj hnub no tsuas yog zos dab lawm xab.

Student Edition pages 638–649

| Week at a Glance | Customize instruction every day for your English Language Learners. | | | | |
|---|---|---|---|---|---|
| | **Day 1** | **Day 2** | **Day 3** | **Day 4** | **Day 5** |
| **Teacher's Edition** | Use the ELL Notes that appear throughout each day of the lesson to support instruction and reading. | | | | |
| **ELL Poster 26** | • Assess Prior Knowledge<br>• Develop Concepts and Vocabulary | • Preteach Tested Vocabulary | • Actions and Consequences | • Tide Pool Mural | • Monitor Progress |
| **ELL Teaching Guide** | • Picture It! Lesson, pp. 176–177<br>• Multilingual Summaries, pp. 180–182 | • ELL Reader Lesson, pp. 262–263 | • Vocabulary Activities and Word Cards, pp. 178–179<br>• Multilingual Summaries, pp. 180–182 | | |
| **ELL Readers** | • Reread *Gold in the American River* | • Teach *Nighttime Under the Sea* | • Reread *Nighttime Under the Sea* and other texts to build fluency | | |
| **ELL and Transition Handbook** | Use the following as needed to support this week's instruction and to conduct alternative assessments:<br>• Phonics Transition Lessons<br>• Grammar Transition Lessons<br>• Assessment | | | | |

**Picture It!** Comprehension Lesson

# Drawing Conclusions

Use this lesson to supplement or replace the skill lesson on pages 634–635 of the Teacher's Edition.

## Teach

Distribute copies of the Picture It! blackline master on page 177.
• Tell students to look at the picture and read the title. Ask students whether they have ever eaten curry. Tell them it is a dish from India. Do not mention that it is spicy, since this is a conclusion that students will draw from the text.
• Share the Skill Points (at right) with students.
• Read the paragraph aloud.

## Practice

Read aloud the directions on page 177. Have students read the paragraph and then answer the questions that follow. Remind students to circle the letter next to the best answer to each question. Have students keep their work for later reteaching.

**Answers for page 177: 1. A.** Curry is very spicy. **2. D.** Curry has a lot of spices in it. **3. C.** coriander, turmeric, red pepper, and curry

> ### Skill Points
> ✓ When you **draw conclusions,** you make a decision based on information in the text.
> ✓ Details from the text should support your conclusion.

**Read** the paragraph, and then **read** the questions. **Circle** the best answer for each question.

## Making Curry

Curry is an Indian dish. It is a kind of sauce with vegetables or meat. People like to have it with white rice. To make curry, you need a lot of spices. Coriander and turmeric are good to have. You should also have some red pepper. And of course, you need curry. A good cook keeps adding spices and tasting the sauce. Curry has to have the right combination of spices.

**1.** What is a reasonable conclusion you can draw from this paragraph?

   **A.** Curry is very spicy.

   **B.** Indian food takes a long time to make.

   **C.** Curry is the most important spice in Indian cooking.

   **D.** Most Indian dishes include white rice.

**2.** Why is this a reasonable conclusion?

   **A.** It is hard to make curry.

   **B.** Curry is usually served with white rice.

   **C.** Only good cooks can make curry.

   **D.** Curry has a lot of spices in it.

**3.** What are some of the spices in curry?

   **A.** white rice

   **B.** vegetables and meat

   **C.** coriander, turmeric, red pepper, and curry

   **D.** a secret Indian blend

# Vocabulary Activities and Word Cards

Copy the Word Cards on page 179 as needed for the following activities.
Use the blank cards for additional words that you want to teach.
Also see suggestions for teaching vocabulary in the ELL and Transition Handbook.

| Poster Clues | Group Story | Draw Me a Picture |
|---|---|---|
| • Distribute sets of Word Cards to students. Then, from another set of Word Cards, have a student pick a card without letting others see it.<br><br>• The student stands at the ELL Poster, points to the relevant area on it, and uses the Poster to give hints about the word.<br><br>• Other students try to guess which vocabulary word the student has. The first person to guess correctly is allowed to choose the next Word Card and make up clues about it.<br><br>• Continue until all vocabulary words have been used. | • Form groups of students. Put a set of Word Cards in a bag for each group.<br><br>• Have group members take turns drawing a card and making a sentence with the word. The sentences should tell a story. The first student should create a good story starter, for example: *A pirate concealed a treasure chest in a cave.*<br><br>• The next student then creates the next sentence, until all the words have been used.<br><br>• If possible, ask a group member to write the story down. Invite each group to present its story to the others. | • Create enough Word Cards so that you can give two or three cards to each student. Distribute the cards at random.<br><br>• Ask students to create a sketch, drawing, or symbol to illustrate their assigned words. Students should put each illustration on a separate piece of paper.<br><br>• Students should take turns explaining their illustrations to the rest of the students, or within small groups of students. |

algae

concealed

driftwood

hammocks

lamented

sea urchins

sternly

tweezers

# Multilingual Summaries

## At the Beach

One day Fernando goes to the beach with his family. They all go in Papi's car. The children run into the water as soon as they get there. The adults sit in the shade. The men play dominoes.

Fernando wants to go to the reef. The other children go with him. Their parents had told them not to go. Fernando's little cousin Javi steps on a sea urchin. Sea urchins have sharp spines. Javi is hurt. The children will be in trouble if their parents find out that they went to the reef. Fernando tells a lie when they go back for lunch.

Fernando feels bad about lying. He tells the truth. He thinks Mami will not give him lunch. But Mami thanks him for telling the truth, and Fernando eats his lunch.

## En la playa

Un día, Fernando va a la playa con su familia. Todos van en el auto de Papi. Los niños corren hacia el agua tan pronto llegan allí. Los adultos se sientan en la sombra. Los hombres juegan dominó.

Fernando quiere ir al arrecife. Los otros niños van con él. Sus padres les han dicho que no vayan allí. El primo pequeño de Fernando, Javi, pisa un erizo de mar. El erizo de mar tiene espinas afiladas. Javi se hace daño. Los niños tendrán problemas si sus padres descubren que ellos fueron al arrecife. Fernando dice una mentira cuando regresan a almorzar.

Fernando se siente mal porque ha mentido y finalmente dice la verdad. Él piensa que Mami no le dará el almuerzo. Pero Mami le da las gracias por decirle la verdad, y Fernando se come su almuerzo.

# Multilingual Summaries

## 在海邊

　　一天，費爾南多和家人一起去海邊，爸爸開車帶他們去。孩子們一到海邊，就跑去游泳。大人們坐在遮陽傘下，男人們在玩多米諾牌。

　　費爾南多想去珊瑚礁，雖然父母親不讓去，小朋友們還是跟著他。小表弟加維不小心踩到海膽，被尖銳的刺扎傷了。為了不讓父母發現他們去珊瑚礁玩了，費爾南多回來吃午餐時，沒有說實話。

　　撒謊之後，費爾南多心裏總發慌，最後還是說了實話。他想媽咪肯定不會給他吃午餐。可為了獎勵他的誠實，媽咪還是讓費爾南多吃了午餐。

## Trên Bãi Biển

　　Ngày nọ Fernando đi ra bãi biển với gia đình. Cả gia đình đi trên xe của Papi. Các đứa trẻ chạy xuống nước ngay khi đến nơi. Người lớn ngồi dưới bóng râm. Các ông thì chơi cờ đô-mi-nô.

　　Fernando muốn đi ra dãy đá ngầm. Các đứa trẻ khác muốn đi với cậu ấy. Cha mẹ chúng đã bảo chúng đừng đi. Đứa em họ của Fernando là Javi đạp trúng một con nhím biển. Những con nhím biển có các gai nhọn. Javi bị đau. Các đứa trẻ sẽ bị rầy rà nếu cha mẹ chúng biết được chúng đã đi ra dãy đá ngầm. Fernando đã nói dối khi chúng quay về ăn trưa.

　　Fernando cảm thấy ân hận vì đã nói dối. Cậu nói lên sự thật. Cậu bé nghĩ là Mami sẽ không cho cậu ăn trưa. Nhưng Mami cám ơn cậu bé đã nói thật, và Fernando được ăn bữa ăn trưa của mình.

# Multilingual Summaries

## 해변에서

어느 날 페르난도는 아빠의 차를 타고 가족과 함께 바다에 간다. 아이들은 도착하자마자 물로 뛰어들고 어른들은 그늘에 앉는다. 남자들은 도미노 게임을 한다.

페르난도는 암초에 가고 싶어해서 다른 아이들과 함께 암초에 간다. 하지만 아이들 부모님들은 암초에 가지 말라고 미리 주의를 주었다. 페르난도의 어린 사촌인 하비가 성게를 밟는다. 성게 표면에 뾰족한 가시가 있어 하비는 상처를 입는다. 아이들이 암초에 갔었다는 걸 부모님들이 알게 된다면 아이들은 벌을 받게 될 것이다. 페르난도는 아이들과 점심을 먹으러 돌아갔을 때 거짓말을 한다.

페르난도는 거짓말한 것을 뉘우치며 사실을 말하고 엄마가 점심을 주지 않을 것이라고 생각한다. 하지만 엄마는 사실을 말해 준 것에 대해 고마워하고 페르난도는 점심을 먹는다.

## Tom Ntug Dej Hiav Txwv

Muaj ib hnub Fernando thiab nws tsev neeg mus tom ntug dej ntawm cov dej hiav txwv. Sawvdaws huv tib si mus rau hauv Papi ib lub tshevb. Thaum mus txog ntug dej lawm ces cov menyuam txawm khiav mus nkag rau hauv cov dej. Cov tiav hlob zaum hauv qhov chaw uas ntxoov ntxoo li. Cov txiv neej ua si dominoes.

Fernando xav mus tom cov pob zeb ntse uas nyob ntug dej. Luag lwm cov meny7uam nrogg nws mus thiab. Sawvdaws cov niam thiav txiv qhia tias tsis txhob mus qhov ntawd. Fernando tus kwvtij yau Javi, tsuj nthi ib tug ntses Urchin uas nyob lub hiav txwv. Cov ntses Urchin uas nyob lub hiav txwv, muaj cov koob ntse uas nyob ntawm lawv txoj nqaj qaum. Javi raug mob. Cov niam, txiv yuav chim siab yog alwv paub tias lawv cov menyuam mus xyuas cov pob zeb ntse nyob ntug dej hiav txwv. Thaum cov menyuam rov qab mus noj su, ces Fernando hais lus dag.

Fernando nyob tsis zoo hauv lub siab rau qhov nws hais lus dag. Nws cia li rov qab hai lus tseeb. Fernando xav tias Mami yuav tsis pub su rau nws noj. Tiamsis Mami ua Fernando tsaug vim rau qhov nws hais lus tseeb, Fernando cia li noj nws cov mov.

# The Mystery of St. Matthew Island

Student Edition pages 658–667

| Week at a Glance | Customize instruction every day for your English Language Learners. | | | | |
|---|---|---|---|---|---|
| | **Day 1** | **Day 2** | **Day 3** | **Day 4** | **Day 5** |
| **Teacher's Edition** | Use the ELL Notes that appear throughout each day of the lesson to support instruction and reading. | | | | |
| **ELL Poster 27** | • Assess Prior Knowledge<br>• Develop Concepts and Vocabulary | • Preteach Tested Vocabulary | • Local Effects | • Tundra Mural | • Monitor Progress |
| **ELL Teaching Guide** | • Picture It! Lesson, pp. 183–184<br>• Multilingual Summaries, pp. 187–189 | • ELL Reader Lesson, pp. 264–265 | • Vocabulary Activities and Word Cards, pp. 185–186<br>• Multilingual Summaries, pp. 187–189 | | |
| **ELL Readers** | • Reread *Nighttime Under the Sea* | • Teach *All Things in Balance* | • Reread *All Things in Balance* and other texts to build fluency | | |
| **ELL and Transition Handbook** | Use the following as needed to support this week's instruction and to conduct alternative assessments:<br>• Phonics Transition Lessons<br>• Grammar Transition Lessons<br>• Assessment | | | | |

**Picture It!** Comprehension Lesson

## Main Idea and Details

Use this lesson to supplement or replace the skill lesson on pages 654–655 of the Teacher's Edition.

### Teach

Distribute copies of the Picture It! blackline master on page 184.
- Point to the illustration. Tell students that it shows Stonehenge, an ancient place in England.
- Share the Skill Points (at right) with students.
- Read the passage aloud. Ask: *What is this passage about?* (Stonehenge)

### Practice

Read aloud the directions on page 184. Have students read the passage and then answer the questions that follow. Encourage students to use complete sentences. Have students keep their work for later reteaching.

**Answers for page 184:** Possible answers: **1.** Stonehenge must have been very important to the people who built it. **2.** They built it without machines. They lifted rocks weighing up to 50 tons. They moved the rocks up to 240 miles.

> ### Skill Points
>
> ✓ The **main idea** is the most important idea in a paragraph. The author often states it at the beginning or end of the paragraph. But sometimes the main idea is not directly stated.
>
> ✓ **Details** are pieces of information that tell more about the main idea.

# Main Idea and Details

Name _____

**Read** the passage. **Answer** the questions that follow.

## The Mystery of Stonehenge

Stonehenge is a mysterious place in Southern England. It consists of a circle of very large stone slabs. The stones were erected thousands of years ago, before people had machines to help them build and lift. The stones weigh as much as 50 tons (100,000 pounds) each. Even more amazing, the stones were brought from places up to 240 miles away! Nobody is sure why the stones were placed here. But one thing is certain: Stonehenge must have been very important to the ancient people who built it.

**1.** What is the main idea?

_____

_____

**2.** What are three examples that support the main idea?

_____

_____

_____

_____

_____

_____

# Vocabulary Activities and Word Cards

Copy the Word Cards on page 186 as needed for the following activities.
Use the blank cards for additional words that you want to teach.
Also see suggestions for teaching vocabulary in the ELL and Transition Handbook.

| Cloze Sentences | Matching Game | Scrambled Sentences |
|---|---|---|
| • Form four groups of students. Give each group two Word Cards and paper strips. | • On blank cards, write a definition for each vocabulary word. | • Form groups of students. Give each group one Word Card and many index cards. |
| • Groups create cloze sentences for each of their words, leaving a blank in place of the word. | • Give a Word Card and its matching definition card to two different students. (Distribute as many vocabulary and definition card pairs as you have pairs of students. You may not be able to use all cards in one round.) Tell students to memorize the words on their cards. | • Tell groups to create sentences with their assigned words and write each word of the sentence (except the word on the Word Card) on a separate card. |
| • When they have finished, redistribute the Word Cards. | | • Invite a group to put its cards in scrambled order. Challenge the other students to arrange the cards in the correct order. |
| • Invite each group to take turns displaying their cloze sentences. The group with the missing word must put the correct Word Card on the line to complete the sentence. | • Collect the cards and have the students circulate in the classroom saying their word or definition aloud to each person until they find a match. | • Continue until all groups have presented their sentences. |
| • Continue until all groups have presented their sentences. | | |

bleached

carcasses

decay

parasites

scrawny

starvation

suspicions

tundra

# Multilingual Summaries

English

## The Mystery of Saint Matthew Island

Scientists released twenty-nine reindeer on Saint Matthew Island in 1944. There were no predators on the island. Saint Matthew Island had plenty of food for the reindeer. The herd quickly expanded. By 1963, there were more than six thousand reindeer.

The reindeer began to die. No one knew why. A scientist named David Klein went to the island to investigate. He knew the reindeer had not been exposed to parasites. There were no predators on the island. Why did they die?

Dr. Klein examined the bones. They had no fat in their bone marrow. Dr. Klein realized that the animals had too little to eat. They had died during a hard winter. The herd had grown too fast. They had eaten all the food on the island and died of starvation.

Spanish

## El misterio de la isla de Saint Matthew

En 1944, los científicos llevaron veintinueve renos a la isla de Saint Matthew y los dejaron en libertad. No había depredadores en la isla. La isla de Saint Matthew tenía suficiente comida para los renos. La manada se expandió rápidamente. Para 1963, había más de seis mil renos.

Los renos comenzaron a morir. Nadie sabía por qué. Un científico llamado David Klein fue a la isla para investigar. Él sabía que los renos no estaban expuestos a los parásitos. No había depredadores en la isla. Entonces, ¿por qué murieron?

El Dr. Klein examinó los huesos. No tenían grasa en la médula. El Dr. Klein se dio cuenta de que ellos habían tenido muy poco que comer. Habían muerto durante un duro invierno. La manada había crecido muy rápido. Los renos se habían comido toda la comida de la isla y murieron de hambre.

# Multilingual Summaries

## 聖馬修島的秘密

1944年，科學家把29頭馴鹿放到聖馬修島上。那裏沒有凶猛的食肉動物，而且食物充足，因此馴鹿急劇增長。到1963年，島上的馴鹿數目已經超過6000多。

可是馴鹿開始莫名其妙地死去，沒有人知道原因。科學家克萊因去島上研究。他知道這裏沒有寄生蟲，也沒有食肉動物。為什麼馴鹿會神秘地死亡？

克萊因仔細研究馴鹿殘骸，發現骨髓中沒有脂肪。他終於明白，原因是食物太少，在嚴寒的冬天，就會造成死亡。馴鹿繁殖迅速，吃光島上所有食物，活活餓死了。

## Điều Bí Ẩn ở Đảo Saint Matthew

Các nhà khoa học đã thả hai mươi chín con nai tuyết trên Đảo Saint Matthew vào năm 1944. Không có những con dã thú săn bắt mồi trên đảo này. Đảo Saint Matthew có nhiều thức ăn cho các con nai tuyết này. Đàn nai gia tăng mau chóng. Đến năm 1963, đã có trên sáu ngàn con nai tuyết.

Những con nai tuyết bắt đầu chết. Không ai biết vì lý do gì. Một nhà khoa học tên David Klein đi đến đảo này để điều tra. Ông biết là các con nai tuyết này không có bị ký sinh trùng. Trên đảo cũng không có dã thú săn mồi. Tại sao những con nai này chết?

Klein khám nghiệm những mảnh xương. Các mảnh xương không có chất mỡ trong tủy xương. Bác sĩ Klein hiểu ra là những con thú này đã không có đủ ăn. Chúng chết trong một mùa đông khắc nghiệt. Đàn nai đã gia tăng quá nhanh. Chúng đã ăn hết mọi thức ăn trên đảo, và chết vì đói.

# Multilingual Summaries

## 세인트 매튜섬의 미스터리

1944년 과학자들은 세인트 매튜섬에 순록 29마리를 풀어주었다. 섬에는 어떤 맹수도 없었으며 먹을 것도 풍부했다. 순록 무리는 빠른 속도로 성장했다. 1963년까지 그곳엔 6천마리 이상의 순록이 있었다.

그런데 순록이 죽기 시작했고 누구도 그 이유를 알지 못했다. 데이비드 클라인이라는 한 과학자가 섬에 들어가 조사를 시작했다. 그는 순록이 기생충에 노출되지 않았고 섬에는 맹수도 없었다는 사실을 알게 되었다. 그렇다면 순록들은 왜 죽은 것일까?

클라인은 순록의 뼈를 조사했는데 그들의 골수에는 지방이 하나도 없었고, 섬에 먹을 것이 너무나 없었다는 것을 알아냈다. 이들은 혹독한 겨울에 죽었다. 즉 순록 무리가 너무도 빨리 늘어나 섬의 모든 먹을 것을 먹어 치우고는 굶어 죽었던 것이다.

## Txoj Kev Xav Tsis Thoob Txog Lub Koog Povtxwv Saint Matthew

Nyob xhoo ib txhiab cuaj puas plaub caug plaub cov kws Scientists tso nees nkaum cuaj cov muas lwj tom lub koog pov txwv Saint Matthew. Nyob lub koog povtxwv ntawd tsis tau muaj lwm cov tsiaj txhu zoo li lawv. Lub koog povtxwv Saint Matthew tau muaj cov mov txaus rau cov muas lwj noj. Lub pab muas lwj tau loj hlob sai sai li. Txog xyoo ib txhiab cuaj puas rau caum peb, tau muaj rau ;hav cov muas lwj.

Cov muas lwj pib tas sim neej. Tsis tau muaj leejtwg paub ua li cas. Ib tug kws scientisit hu ua David Klein mus xyuas lub koog pov txwv nrhiav kawm saib. Nws twb paub tias cov muas lwj tsis tau ntsib kab mob hlo li. Tsis tau muaj lwm cov tsiaj txhu sib twv tom lub koog pov txwv. Ua licas lawv tuag?

Klein kawm saib cov pob txha. Cov muas lwj tsis muaj cov roj rau hauv lawv pob txha hlwb. Tus kws Klein twb tau nrhiav cov tsiaj txhu tsis muaj cov mov txaus rau lawv noj. Lawv tau tam sim neej thaum lub ciaj nyuj no no heev. Lub pab tau loj hlob sai sai dhau lawm. Lawv tau hoj txhua yam mov nyob rau lub koog pov txwv, lawv thiaj li tau tuag.

# King Midas and the Golden Touch
Student Edition pages 678–695

| Week at a Glance | Customize instruction every day for your English Language Learners. | | | | |
|---|---|---|---|---|---|
| | **Day 1** | **Day 2** | **Day 3** | **Day 4** | **Day 5** |
| **Teacher's Edition** | Use the ELL Notes that appear throughout each day of the lesson to support instruction and reading. | | | | |
| **ELL Poster 28** | • Assess Prior Knowledge<br>• Develop Concepts and Vocabulary | • Preteach Tested Vocabulary | • Interview with the Mummy | • A Chain of Good Actions | • Monitor Progress |
| **ELL Teaching Guide** | • Picture It! Lesson, pp. 190–191<br>• Multilingual Summaries, pp. 194–196 | • ELL Reader Lesson, pp. 266–267 | • Vocabulary Activities and Word Cards, pp. 192–193<br>• Multilingual Summaries, pp. 194–196 | | |
| **ELL Readers** | • Reread *All Things in Balance* | • Teach *A Tale of Gold and Glory* | • Reread *A Tale of Gold and Glory* and other texts to build fluency | | |
| **ELL and Transition Handbook** | Use the following as needed to support this week's instruction and to conduct alternative assessments:<br>• Phonics Transition Lessons<br>• Grammar Transition Lessons<br>• Assessment | | | | |

**Picture It!** Comprehension Lesson

# Compare and Contrast

Use this lesson to supplement or replace the skill lesson on pages 674–675 of the Teacher's Edition.

## Teach

Distribute copies of the Picture It! blackline master on page 191.
• Direct students' attention to the two pictures. One shows the Parthenon in ancient times. The other shows the Parthenon as it is today. Invite students to describe the pictures.
• Share the Skill Points (at right) with students.
• Read the paragraph aloud. Ask: *How has the Parthenon changed over time?*

## Practice

Read aloud the directions on page 191. Have students read the paragraph and then complete the chart. Tell them to look at the pictures for help if they need to. Have students keep their organizers for later reteaching.

**Answers for page 191:** *Then:* The Parthenon had a roof and many statues. Teachers gave lectures. Boys and young men came to listen. *Now:* The roof and most of the statues are gone. Tourists come to take pictures.

> ### Skill Points
> ✓ When you **compare and contrast**, you show how things are similar and how they are different.
>
> ✓ You can compare two different things, or you can compare the same thing in the past and in the present, showing how it has changed.

© Scott Foresman 5

Name _____

**Read** the paragraph and study the pictures. Then complete the chart.

- **Write** what the Parthenon was like in ancient times in the *Then* column.
- **Write** what it is like today in the *Now* column.

# The Parthenon

The Parthenon is an ancient Greek temple. The building was completed more than 2,400 years ago. It has gone through many changes since then. Originally, it had a pointed roof, but the roof is gone now. Most of the statues are gone too. In ancient times, teachers gave lectures on the front steps. Boys and young men came to listen. These days you will not see anybody taking classes at the Parthenon. But you can see many tourists taking pictures.

| The Parthenon | |
| --- | --- |
| **Then** | **Now** |
| | |

# Vocabulary Activities and Word Cards

Copy the Word Cards on page 193 as needed for the following activities.
Use the blank cards for additional words that you want to teach.
Also see suggestions for teaching vocabulary in the ELL and Transition Handbook.

| Yes or No? | Word Sort | Charades |
|---|---|---|
| • Divide the students into two teams. Ask a student from Team A to come to the front of the class and take a Word Card without showing it to the other students.<br><br>• The two teams will take turns asking the student yes-or-no questions about the hidden word. For example: *Is it a noun? Is it an adjective?*<br><br>• On a team's turn, if the students think they know what the word is, they ask, *Is it [word]?* If they identify the word, they receive a point. But if they are incorrect, they receive a negative point. Play continues until the word is guessed by either team. Then invite a student from Team B to present the next word.<br><br>• Continue switching between teams as you call on students to take a Word Card. When all words have been guessed, calculate the scores, subtracting any negative points, and declare the winning team. | • Form pairs of students and give each pair a set of Word Cards. Ask students to sort their Word Cards into three categories: adjectives, nouns, and verbs.<br><br>• After five or ten minutes, create a chart on the board with these category headings. Invite one pair of students to share the words that they have written under *Adjectives.* Ask another pair to share the words they have under *Nouns,* and a third pair to say what they have listed under *Verbs.* Complete the chart as dictated by students.<br><br>• Review the three lists and address any errors as necessary. As you do so, check to make sure that students understand the meaning of each word. You can ask students to show understanding by giving a synonym, using the word in a sentence, acting it out, or drawing a picture. | • Divide the students into small groups. Assign each group one or more Word Cards.<br><br>• Have each group discuss how best to act out the meaning of the vocabulary word.<br><br>• The group's first hint should be the number of syllables the word has. The students can indicate this however they choose (for example, clapping or holding up fingers).<br><br>• Groups take turns acting out scenes. Members of the other groups work together to try to guess the word. Award a point to the group that guesses correctly first.<br><br>• Continue until the meanings of all of the vocabulary words have been acted out. |

**adorn**

**cleanse**

**lifeless**

**precious**

**realm**

**spoonful**

# Multilingual Summaries

## King Midas and the Golden Touch

King Midas loved gold. His daughter was the only thing he loved more.

One day, the guards brought in a man they found. He had been sleeping in the garden. King Midas asked the man to stay for dinner.

To thank the king, the man offered him a wish. King Midas wished for all he touched to turn to gold. The next day, the king woke up to find his wish had come true. The king was happy with his wish until he touched his daughter. She turned to gold. King Midas begged for the wish to be undone. He got that wish too. King Midas restored everything he had turned to gold. He saved one gold rose to always remember the curse.

Spanish

## El rey Midas y su don del oro

Al rey Midas le fascinaba el oro. Su hija era lo único que él amaba más.

Un día, los guardias llevaron a su presencia a un hombre que habían encontrado durmiendo en el jardín. El rey Midas le pidió al hombre que se quedara a cenar con él.

Para agradecerle al rey, el hombre se ofreció a concederle un deseo. El rey Midas deseaba que todo lo que él tocara se convirtiera en oro. Al día siguiente, el rey se levantó y supo que su deseo se había hecho realidad. El rey estaba feliz con el don que había adquirido hasta que tocó a su hija y ella también se convirtió en oro. El rey Midas suplicó que su deseo fuera anulado. Ese deseo también le fue concedido. El rey Midas restableció todo lo que él había convertido en oro a su estado original. Sólo dejó una rosa de oro para recordar siempre la maldición.

# Multilingual Summaries

## 邁達斯國王的金手

邁達斯國王著迷金子，女兒是他唯一的珍愛。

有一天，警衛發現有人在花園裏睡覺，把他帶到國王面前。邁達斯不但沒處罰他，而且邀他共進晚餐。

那個人為了感謝國王，說可以滿足他的願望。邁達斯希望，能把碰到的東西都變成金子。第二天醒來，發現他的夢想真的實現了。他非常高興，可是一擁抱女兒，把她也變成了金子。邁達斯國王懊悔萬分，希望收回所說的話。於是，所有東西變回原來的樣子。國王保留了一朵金玫瑰，他要永遠記住這個教訓。

## Vua Midas và Phép Hóa Vàng

Vua Midas yêu vàng. Con gái của ông là điều duy nhất mà ông yêu hơn vàng.

Một ngày nọ, quân cảnh vệ dẫn vào một người đàn ông mà họ tìm gặp. Ông này đang ngủ trong vườn của vua. Vua Midas mời ông này ở lại dùng bữa ăn tối.

Để cám ơn nhà vua, ông này ban cho vua một điều ước. Vua Midas ước là mọi thứ mà ngài đụng vào sẽ biến thành vàng. Qua ngày sau, nhà vua thức giấc và thấy là điều ước của mình trở nên sự thật. Nhà vua vui mừng vì lời ước của mình đến khi ngài đụng vào con gái của mình. Cô con gái trở thành vàng. Vua Midas khẩn xin cho điều ước được xóa bỏ. Nhà vua được điều ước này. Vua Midas phục hồi lại mọi vật mà ngài đã biến thành vàng. Ngài để lại một hoa hồng bằng vàng để luôn nhớ đến lời nguyền.

# Multilingual Summaries

## 마이다스 왕과 황금 손길

마이다스 왕은 황금을 사랑했고 그가 금보다 더 사랑하는 유일한 것은 그의 딸이었다.

하루는 경비병들이 정원에서 잠을 자고 있던 한 남자를 발견하고 궁으로 데리고 왔다. 마이다스 왕은 그 남자에게 남아서 저녁을 먹자고 청했다.

왕에게 감사를 전하기 위해 남자는 왕의 소원을 들어주겠다고 말했다. 마이다스 왕은 그가 만지는 모든 것이 금으로 변하게 해달라고 빌었다. 그 다음날 왕은 잠에서 깨어나 자신의 소원이 실현되었다는 것을 알게 되었다. 왕은 자신의 딸에게 손을 갖다 대서 딸이 금으로 변하기 전까지는 자신의 소원에 대해 행복해했다. 마이다스 왕은 자신의 소원을 되돌리길 간청했고 그 소원 역시 이루어졌다. 왕은 자신이 황금으로 바꾸어 놓았던 모든 것을 되돌려 놓았지만 그 저주를 항상 기억하기 위해 황금 장미 하나를 남겨두었다.

## Vaj ntxwv Midas thiab Kev Kov Kub

Vaj ntxwv Midas nyiam nyiam kub. Nws tus ntxhais yog tib tug nws nyiam nyiam tshaj.

Muaj ib hnub, cov tiv thaiv tau coj ib tug txiv neeg hauv tsev lawv nrhiav. Nws mas pw tom teb. Vaj ntxwv tau caw tus no los noj hmo.

Kom ua kev zoo siab ua tsaug rau tus vaj ntxwv, tus txiv neej hais tias nws mam foom ib yam dabtsi los xij raws li tus vaj ntxwv lub siab xav. Tus vaj ntxwv Midas lub siab xav tau ib lub txiaj ntsim uas pub hwj chim kom ib puas yam tsav nws kov mam txi los ua kub. Hnub tom qab, tus vaj ntxwv sawv los mus nrhiav hais tias nws qhov lub siab xav no twb muaj lawm. Vaj ntxwv zoo zoo siab txog thaum nws kov nws tus ntxhais. Nws ho txi los ua kub. Vaj ntxwv Midas thov thov kom nws qhov lub siab xav no cia ploj mus lawm. Nws txawm tau raws li nws lub siab xav no thiab. Vaj ntxwv Midas rov qab kov ib puas yam tsav nws kov thaum ib kom txhob ua kub ntxiv li lawm. Nws tau ceev ib lub paj kub kom nco ntsoov qhov foom tsis zoo no xawb mawm.

# The Hindenburg

| Week at a Glance | Customize instruction every day for your English Language Learners. | | | | |
|---|---|---|---|---|---|
| | **Day 1** | **Day 2** | **Day 3** | **Day 4** | **Day 5** |
| **Teacher's Edition** | Use the ELL Notes that appear throughout each day of the lesson to support instruction and reading. | | | | |
| **ELL Poster 29** | • Assess Prior Knowledge<br>• Develop Concepts and Vocabulary | • Preteach Tested Vocabulary | • Warning Labels | • Periodic Table of Elements | • Monitor Progress |
| **ELL Teaching Guide** | • Picture It! Lesson, pp. 197–198<br>• Multilingual Summaries, pp. 201–203 | • ELL Reader Lesson, pp. 268–269 | • Vocabulary Activities and Word Cards, pp. 199–200<br>• Multilingual Summaries, pp. 201–203 | | |
| **ELL Readers** | • Reread *A Tale of Gold and Glory* | • Teach *Lighter Than Air* | • Reread *Lighter Than Air* and other texts to build fluency | | |
| **ELL and Transition Handbook** | Use the following as needed to support this week's instruction and to conduct alternative assessments:<br>• Phonics Transition Lessons<br>• Grammar Transition Lessons<br>• Assessment | | | | |

**Picture It!** Comprehension Lesson

## Fact and Opinion

Use this lesson to supplement or replace the skill lesson on pages 700–701 of the Teacher's Edition.

### Teach

Distribute copies of the Picture It! blackline master on page 198.
- Point out the picture and explain that it shows a hot air balloon traveling over the Grand Canyon.
- Share the Skill Points (at right) with students.
- Read the passage aloud. Ask: *What opinion is expressed by the author? Why does the author have that opinion?*

### Practice

Read aloud the directions on page 198. Have students read the paragraph and then complete the chart below. Have students keep their organizers for later reteaching.

**Answers for page 198:** *Statement of Opinion:* The best way to see the Grand Canyon is by balloon. *Support:* Airplanes go too fast. Balloons are quiet. Balloons don't pollute. *Valid or Faulty:* Answers will vary: The first point may be a matter of personal opinion; the second and third points are more objective.

> ### Skill Points
> ✓ A **fact** is a true statement. An **opinion** is not true or false. It is a personal thought or belief. Opinions cannot be proven.
> ✓ **Valid opinions** are supported by good reasons and examples.
> **Faulty opinions** are supported by very personal reasons, or they might not be supported at all.

**Read** the paragraph. Then complete the chart.

- In the first column, **write** an opinion expressed in the passage.
- In the second column, **write** the statements from the passage that support the opinion.
- Do you think the opinion is valid or faulty? **Explain** in the third column.

# The Grand Canyon by Balloon

The best way to see the Grand Canyon is by balloon. Airplanes and helicopters go too fast. If you ride in a balloon, you can take a tour for the whole day. Balloons are quiet too. Sometimes you can hear the wind whistling through the canyon. The biggest advantage of all is that balloons are not bad for the environment. Airplanes pollute the air, but hot air balloons do not.

| Statement of Opinion | Support | Valid or Faulty? |
|---|---|---|
| | | |
| | | |

© Scott Foresman 5

# Vocabulary Activities and Word Cards

Copy the Word Cards on page 200 as needed for the following activities.
Use the blank cards for additional words that you want to teach.
Also see suggestions for teaching vocabulary in the ELL and Transition Handbook.

| Do or Draw | Alphabetizing Game | Helpful Hints |
|---|---|---|
| • Distribute sets of Word Cards to students. Ask them to sort the words into two groups, nouns and verbs.<br><br>• Ask a student to come to the front of the class and choose a Word Card without showing it to anyone. Explain that the student will either act out or draw to demonstrate the meaning of the word. If the word is a noun, the student will draw. If it is a verb, he or she will act it out.<br><br>• As the student either draws or acts out the word, the other students should try to guess it. The first person to correctly guess the word is next to choose a Word Card and either draw or act out to demonstrate the word's meaning. | • Form pairs of students. Give partners a set of Word Cards and have them arrange the cards in alphabetical order.<br><br>• Remind students that words beginning with the same letter are alphabetized according to the second letter.<br><br>• To add an extra challenge, tell students they must make a sentence with each word as it is put in alphabetical order. | • Divide students into small groups and give each group a Word Card. The students work together to think of several hints they could give about their word. The hints should become increasingly specific. For example:<br>*It is a verb.*<br>*It is a present-tense verb.*<br>*It is something a person is doing.*<br>*It is something a person is doing to someone else.*<br>*It means that someone is telling someone that he or she is wrong.*<br>*(criticizing)*<br>Groups should think of four or five hints for their words.<br><br>• Students present their clues, one at a time, to the other groups. After each hint, students can guess. The group that guesses correctly first gets to present its own word next. Make sure all groups present their words.<br><br>• You may choose to give each group of students a complete set of Word Cards to aid them in guessing the hinted word. |

**Vocabulary Activities and Word Cards**

# criticizing

# cruised

# drenching

# era

# explosion

# hydrogen

# Multilingual Summaries

## The *Hindenburg*

Hugo Eckener began to make airships in Germany in 1900. Airships were huge, hollow structures. Gas-filled balloons inside made them float. The gas was very explosive. Sparks and flames could easily set the airship on fire. People traveled across the Atlantic Ocean in the airships.

The biggest airship ever made was the *Hindenburg.* It first flew in 1936. It took two and a half days to cross the Atlantic Ocean. On May 3, 1937, the *Hindenburg* left Germany for what would be its last flight.

When the airship reached the United States, thunderstorms kept it from landing right away. The airship circled and came back. Suddenly, the airship was on fire. No one knew how the fire started. Of the ninety-seven people on the ship, sixty-seven survived. Airships were never again used for travel.

**Spanish**

## El *Hindenburg*

Hugo Eckener empezó a hacer dirigibles en Alemania en 1900. Un dirigible era una estructura hueca enorme. Se llenaba con globos de gas y estos lo hacían flotar. El gas era muy explosivo. Las chispas y las llamas podían provocar un incendio. La gente viajaba a través del océano Atlántico en estos dirigibles.

El dirigible más grande que se había hecho era el *Hindenburg.* Voló por primera vez en 1936. Le tomó dos días y medio atravesar el océano Atlántico. El 3 de mayo de 1937, el *Hindenburg* salió de Alemania en un vuelo que sería el último.

Cuando el dirigible se acercaba a Estados Unidos, una tormenta eléctrica le impidió aterrizar de inmediato. El dirigible daba vueltas y regresaba. De repente se incendió. Nadie sabía cómo había comenzado el fuego. De las noventa y siete personas que estaban a bordo, sobrevivieron sesenta y siete. Los dirigibles nunca más fueron usados para viajar.

# Multilingual Summaries

## 興登堡號飛船

1900年，埃克納開始在德國造飛船。飛船頂上是非常大的氣球，裏面充滿易燃氣體，這樣才能飛行。氫氣很容易爆炸，碰到火星就會著火。但人們駕駛飛船，橫越了大西洋。

最大的飛船叫興登堡號，第一次飛行是在1936年，它用兩天半時間就飛過了大西洋。1937年5月3日，興登堡號飛離德國，這是它最後一次飛行。

飛船到達美國時，因為有雷雨不能降落。它慢慢地盤旋來回，不知道為什麼，突然著火了。飛船上有97人，只有67人生還。從此以後，飛船不再用作載人旅行。

## Tàu Khinh Khí Cầu *Hindenburg*

Hugo Eckener bắt đầu chế tạo những chiếc tàu khinh khí cầu ở Đức Quốc vào năm 1900. Các chiếc tàu khinh khí cầu là những kiến trúc rỗng, khổng lồ. Những quả cầu bơm đầy khinh khí giữ cho chiếc tàu bay trên không. Khinh khí rất dễ nổ. Những tia lửa và lửa ngọn có thể dễ dàng làm cháy chiếc tàu. Người ta du lịch ngang Đại Tây Dương trong những chiếc tàu khinh khí cầu này.

Chiếc tàu khinh khí cầu lớn nhất được chế tạo là chiếc Hindenburg. Chiếc này bay lần đầu vào năm 1936. Phải mất hai ngày rưỡi để băng qua Đại Tây Dương. Vào ngày 3 tháng Năm, năm 1937, chiếc Hindenburg rời Đức Quốc kể như chuyến bay cuối cùng.

Khi chiếc tàu khinh khí cầu đến Hoa Kỳ, mưa bão làm cho chiếc tàu không đáp xuống liền được. Chiếc tàu bay một vòng và quay trở lại. Thình lình, chiếc tàu bị cháy. Không ai biết làm thế nào mà lửa đã bốc cháy. Trong số chín mươi bảy người đi trên tàu, có sáu mươi bảy người sống sót. Tàu khinh khí cầu từ đó không còn được dùng để du lịch nữa.

# Multilingual Summaries

## 힌덴버그 호

휴고 에케너는 1900년 독일에서 비행선을 만들기 시작했다. 그 비행선은 거대했고 속이 빈 구조로 만들어졌다. 내부에 가스를 채운 풍선이 비행선을 뜨도록 만들었는데 그 가스는 폭발성 물질로 불꽃과 화염이 비행선을 쉽사리 태울 수 있었다. 사람들은 비행선을 타고 대서양을 횡단했다.

그때까지 제작된 비행선 중 가장 큰 것은 힌덴버그 호였다. 힌덴버그 호는 1936년 처녀비행을 했는데 대서양을 건너는 데 이틀 반이나 걸렸다. 1937년 5월 3일 힌덴버그 호는 독일을 향해 떠났고 그것이 마지막 비행이 되었다.

비행선이 미국에 도착했을 때 심한 뇌우로 곧바로 착륙하는 것이 어려웠다. 비행선은 선회하다 다시 돌아왔는데 갑자기 선체에 불이 났다. 하지만 아무도 그 불이 어떻게 나게됐는지 알지 못했다. 비행선에 타고 있던 97명 중 67명이 살아 남았다. 그 이후로 비행선은 여행을 목적으로 사용되지 않았다.

## Lub *Hindenburg*

Thaum xyoo ib txhiab cuaj puas (1900) hauv teb chaws Yelemes Hugo Eckner pib txua cov zais nyob hoom. Cov zais nyob hoom no yog khoob thiab loj kawg nkaus. Lawv muaj cov zais loj rau hauv kom thiaj ntab saum cua. Cov roj rau hauv hlaws tau yoojyim. Cov txim taws, thiab cov nplaim taws muaj peevxwm kom lub zais nyob hoom raug hluavtaws. Cov neeg caij nyob hoom no, hla lub dej hiav txwv Atlantic.

Lub zais nyob hoom loj tshaj yog lub Hindenburg. Ib txhiab cuaj puas peb caug rau (1936) yog thawj thawj zaug lub no ya ya. Nws siv sijhawm npaum li ob thiab ib nrag hnub hla lub hiav txwv Atlantic. Thaum lub tsib hlis ntuj, hnub tim peb, xyoo ib txhiab cuaj puas peb caug xya (193) Lub Hindenburg tau ncaim tebchaws Yelemees zaum kawg.

Thaum lub zais nyob hoom tuaj txog tebchaws Ameslikas, nag xob nag cua tiv thaiv Lub ntawd kom nws tsaws tsis tau zaum. Lub zais nyob hoom sim tsaws ib zaug ntxiv. Lub zais nyob hoom txawm raug hluav taws. Tsis muaj leejtwg paub lub zais nyob hoom ntawd raug hluavtaws li cas. Cuaj kaum xya neeg caij lub zais nyob hoom ntawd, tau muaj peb caug neeg tuag.

# Sweet Music in Harlem

| Week at a Glance | Customize instruction every day for your English Language Learners. | | | | |
|---|---|---|---|---|---|
| | **Day 1** | **Day 2** | **Day 3** | **Day 4** | **Day 5** |
| **Teacher's Edition** | Use the ELL Notes that appear throughout each day of the lesson to support instruction and reading. | | | | |
| **ELL Poster 30** | • Assess Prior Knowledge<br>• Develop Concepts and Vocabulary | • Preteach Tested Vocabulary | • Categorizing Instruments | • Review Sequence of Events | • Monitor Progress |
| **ELL Teaching Guide** | • Picture It! Lesson, pp. 204–205<br>• Multilingual Summaries, pp. 208–210 | • ELL Reader Lesson, pp. 270–271 | • Vocabulary Activities and Word Cards, pp. 206–207<br>• Multilingual Summaries, pp. 208–210 | | |
| **ELL Readers** | • Reread *Lighter Than Air* | • Teach *What Do You See, James Van Der Zee?* | • Reread *What Do You See, James Van Der Zee?* and other texts to build fluency | | |
| **ELL and Transition Handbook** | Use the following as needed to support this week's instruction and to conduct alternative assessments:<br>• Phonics Transition Lessons<br>• Grammar Transition Lessons<br>• Assessment | | | | |

## Picture It! Comprehension Lesson
## Sequence

Use this lesson to supplement or replace the skill lesson on pages 726–727 of the Teacher's Edition.

### Teach

Distribute copies of the Picture It! blackline master on page 205.
• Point to the picture. Tell students it shows the Apollo Theater in New York City. Students are going to read about the history of the Apollo Theater.
• Share the Skill Points (at right) with students.
• Read the passage aloud

### Practice

Read aloud the directions on page 205. Tell students to pay attention to dates in the paragraph. When they are finished, have them complete the time line. Have students keep their time lines for later reteaching.

**Answers for page 205:** 1913: Apollo opens. 1934: Sid Cohen buys the Apollo and invites African American artists to perform. 1934–1950s: Apollo is a popular place. 1971: The theater is forced to close. 1983: It reopens. 1988: The Apollo is declared a national landmark.

### Skill Points

✓ The **sequence of events** is the order in which events happen.

✓ The author does not always tell you events in the order they happen.

✓ You can keep track of events by making a time line.

Name _____

**Read** the passage and then complete the time line. **Write** an event in the history of the Apollo Theater next to the date when it took place.

# Harlem's Apollo Theater

The Apollo Theater is a New York City landmark. It is located on 125th Street in Harlem. When it opened in 1913, only white people could go there. But in 1934 a man named Sid Cohen bought the theater. He invited African American artists to perform at the Apollo. More and more people began to come. For the first time, blacks and whites sat together in the same audience.

The Apollo was a popular place for almost 20 years. But in early 1971, it was forced to close. Many people asked for it to reopen, and so it did, in 1983. Five years later, it was declared a national landmark. People still go there, especially to see amateurs and young performers.

| 1910 | 1913 _____ |
| 1920 | |
| 1930 | 1934 _____ |
| 1940 | |
| 1950 | 1934–1950s _____ |
| 1960 | |
| 1970 | 1971 _____ |
| 1980 | 1983 _____ |
| 1990 | 1988 _____ |

# Vocabulary Activities and Word Cards

Copy the Word Cards on page 207 as needed for the following activities.
Use the blank card for an additional word that you want to teach.
Also see suggestions for teaching vocabulary in the ELL and Transition Handbook.

| Sorting Activity | Group Story | Picture-Word Concentration |
|---|---|---|
| • Form groups of students. Give each group a set of Word Cards.<br><br>• Ask groups to sort their cards into different categories. Tell them that they are free to decide what the categories are, but that they will be asked to explain their categories to the class.<br><br>• When groups are finished, invite groups to take turns presenting their word sorts to the class. Remind students to explain the rationale behind their categories. | • Form groups with equal numbers of students. Put a set of Word Cards in a paper bag for each group.<br><br>• Members of each group take turns drawing a card out of the bag and making a sentence with the word. Together, the sentences should tell a story. Explain that the first student should create a good story starter; for example: *It was nighttime, and a band got together on a street corner.*<br><br>• The next student then draws a card and creates the next sentence of the story. Groups continue in this way until all the words have been used.<br><br>• If possible, ask one member of the group to write the story down as it is dictated by the group. Then ask each group to share its story with the others. | • Give pairs of students sets of Word Cards and an equal number of blank cards.<br><br>• Ask students to work together to draw a picture on each blank card to illustrate each of the vocabulary words. Students should discuss their illustrations with one another.<br><br>• Students then shuffle the two sets of cards together and lay them face down in a grid pattern. They take turns choosing two cards. If they are a word and its matching picture, they keep the cards. If not, they put the cards back. Students continue taking turns until all of the cards have been matched. The winner is the student with more cards.<br><br>• For variety, this game can also be played by two teams of students. |

bass

clarinet

fidgety

forgetful

jammed

nighttime

secondhand

# Multilingual Summaries

## Sweet Music in Harlem

C.J.'s Uncle Click is a jazz musician. C.J. wants to be one too. One afternoon, a photographer comes to take Uncle Click's picture for a magazine. Uncle Click cannot find his special hat.

C.J. goes to look for the hat. It's not at the barbershop, but the barber wants to be in the picture. It's not at the diner, but the diner's waitress wants to be in the picture. It's not at the music club, but the club's singer wants to be in the picture too.

C.J. goes home without the hat. He is sorry he did not find it. The photographer comes. His uncle is happy that so many people came to be in the picture. That night, Uncle Click gave C.J. his birthday present a week early. Inside the box was a new clarinet and also Uncle Click's hat!

## La dulce música de Harlem

El tío de C.J., tío Click, es un músico de jazz. C.J. también quiere ser músico. Una tarde, un fotógrafo llega a tomarle una foto al tío Click para una revista. Tío Click no puede encontrar su sombrero especial.

C.J. va a buscar el sombrero. No está en la barbería, pero el barbero quiere salir en la foto. No está en el restaurante, pero la mesera quiere salir en la foto. No está en el club de música, pero el cantante del club también quiere salir en la foto.

C.J. se va a casa sin el sombrero. Está triste porque no lo encontró. El fotógrafo llega. Su tío está feliz de que viniera tanta gente para salir en la foto. Esa noche, una semana antes de su cumpleaños, el tío Click le da a C.J. su regalo. Dentro de la caja había un clarinete nuevo, ¡y también el sombrero del tío Click!

# Multilingual Summaries

## 哈萊姆的動聽樂曲

　　克裏克的叔叔是個爵士音樂家，克裏克很想和叔叔一樣。有一天下午，攝影師要來為叔叔拍照，登在雜誌上。叔叔怎麼也找不到他那頂特別的帽子。

　　克裏克四處去找叔叔的帽子。理髮店裏沒有帽子，可理髮師說，他也想拍照。餐館裏沒有帽子，可女招待員說，她也想拍照。音樂俱樂部也沒有帽子，可歌手說，他也想拍照。

　　克裏克沒有找到帽子，心裏非常抱歉。攝影師來了，叔叔看到有這麼多人一起拍照，非常開心。那天晚上，叔叔特意提前一個星期，把生日禮物送給克裏克。禮盒裏有全新的單簧管，還有叔叔的帽子！

## Nhạc Du Dương Ở Harlem

　　Chú Click của C.J. là một nhạc sĩ nhạc jazz. C.J. cũng muốn được là một nhạc sĩ như vậy. Một buổi chiều nọ, một nhiếp ảnh gia đến chụp ảnh Chú Click để đăng lên một tạp chí. Chú Click không tìm thấy chiếc nón đặc biệt của mình.

　　C.J. đi tìm chiếc nón. Chiếc nón không có ở tiệm hớt tóc, nhưng ông thợ hớt tóc muốn được chụp trong ảnh. Nón không có ở tiệm ăn, nhưng cô hầu bàn ở tiệm ăn muốn được chụp trong ảnh. Nón không có ở câu lạc bộ âm nhạc, nhưng ca sĩ của câu lạc bộ cũng muốn được chụp trong ảnh nữa.

　　C.J. về nhà mà không có nón. Cậu bé hối tiếc là cậu không tìm được chiếc nón. Nhiếp ảnh gia đến. Chú của cậu bé vui mừng là nhiều người đã đến để được chụp trong ảnh. Tối hôm đó, Chú Click tặng C.J. món quà sinh nhật sớm đến một tuần. Trong hộp là cây kèn clarinet mới, và cả chiếc nón của Chú Click nữa!

# Multilingual Summaries

## 할렘의 달콤한 음악

C.J.의 삼촌인 클릭은 재즈 음악가다. C.J.는 자신도 재즈 음악가가 되고 싶어한다. 어느 날 오후 잡지에 실을 클릭 삼촌 사진을 찍으러 사진사 하나가 온다. 클릭 삼촌은 사진 촬영 때 쓸 그의 특별한 모자를 찾을 수가 없다.

C.J.는 그 모자를 찾으러 간다. 이발소에서 모자를 찾을 수 없었지만 이발사는 사진을 같이 찍고 싶어한다. 식당에서도 모자를 찾을 수 없었지만 식당의 웨이트리스도 사진을 같이 찍고 싶어한다. 음악 클럽에서도 모자를 찾을 수 없었지만 클럽의 가수 역시 사진을 같이 찍고 싶어한다.

C.J.는 모자를 찾지 못하고 집으로 돌아왔고 그 점에 대해 미안해 한다. 이제 사진사가 온다. 삼촌은 많은 사람들이 사진을 같이 찍으려고 온 것을 보고 기뻐한다. 그날 밤, 클릭 삼촌은 C.J.에게 생일 선물을 1주일이나 먼저 준다. 상자 안에는 새 클라리넷이 있었고 클릭 삼촌의 모자도 있는 것이 아닌가!

## Kev Hu Nkauj Zoo Mloog Hauv Harlem

C.J.'s tus dab laug Click yog ib tug kws nkauj jazz. C.J. xav ua ntawd thiab. Muaj ib tav su ib tug thaij koob los thaij tus dab laug Click duab kom ntxiv tau rau hauv phau ntawv magazine. Dab laug Click nrhiav tsi laib nws kaub mom tshwj xeeb.

C.J. tau mus nrhiav kaub mom. Nws tsi nyob tim lub tsev txiav plaub hau, tiam si tu txiav plaub hau xav kom nws lub duab nyob ntawm daim duab. Nws tsi nyob hauv tsev ua mov noj, tiam si tu muab mov noj xav kom nws lub duab nyob ntawm daim duab. Nws tsi nyob hauv tsev ua nkauj, tiam si tsev nkauj tus hu nkauj xav kom nws lub duab nyob ntawm daim duab thiab.

C.J. mus tsev tsis muaj lub kaub mom. Nws tu siab nws nrhiav tsis laib. Tus thaij duab tuaj lawm. Nws tus dab laug zoo siab tias neeg coob xav tuaj kom lawv cov duab nyob ntawm daim duab thiab. Hmo ntawd, dab laug Click tau pub C.J. nws hnub yug khoom plig ib as thiv ntxov. Nyob hauv lub thawb muaj ib lub tshuaj clarinet, thiab kuj muaj tus dab laug lub kaub mom thiab.

# ELL Reader Lessons and Study Guides

# Hana Gets Serious

by Richard Tobolka

ELL Reader 5.1.1   Fiction

## INTRODUCE THE BOOK

**Activate Prior Knowledge/Build Background** Read the title, and explain the meaning of the idiom *to get serious*. In the context of this book, it means "to stop playing games and start working hard."

**Preview/Use Text Features** Preview the reader by talking about the illustrations together and naming the labeled items. Ask students to make predictions based on the illustrations. As you point to each picture, ask: *Is Hana being a good student? What is she doing?*

**Preteach Vocabulary** Review the tested vocabulary words that appear in this book: **reputation** and **assignment**. Introduce these key words from the book: **pranks** (p. 2), **report** (p. 7), and **education** (p. 8). Discuss these words and add them to a Word Wall.

## READ THE BOOK

Choose among these options for reading to support students at all English proficiency levels.

**Read Aloud** Read the book aloud as students follow along. Pause to verify comprehension and to explain unfamiliar concepts.

**Monitored Reading** Have students silently read a few pages at a time. Use the following questions to support comprehension:

- **Pages 2–3** What did Hana do in Mr. Diaz's class that got her in trouble? (She whistled in class.)
- **Pages 4–5** What did she do in Mrs. Willow's class that got her in trouble? (She filled a closet full of balloons.)
- **Pages 6–8** How is Hana different now that she's in the fifth grade? (She has become a serious student.)

**Reread** Have students reread the book with a partner, in small groups, or independently. Have them complete the Study Guide on page 213.

## RESPOND

Answers to the Reader's Inside Back Cover:

**Talk About It**
**1.** Possible responses: Hana was always getting into trouble. She probably did not like school *or* She did not think school was important. (Character)
**2.** She read about George Washington Carver during the summer. Now she wants to follow in his footsteps. (Plot)

**Write About It**
**3.** Possible responses: likes to draw; tells good stories; has a good sense of humor; gets serious in fifth grade (Character)
Support writers at various English proficiency levels.

    **Beginning** Provide sentence frames such as *She likes to _____; She is good at _____.* Have students dictate words to complete each sentence.
    **Intermediate** Provide the same sentence frames, but have students copy and complete them on their own.
    **Advanced** Ask students to think about things that Hana likes and is good at. They can add more ovals to their webs as needed.

**Extend Language** A class clown is a student who gets into trouble and jokes around a lot.

Answers to page 213:
*What:* gets serious
*When:* beginning in fifth grade
*Where:* school; Mr. Pierre's class
*Why:* She read about George Washington Carver and realized that education is important.

**Family Link** Read aloud the Family Link activity on page 213 before sending copies of the Study Guide home with students. Later, invite students to talk about their personal heroes.

**212** *Hana Gets Serious*  Unit 1, Week 1

ELL Teaching Guide

- **Read** *Hana Gets Serious* again.
- Use the information from the story to **complete** the chart below.

| | |
|---|---|
| **Who?** | Hana Hong |
| **What?** | |
| **When?** | |
| **Where?** | |
| **Why?** | |

## Family Link

Hana's hero is George Washington Carver. Who is your hero?
Talk to family members about your heroes.

# Tommy and the Tornado

by Darleen Ramos

ELL Reader 5.1.2   Fiction

## INTRODUCE THE BOOK

**Activate Prior Knowledge/Build Background** Read the title, and call attention to the word *tornado*. Ask students if they know what it means. If not, point to the picture on the front of the book and draw a sketch of a tornado on the board. Explain that it is a very dangerous type of storm.

**Preview/Use Text Features** Preview the reader by talking about the illustrations together and naming the labeled items. Point out the *Extend Language* features on pages 3 and 6 and the *Did You Know?* box on page 7.

**Preteach Vocabulary** Review the tested vocabulary words that appear in this book: **constructed** and **resourceful**. Introduce these key words from the book: **hayloft** (p. 4), **storm cellar** (p. 5), and **twister** (p. 8). Discuss these words and add them to a Word Wall.

## READ THE BOOK

Choose among these options for reading to support students at all English proficiency levels.

**Read Aloud** Read the book aloud as students follow along. Pause to verify comprehension and to explain unfamiliar concepts.

**Monitored Reading** Have students read aloud a few pages at a time. Use the following questions to support comprehension:
- **Pages 2–3** Where does the story take place? (on a farm in Oklahoma)
- **Pages 4–5** What is the "hiding hole"? (It's the storm cellar.)
- **Pages 6–8** What was the damage from the storm? (It ruined the cornfields and tore down telephone lines.)

**Reread** Have students reread the book with a partner, in small groups, or independently. Have them complete the Study Guide on page 215.

## RESPOND

Answers to the Reader's Inside Back Cover:

**Talk About It**
**1.** The sky was green with dark clouds; bugs flew into the attic; rain started to fall. (Draw Conclusions)
**2.** Christopher fell and hurt his ankle. (Cause and Effect)

**Write About It**
**3.** *Things to Do:* Know the signs of an approaching tornado; go to a shelter such as an underground room with a solid door. *Things to Avoid:* being outside; panicking
Support writers at various English proficiency levels.

**Beginning** Give students sentence starters such as *You should* _____ and *You should not* _____. Have students dictate the rest of each sentence.
**Intermediate** Give students the same sentence starters, but have them state and write the complete sentences on their own.
**Advanced** Encourage students to complete the chart using complete sentences.

**Extend Language** *Joyous* is the opposite of sad; *thunderous* describes a loud storm.

Answers to page 215:
Possible responses:
*Before the Storm:* Tommy and Christopher went into the hayloft. They looked at pictures.
*During the Storm:* The tornado tore up cornfields. The boys hid in the storm cellar.
*After the Storm:* The boys went back to the house. Tommy's parents came home.

**Family Link** Read aloud the Family Link activity on page 215 before sending copies of the Study Guide home with students. Later, invite students to share the storm stories that they heard at home.

Name _____

- **Read** *Tommy and the Tornado* again.
- **Complete** the story map. **Write** what happened before, during, and after the storm.

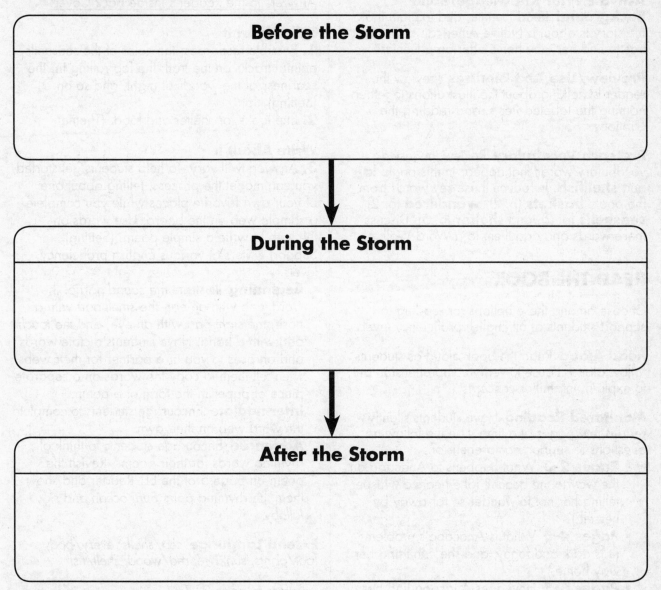

## Before the Storm

## During the Storm

## After the Storm

## Family Link

Has anyone in your family been through a storm? What was it like?
Ask family members to share what they know about storms.

# Finding Home

by Diane Jerome

ELL Reader 5.1.3   Fiction

## INTRODUCE THE BOOK

**Activate Prior Knowledge/Build Background** Read the title, and explain that the story is about a Native American girl who has to find her way home after an adventure.

**Preview/Use Text Features** Preview the reader by talking about the illustrations together, naming the labeled items, and reading the captions.

**Preteach Vocabulary** Review the tested vocabulary words that appear in this book: **lair** and **shellfish**. Introduce these key words from the book: **baskets** (p. 2), **wandered** (p. 2), **seashells** (p. 2), and **shelter** (p. 5). Discuss these words and add them to a Word Wall.

## READ THE BOOK

Choose among these options for reading to support students at all English proficiency levels.

**Read Aloud** Read the book aloud as students follow along. Pause to verify comprehension and to explain unfamiliar concepts.

**Monitored Reading** Have students silently read a few pages at a time. Use the following questions to support comprehension:

- **Pages 2–3** What happens to Anacapa on the way to the beach? (She hears a whisper telling her not to wander so far away by herself.)
- **Pages 4–5** What is Anacapa's problem? (It is dark and foggy, and she can't find her way home.)
- **Pages 6–8** How does Anacapa find her way home? (She waits until it is morning; she follows the condor.)

**Reread** Have students reread the book with a partner, in small groups, or independently. Have them complete the Study Guide on page 217.

## RESPOND

Answers to the Reader's Inside Back Cover:

**Talk About It**
**1.** Possible responses: the color of the seashells; animal tracks on the trail; the fog rolling in; the scariness of the woods at night, and so on. (Setting)
**2.** She looks for shelter and food. (Theme)

**Write About It**
**3.** Answers will vary. To help students get started, you can model the process, telling about one of your own favorite places while you complete a sample web on the board. Use words on the web to write a simple poem. (Setting) Support writers at various English proficiency levels.

**Beginning** Illustrate the *sound* part of the word web with an ear, the *smell* part with a nose, the *sight* part with an eye, and the *touch* part with a hand. Have students dictate words and phrases to you or a partner for their webs. Then tell them to copy the words on a separate piece of paper in the form of a poem.
**Intermediate** Encourage students to complete the word web on their own.
**Advanced** Encourage students to think of rhyming words for their poems. Revisit the poem on page 5 of the ELL Reader and show them the rhyming pairs *Sun, ocean* and *sky, lullaby.*

**Extend Language** *sea/shells; every/body; foot/prints; sun/rise; red/wood; shell/fish*

Answers to page 217:
Check to make sure students have labeled Anacapa's village, the forest, the beach, and the path. The path should go from Anacapa's village to the beach.

**Family Link** Read aloud the Family Link activity on page 217 before sending copies of the Study Guide home with students. Later, invite students to share about a camping trip they have taken with their families or would like to take.

Name _____

- **Read** *Finding Home* again. **Look** at the illustrations and pay attention to the descriptions of the settings.
- **Draw** a map that shows Anacapa's village, the forest, the beach, and the path that Anacapa followed. **Label** each part of your map.

## Family Link

Have you or anybody in your family gone on a camping trip? What was it like? Talk to family members about a camping trip you took or would like to take.

# Roberto Clemente

by Johnnie Burton

## INTRODUCE THE BOOK

### Activate Prior Knowledge/Build Background
Read the title, and direct students' attention to the photo on the cover. Tell students this is a picture of Roberto Clemente, a famous baseball player.

### Preview/Use Text Features
Preview the reader by talking about the photographs together and reading the captions. Point out the Batting Average Chart on page 8.

### Preteach Vocabulary
Review the tested vocabulary words that appear in this book: **weakness** and **outfield**. Introduce these key words from the book: **scouts** (p. 4), **contract** (p. 5), and **average** (p. 8). Discuss these words and add them to a Word Wall.

## READ THE BOOK

Choose among these options for reading to support students at all English proficiency levels.

### Read Aloud
Read the book aloud as students follow along. Pause to verify comprehension and to explain unfamiliar concepts.

### Monitored Reading
Have students read aloud a few pages at a time. Use the following questions to support comprehension:

- **Pages 2–5** What was the Puerto Rican Winter League? (It was a group of baseball teams that played in Puerto Rico in the winter. Scouts from the major league teams would go there to look for new players.)
- **Pages 6–9** What was Roberto's greatest weakness as a player? (He was impatient and swung at the ball even when it was a bad pitch.)
- **Pages 10–12** What are some facts that support this opinion: *Roberto Clemente was one of the greatest baseball players of all time?* (Possible responses: He had 3,000 hits. He was the first Spanish-speaking player elected to the Baseball Hall of Fame. He played 18 years in the major leagues. He had a .414 batting average in the 1971 World Series.)

### Reread
Have students reread the book with a partner, in small groups, or independently. Have them complete the Study Guide on page 219.

## RESPOND

Answers to the Reader's Inside Back Cover:

### Talk About It
**1.** Roberto had to overcome racism. Some people treated him poorly because of his color. (Draw Conclusions)
**2.** Answers will vary. Encourage students to elaborate on their responses.

### Write About It
**3.** Students should write about some qualities of Roberto Clemente that they admire. Support writers at various English proficiency levels.
   **Beginning** Provide the following sentence frame: *Roberto Clemente was _____.* Then make a list of adjectives on the board: *brave, talented, generous, kind, hard working, athletic,* and so on. Ask students to complete the sentence frame using one of the adjectives.
   **Intermediate** Provide the same sentence frame. Ask students to write three sentences in the same pattern, using adjectives that they find in the text.
   **Advanced** For each quality that they write about, ask students to provide an example from the text that illustrates that quality.

### Extend Language
To *strike out* means to fail to meet one's goal.

Answers to page 219:
4; 6; 2; 1; 3; 5

### Family Link
Read aloud the Family Link activity on page 219 before sending copies of the Study Guide home with students. Later, invite students to talk with the class about their own and their family members' favorite sports.

- **Read** *Roberto Clemente* again.
- Which event happened first? Which happened next? **Number** the events in order from 1 to 6.

___ In 1954, he joins the Pittsburgh Pirates.

___ Roberto Clemente dies in a plane crash on December 31, 1972.

___ He plays for the Puerto Rican Winter League.

___ Roberto Clemente is born on August 18, 1934, in Carolina, Puerto Rico.

___ The Dodgers offer him $10,000 to join their team.

___ Roberto helps the Pirates win the World Series.

## Family Link

What is your favorite sport? Talk to your family about it. Ask family members what sports they liked when they were your age.

# Love, Enid

by Doris Leslie

ELL Reader 5.1.5   Fiction

## INTRODUCE THE BOOK

**Activate Prior Knowledge/Build Background** Read the title, and tell students this book is about a girl who came to the United States from Belize, a nation in Central America.

**Preview/Use Text Features** Preview the reader by talking about the illustrations together and reading the captions. Point out the elements of a friendly letter and the map on page 2.

**Preteach Vocabulary** Review the tested vocabulary words that appear in this book: **immigrants**, **newcomer**, and **advice**. Introduce these key words from the book: **skyscrapers** (p. 2) and **homesick** (p. 4). Discuss these words and add them to a Word Wall.

## READ THE BOOK

Choose among these options for reading to support students at all English proficiency levels.

**Read Aloud** Read the book aloud as students follow along. Pause to verify comprehension and to explain unfamiliar concepts.

**Monitored Reading** Have students silently read a few pages at a time. Use the following questions to support comprehension:
- **Pages 2–3** Do you think Enid likes living in Milwaukee? (Possible response: Yes, she is happy to be reunited with her mother.)
- **Pages 4–7** What are some things Enid enjoys in Milwaukee? (Possible responses: being with her mother; making a new friend; a rainstorm; looking forward to snow)
- **Page 8** What can you tell by looking at the chart? (Responses will vary. Possible responses: Most of the immigrants in 2003 were from Mexico. Five of the top ten countries are in Latin America.)

**Reread** Have students reread the book with a partner, in small groups, or independently. Have them complete the Study Guide on page 221.

## RESPOND

Answers to the Reader's Inside Back Cover:

**Talk About It**
**1.** Answers will vary. Possible responses: sunglasses, shorts, sun lotion, insect repellent, travel guide, bathing suit
**2.** Possible response: Enid probably misses her friends and relatives more than anything else. (Character)

**Write About It**
**3.** *Same:* speak English, near water, buildings are close together; *Different:* weather, food, buildings (Compare and Contrast)
Support writers at various English proficiency levels.
   **Beginning** Draw a two-column chart labeled *Same* and *Different* on the board. Encourage students to dictate words and phrases for each column.
   **Intermediate** Show students a two-column *Same-and-Different* chart, and ask them to complete one like it on their own.
   **Advanced** Encourage students to use complete sentences to describe things that are the same and different.

**Extend Language** *Belizeans* are from Belize; *Columbians; Koreans, Nigerians,* and *Russians;* Answers will vary.

Answers to page 221:
*August 30:* Enid just moved to Milwaukee from Belize. Things are very different; *September 5:* Enid starts school; *September 9:* Enid helps her mother cook; *September 17:* Enid shows off her basketball skills and makes a new friend; *October 2:* Enid finds Milwaukee different from home and misses many things; *October 22:* Enid enjoys a rainstorm and looks forward to snow.

**Family Link** Read aloud the Family Link activity on page 221 before sending copies of the Study Guide home with students. Later, students can share family stories with the class.

- **Read** *Love, Enid* again.
- What does Enid write about to her aunt? **Summarize** each letter. Tell about the most important thing Enid talks about in each one.

| August 30 | September 5 |
|---|---|
| September 9 | September 17 |
| October 2 | October 22 |

# Family Link

Has anyone in your family moved a long distance, from one region to another? Ask family members to talk about moving.

# Butterfly Garden

by Grace McMurphy

ELL Reader 5.2.1   Realistic Fiction

## INTRODUCE THE BOOK

**Activate Prior Knowledge/Build Background** Read the title, and invite students to make a prediction about the story based on the title and the cover illustration.

**Preview/Use Text Features** Preview the reader by talking about the illustrations together, naming the labeled items, and reading the captions.

**Preteach Vocabulary** Review the tested vocabulary words that appear in this book: **caterpillar**, **sketched**, and **cocoon**. Introduce these key words from the book: **seniors** (p. 4), **cycle** (p. 6), and **diagram** (p. 9). Discuss these words and add them to a Word Wall.

## READ THE BOOK

Choose among these options for reading to support students at all English proficiency levels.

**Read Aloud** Read the book aloud as students follow along. Pause to verify comprehension and to explain unfamiliar concepts.

**Monitored Reading** Have students read aloud a few pages at a time. Use the following questions to support comprehension:

- **Pages 2–5** How did the idea for the butterfly garden start? (A group of seniors said that they were planning one. They asked students to help.)
- **Pages 6–9** How did the Butterfly Band get ready to grow the garden? (They read books. They sketched a diagram.)
- **Pages 10–12** What work needed to be done to create the garden? (Dirt had to be plowed. Rocks had to be put in the right place. Then plants could be planted.)

**Reread** Have students reread the book with a partner, in small groups, or independently. Have them complete the Study Guide on page 223.

## RESPOND

Answers to the Reader's Inside Back Cover:

**Talk About It**
**1.** They wanted to get involved to improve their community. (Draw Conclusions)
**2.** Both the seniors and the children are friendly, like to help others, like to work together, and like the butterfly garden. But the seniors are much older than the children. (Compare and Contrast)

**Write About It**
**3.** Answers will vary. Prompt students if necessary by making suggestions.
Support writers at various English proficiency levels.

> **Beginning** Ask yes/no questions such as: *Can we help our community by cleaning the park?* Record ideas in the appropriate section of the chart.
> **Intermediate** Prompt students by pointing out opportunities in your community, for example: *The shelter for homeless people needs canned food. What can we do?* Record students' ideas in the appropriate section of the chart.
> **Advanced** Pair students to complete the chart together.

**Extend Language** Milkweed contains a white, milky liquid; black-eyed Susans have a black center; blueberries are blue; marigolds are a golden orange.

Answers to page 223:
*Characters:* Yolanda, Devon, Dawn, Ms. Wallace, other students, Mr. Wright, other seniors; *Setting:* Greenville School, Sunrise Center; *First:* Greenville School students decide to visit the Sunrise Center. *Next:* The seniors ask the students to help them plant a butterfly garden. *Then:* Students research, sketch, and then work with the seniors to make the garden. *Last:* The community enjoys the garden.

**Family Link** Read aloud the Family Link activity on page 223 before sending copies of the Study Guide home with students. Later, students can share what they learned about garden insects.

Name _____

- **Read** *Butterfly Garden* again.
- **Complete** the chart. **Write** the characters in the story. **Write** the settings of the story.
- Next, **write** the main events of the story in order.

| **Characters** | **Settings** |
|---|---|
| | |

## Events

| | |
|---|---|
| **First** | |
| **Next** | |
| **Then** | |
| **Last** | |

## Family Link

Does your family have a garden? Talk with your family members about the insects that live in gardens.

# Making a Difference in Denmark

by Levi Weimer

ELL Reader 5.2.2    Nonfiction

## INTRODUCE THE BOOK

**Activate Prior Knowledge/Build Background** Read the title. Tell students that this book tells what the people of Denmark did to help Danish Jews during World War II. Ask students to share what they know about that war.

**Preview/Use Text Features** Preview the reader by talking about the photographs together and reading the captions. Have students examine the maps on pages 2–3.

**Preteach Vocabulary** Review the tested vocabulary words that appear in this book: **diplomat** and **agreement**. Introduce these key words from the book: **escape** (p. 6), **rescue** (p. 7), and **captured** (p. 7). Discuss these words and add them to a Word Wall.

## READ THE BOOK

Choose among these options for reading to support students at all English proficiency levels.

**Read Aloud** Read the book aloud as students follow along. Pause to verify comprehension and to explain unfamiliar concepts.

**Monitored Reading** Have students silently read a few pages at a time. Use the following questions to support comprehension:
- **Pages 2–3** What was the agreement between the Germans and the Danish government? (The Danes could govern themselves if they did not fight against the Germans.)
- **Pages 4–5** Who was Georg F. Duckwitz? (He was a German diplomat in Denmark who helped the Danish government.)
- **Pages 6–8** What were the risks for Danes caught helping Jews? (They could go to jail or be killed.)

**Reread** Have students reread the book with a partner, in small groups, or independently. Have them complete the Study Guide on page 225.

## RESPOND

Answers to the Reader's Inside Back Cover:

**Talk About It**
**1.** Possible responses: Danes hid Jews in their homes. They helped the Jews escape. They paid for their passage to Sweden. They asked that captured Jews be treated fairly. (Main Idea and Details)
**2.** Jews were in danger because Hitler wanted to destroy Jewish communities throughout Europe. (Cause and Effect)

**Write About It**
**3.** Possible facts include: Millions of Jews were killed in World War II. About 8,000 Jews lived in Denmark. Danes helped Jews to escape Nazis. *My feelings:* Student reactions will vary. (Fact and Opinion)
Support writers at various English proficiency levels.

> **Beginning** Copy the chart on the board and write a list of facts in the first column. Ask students how they feel about each event. Record their responses in the second column.
> **Intermediate** Help students complete the first column of the chart if necessary. Encourage them to complete the second column on their own.
> **Advanced** Encourage students to complete both columns of the chart on their own, using complete sentences.

**Extend Language** The Swedish are from Sweden.

Answers to page 225:
*In April of 1940,* the Nazis march into Denmark. *Within three years,* the Nazis have more control of Denmark and plan to deport Jewish Danes. *During the Jewish New Year,* the Jews leave in secret. *In just a few days,* over 7,000 Jews safely reach Sweden. *In May of 1945,* the war in Europe ends.

**Family Link** Read aloud the Family Link activity on page 225 before sending copies of the Study Guide home with students. Later, ask students to share what they learned about World War II from family members.

- **Read** *Making a Difference in Denmark* again.
- **Complete** each sentence. Use information from the book to **write** what happened in the correct sequence.

In April of 1940, _____

_____

Within three years, _____

_____

During the Jewish New Year, _____

_____

In just a few days, _____

_____

In May of 1945, _____

_____

## Family Link

Tell your family what you have learned about Denmark during World War II. Ask family members to tell what they know about that war.

# Friends Across the Ocean

by Ruby Stein

ELL Reader 5.2.3 Realistic Fiction

## INTRODUCE THE BOOK

**Activate Prior Knowledge/Build Background** Read the title, and talk about the two photos on the cover. Tell students that they show the Great Wall of China and a Mayan pyramid in Guatemala.

**Preview/Use Text Features** Preview the reader by talking about the photographs together, naming the labeled items, and reading the captions. Point out the map on pages 2–3 and the *Extend Language* feature on page 7.

**Preteach Vocabulary** Review the tested vocabulary words that appear in this book: **sacred**, **procession**, and **gratitude**. Introduce these key words from the book: **ancient** (p. 3), **crafts** (p. 4), and **celebrations** (p. 7). Discuss these words and add them to a Word Wall.

## READ THE BOOK

Choose among these options for reading to support students at all English proficiency levels.

**Read Aloud** Read the book aloud as students follow along. Pause to verify comprehension and to explain unfamiliar concepts.

**Monitored Reading** Have students read aloud a few pages at a time. Use the following questions to support comprehension:

- **Pages 2–3** How are the Great Wall of China and the pyramids at Tikal similar? (They are both very old and made of stone.)
- **Pages 4–5** What would you see at a Guatemalan market? (woven blankets, tablecloths, and clothes)
- **Pages 6–7** How are dumplings and tamales similar? How are they different? (They are both filled with meat or vegetables, but the wrapper for a dumpling is made of dough, and the wrapper for a tamale is made of cornmeal. Dumplings are fried, but tamales are steamed.)

**Reread** Have students reread the book with a partner, in small groups, or independently. Have them complete the Study Guide on page 227.

## RESPOND

Answers to the Reader's Inside Back Cover:

**Talk About It**
**1.** Possible response: They both like traditional music, crafts, and food. (Compare and Contrast)
**2.** Possible responses: China has a Great Wall, while Guatemala has ancient pyramids. China has the pipa, and Guatemala has the marimba. (Compare and Contrast)

**Write About It**
**3.** Answers will vary. Circulate as students work to ensure they understand how to complete the diagram. (Compare and Contrast)
Support writers at various English proficiency levels.

> **Beginning** Draw a Venn diagram on the board and explain as you complete it with personal information. Then help students label their diagrams with personal information and information about Marisa or Luk Sun.
> **Intermediate** Provide similar assistance for intermediate students, but encourage them to work more independently.
> **Advanced** Have students complete the activity independently.

**Extend Language** Answers will vary. Possibilities include *baton* (French), *canyon* (Spanish), and *kiosk* (Turkish).

Answers to page 227:
*Arts and Music: China:* landscape paintings, the pipa; *Guatemala:* woven blankets and clothes, the marimba
*Food: China:* fried dumplings; *Guatemala:* tamales, tropical fruit
*Festivals: China:* Chinese New Year

**Family Link** Read aloud the Family Link activity on page 227 before sending copies of the Study Guide home with students. Later, have students share with the class the traditions their families talked about.

# Friends Across the Ocean

Name _____

- **Read** *Friends Across the Ocean* again.
- **Complete** the chart as you read. **Take notes** on the cultures of China and Guatemala. Follow the example.

|  | **China** | **Guatemala** |
|---|---|---|
| **Ancient Civilizations** | the Great Wall of China, built to protect China from invaders | ancient cities and pyramids, such as the Temple of the Grand Jaguar |
| **Arts and Music** |  |  |
| **Food** |  |  |
| **Festivals** |  |  |

## Family Link

Ask family members to share their own favorite cultural traditions. Do they still celebrate these traditions now? Has the way of celebrating changed over the years?

# Gorillas: The Real Story

by Chloe Garcia

ELL Reader 5.2.4   Expository Nonfiction

## INTRODUCE THE BOOK

**Activate Prior Knowledge/Build Background** Read the title, and look at the photo on the front cover. Ask students what they know about gorillas and what they want to know.

**Preview/Use Text Features** Preview the reader by talking about the illustrations and photographs together and reading the captions. Point out the *Extend Language* feature on page 5.

**Preteach Vocabulary** Review the tested vocabulary words that appear in this book: **environment** and **conservation**. Introduce these key words from the book: **apes** (p. 3), **communicate** (p. 8), and **habitats** (p. 10). Discuss these words and add them to a Word Wall.

## READ THE BOOK

Choose among these options for reading to support students at all English proficiency levels.

**Read Aloud** Read the book aloud as students follow along. Pause to verify comprehension and to explain unfamiliar concepts.

**Monitored Reading** Have students silently read a few pages at a time. Use the following questions to support comprehension:

- **Pages 2–3** What are the differences between gorillas and monkeys? (Gorillas are great apes. Monkeys are smaller and have tails.)
- **Pages 4–7** How do gorilla parents raise their young? (They are protective and teach them how to look for food and how to make their nests. Parents can be stern.)
- **Pages 8–10** Why are gorillas in danger? (People are tearing down the forests where they live. Also, hunters sometimes kill gorillas.)

**Reread** Have students reread the book with a partner, in small groups, or independently. Have them complete the Study Guide on page 229.

## RESPOND

Answers to the Reader's Inside Back Cover:

### Talk About It

**1.** They stand up, stamp their feet, pound the ground, throw plants, scream, and charge.
**2.** It is a fact, because it says something that can be proved. It is not a personal belief. (Fact and Opinion)

### Write About It

**3.** Possible responses: Gorillas use their faces, bodies, and voices to communicate. Babies whimper to get their mothers' attention. Adults chuckle, growl, and scream. One gorilla can use over 1,000 signs. (Main Idea and Details) Support writers at various English proficiency levels.

    **Beginning** Ask students to pantomime the gestures, expressions, and sounds that they have read about. Help them write the words for these actions and sounds.
    **Intermediate** Students can write about gorilla communication using single words and phrases.
    **Advanced** Ask students to write a short paragraph about gorilla communication.

**Extend Language** Verbs used in the book include *walk, stand, stamp, pound, beat, tear, charge, throw, care, learn, look, whimper, purr, chuckle, roar, growl, understand.*

Answers to page 229:
*What They Look Like:* thick black hair, large head, brown eyes, longer arms than legs, up to 6 feet tall and 600 pounds
*How They Act:* sometimes aggressive, mostly gentle
*What They Eat:* fruits, vegetables, insects, worms
*Where They Live:* tropical rain forests and high-altitude forests in Africa

**Family Link** Read aloud the Family Link activity on page 229 before sending copies of the Study Guide home with students. Later, students can tell the class what family members shared with them about other wild animals.

Name _____

- **Read** *Gorillas: The Real Story* again.
- **Complete** the diagram. **Write** words and phrases under each heading.

## What They Look Like

_____

_____

_____

## How They Act

_____

_____

_____

_____

( **Gorillas** )

## What They Eat

_____

_____

_____

## Where They Live

_____

_____

_____

## Family Link

Tell your family members what you learned about gorillas. Ask family members to share what they know about other wild animals.

# After the Midnight Ride

by Anita Rochelle

## INTRODUCE THE BOOK

**Activate Prior Knowledge/Build Background** Read the title, and talk to students about the illustration on the cover. It shows a group of Minutemen rushing toward British troops during the Revolutionary War.

**Preview/Use Text Features** Preview the reader by talking about the illustrations together and reading the captions.

**Preteach Vocabulary** Review the tested vocabulary words that appear in this book: **fearless** and **fate**. Introduce these key words from the book: **supplies** (p. 4), **retreating** (p. 7), and **colonists** (p. 7). Discuss these words and add them to a Word Wall.

## READ THE BOOK

Choose among these options for reading to support students at all English proficiency levels.

**Read Aloud** Read the book aloud as students follow along. Pause to verify comprehension and to explain unfamiliar concepts.

**Monitored Reading** Have students read aloud a few pages at a time. Use the following questions to support comprehension:

- **Pages 2–5** Who rode with Paul Revere, and what happened to them? (William Dawes and Samuel Prescott rode with Paul Revere. They were all captured by the British, but Samuel Prescott escaped.)
- **Pages 6–9** Why were the colonists prepared for the British attack? (Samuel Prescott warned them before the British arrived.)
- **Pages 10–12** Which side seemed to "win" the Battle of Concord? (The Minutemen seemed to win the battle, since the British retreated and so many of them were killed.)

**Reread** Have students reread the book with a partner, in small groups, or independently. Have them complete the Study Guide on page 231.

## RESPOND

Answers to the Reader's Inside Back Cover:

**Talk About It**
**1.** They wanted to arrest John Hancock and Samuel Adams in Lexington and destroy colonists' supplies in Concord. (Plot)
**2.** Hundreds of Minutemen came when they thought Concord was being burned. The Minutemen chased the British Regulars from the North Bridge to the streets of Concord. The British retreated to Boston. (Sequence)

**Write About It**
**3.** *Lexington:* unknown who fired first, Minutemen outnumbered; *Both:* fought between colonists and British Regulars, took place on April 19, 1775; *Concord:* British outnumbered; British fired first (Compare and Contrast)
Support writers at various English proficiency levels.

**Beginning** Direct students' attention to pages 6–7 to complete the left half of the diagram. Then tell them to look at pages 10–11 to complete the right half. Help them complete the middle section.
**Intermediate** Give similar assistance to intermediate students, but ask them to complete the middle section on their own.
**Advanced** Ask students to complete the activity on their own.

**Extend Language** *nameless:* without a name; *shameless:* without shame; *colorless:* having no color; *hopeless:* without hope

Answers to page 231
3, 5, 4, 1, 6, 2

**Family Link** Read aloud the Family Link activity on page 231 before sending copies of the Study Guide home with students. Later, students can tell the class what they learned about the American Revolution from family members.

- **Read** *After the Midnight Ride* again.
- Which event happened first? Which happened next?
  **Number** the events in order from 1 to 6.

____ Somebody fires a shot on the Lexington village green.

____ The British decide to go back to Boston.

____ Minutemen attack British soldiers on the North Bridge of Concord.

____ Samuel Prescott warns colonists that the British are coming.

____ Minutemen shoot at the British as they retreat to Boston.

____ British Regulars arrive at Lexington on their way to Concord.

## Family Link

Tell your family what you learned about the American Revolution.
Ask them to tell you what they know about the Revolution.

# Scientific Methods in Action

by D. Michael Kim

## INTRODUCE THE BOOK

**Activate Prior Knowledge/Build Background** Read the title, and talk about the cover illustration. Explain that it shows an experiment. Students will learn about the experiment when they read the book.

**Preview/Use Text Features** Preview the reader by talking about the illustrations together, naming the labeled items, and reading the captions.

**Preteach Vocabulary** Review the tested vocabulary words that appear in this book: **scoundrel** and **subjects**. Introduce these key words from the book: **hypothesis** (p. 3), **observe** (p. 3), **experiment** (p. 3), and **data** (p. 3). Discuss these words and add them to a Word Wall.

## READ THE BOOK

Choose among these options for reading to support students at all English proficiency levels.

**Read Aloud** Read the book aloud as students follow along. Pause to verify comprehension and to explain unfamiliar concepts.

**Monitored Reading** Have students silently read a few pages at a time. Use the following questions to support comprehension:

- **Pages 2–3** What do scientists around the world have in common? (They use the scientific method.)
- **Pages 4–5** Who was Benjamin Franklin? (He was an American inventor, writer, printer, and scientist.)
- **Pages 6–8** Why was Ben's experiment dangerous? (He experimented with lightning, which can kill people.)

**Reread** Have students reread the book with a partner, in small groups, or independently. Have them complete the Study Guide on page 233.

## RESPOND

Answers to the Reader's Inside Back Cover:

**Talk About It**
**1.** The author wrote the book to explain ideas and give information. (Author's Purpose)
**2.** He defined the problem, formed a hypothesis, experimented, drew conclusions, and "published" his results by telling people about the experiment. He did not record and organize his data. (Summarize)

**Write About It**
**3.** Responses for Franklin's experiment: *Define the problem:* Houses burn from lightning. *Form a hypothesis:* An iron rod on top of a building will attract lightning. *Experiment:* Ben flew a kite attached to a wire and a key. *Record data:* Explain the experiment and the results. (Ben did not do this.) *Draw conclusions:* Lightning is electricity and an iron rod can protect houses from lightning. *Publish results:* Ben told people about the lightning rod. (Summarize)
Support writers at various English proficiency levels.

> **Beginning** Copy the chart on the board and verbalize as you complete it. Have students echo you and then copy the chart.
> **Intermediate** Use prompts to help students complete the chart. For example: *What happened to houses when they were hit by lightning? That was the problem Ben wanted to solve.*
> **Advanced** Encourage students to complete the chart on their own.

**Extend Language** scientific

Answers to page 233:
**1.** He used it to decide where to build a hospital.
**2.** He wanted to know how to protect people and buildings from lightning.
**3.** Iron would attract the lightning.
**4.** The king preferred round rods, and most people did not like the king.

**Family Link** Read aloud the Family Link activity on page 233 before sending copies of the Study Guide home with students. Later, students can share what they learned about other scientists.

Name _____

- **Read** *Scientific Methods in Action* again.
- Use the information in the book to **answer** the questions. Use complete sentences if you can.

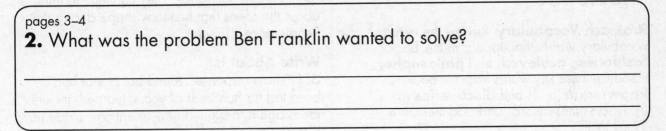

page 2
**1.** What did Al-Razi use the scientific method for?

_____

_____

pages 3–4
**2.** What was the problem Ben Franklin wanted to solve?

_____

_____

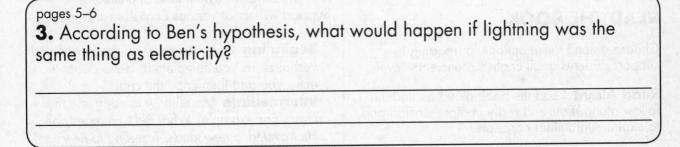

pages 5–6
**3.** According to Ben's hypothesis, what would happen if lightning was the same thing as electricity?

_____

_____

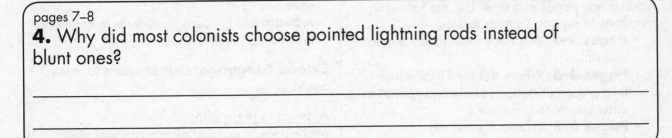

pages 7–8
**4.** Why did most colonists choose pointed lightning rods instead of blunt ones?

_____

_____

## Family Link

Tell your family what you learned about the scientific method and Benjamin Franklin. Ask family members to tell you about another scientist they know.

# The Renaissance

by Claire Barberini

ELL Reader 5.3.2   Nonfiction

## INTRODUCE THE BOOK

**Activate Prior Knowledge/Build Background** Read the title, and tell students that *Renaissance* is the name of a period in history. Ask students to share anything they may know about the Renaissance.

**Preview/Use Text Features** Preview the reader by talking about the illustrations together, naming the labeled items, and reading the captions. Point out the *Extend Language* features on pages 3 and 6.

**Preteach Vocabulary** Review the tested vocabulary words that appear in this book: **fashioned**, **achieved**, and **philosopher**. Introduce these key words from the book: **knowledge** (p. 3) and **discoveries** (p. 8). Discuss these words and add them to a Word Wall.

## READ THE BOOK

Choose among these options for reading to support students at all English proficiency levels.

**Read Aloud** Read the book aloud as students follow along. Pause to verify comprehension and to explain unfamiliar concepts.

**Monitored Reading** Have students read aloud a few pages at a time. Use the following questions to support comprehension:
- **Pages 2–3** What does *Renaissance* mean? (rebirth)
- **Pages 4–5** Where did the Renaissance take place? (It started in Italy and spread to other countries in Europe.)
- **Pages 6–8** What influence did Shakespeare and Michelangelo have on art today? (They both helped to bring art to ordinary people.)

**Reread** Have students reread the book with a partner, in small groups, or independently. Have them complete the Study Guide on page 235.

## RESPOND

Answers to the Reader's Inside Back Cover:

**Talk About It**
**1.** The Renaissance was a period of history that started in the fourteenth century and lasted until about 1650. It was a time of creativity and discovery. (Main Idea and Details)
**2.** People are still inspired when they look at the great works of art that were created during the Renaissance. They continue to think about the ideas that first took shape during the Renaissance. (Theme)

**Write About It**
**3.** Possible responses: found books that had been lost for hundreds of years; learned ancient ideas again; designed new inventions; made new discoveries; created great works of art; developed new philosophies (Main Idea and Details) Support writers at various English proficiency levels.
   **Beginning** Copy the chart on the board and verbalize as you complete it. Have students echo you and then copy the chart.
   **Intermediate** Model how to complete the chart. For example: *What did Columbus do? He traveled to new lands. Traveling to new lands was something people did during the Renaissance.*
   **Advanced** Encourage students to complete the chart on their own.

**Extend Language** *Redraw* means to draw again.

Answers to page 235:
*Michelangelo:* painted pictures on walls and ceilings
*Copernicus:* astronomer who studied planets;
*Descartes:* philosopher who thought about right and wrong
*da Vinci:* artist and inventor
*Shakespeare:* wrote plays

**Family Link** Read aloud the Family Link activity on page 235 before sending copies of the Study Guide home with students. Later, students can share what they learned at home about other thinkers, scientists, and artists.

- **Read** *The Renaissance* again.
- What did you learn about the people of the Renaissance?
  **Take notes** on these scientists, thinkers, and artists.

**Michelangelo**

_____

_____

_____

**Copernicus**

_____

_____

_____

**Descartes**

_____

_____

_____

**da Vinci**

_____

_____

_____

**Shakespeare**

_____

_____

_____

## Family Link

Tell your family what you learned about these people. Ask them to
tell you about other famous scientists, thinkers, or artists.

# Dinosaur Time Line

by Carl Escobedo

ELL Reader 5.3.3   Poetry

## INTRODUCE THE BOOK

**Activate Prior Knowledge/Build Background** Read the title, and direct students' attention to the illustration on the cover. It shows a boy pointing to a dinosaur. Invite students to share what they know about dinosaurs.

**Preview/Use Text Features** Preview the reader by talking about the illustrations together, naming the labeled items, and reading the captions.

**Preteach Vocabulary** Review the tested vocabulary words that appear in this book: **proportion** and **occasions**. Introduce these key words from the book: **reptiles** (p. 2), **dinosaurs** (p. 2), and **paleontologists** (p. 3). Discuss these words and add them to a Word Wall.

## READ THE BOOK

Choose among these options for reading to support students at all English proficiency levels.

**Read Aloud** Read the book aloud as students follow along. Pause to verify comprehension and to explain unfamiliar concepts.

**Monitored Reading** Have students silently read a few pages at a time. Use the following questions to support comprehension:
- **Pages 2–3** How are today's reptiles like dinosaurs? (They are cold-blooded.)
- **Pages 4–5** What did many dinosaurs have in common? (Many of them were much larger than animals today.)
- **Pages 6–8** Why did dinosaurs die? (They might have died because of a volcano eruption or an asteroid from outer space. Scientists are not sure, but it appears they died from a dramatic weather change.)

**Reread** Have students reread the book with a partner, in small groups, or independently. Have them complete the Study Guide on page 237.

## RESPOND

Answers to the Reader's Inside Back Cover:

**Talk About It**
**1.** Answers will vary. Check student answers against information in the book. (Main Idea and Details)
**2.** Answers will vary.

**Write About It**
**3.** Possible responses if Stegosaurus and Tyrannosaurus are chosen: *Stegosaurus:* plant-eater, 150 million years ago, walked on four legs, plates and spikes; *Tyrannosaurus:* meat-eater, 100 million years ago, walked on two legs, fierce; *Both:* dinosaurs, large, could fight (Compare and Contrast)
Support writers at various English proficiency levels.
> **Beginning** Draw sketches of two different dinosaurs on the board. Label their body parts and write descriptive words and phrases about them. Have students use your sketches to complete the diagram.
> **Intermediate** Ask students to write about two dinosaurs that lived in the same period, such as Saltopus and Eoraptor.
> **Advanced** Have students choose the two dinosaurs they want to compare.

**Extend Language** Possible responses: *Stegosaurus* means something like a lizard with a ridge of plates, and *Tyrannosaurus Rex* might mean cruel king of the lizards.

Answers to page 237:
**2.** 230, do not know
**3.** 150, meat
**4.** 150, plants
**5.** 100, plants
**6.** 230, do not know

**Family Link** Read aloud the Family Link activity on page 237 before sending copies of the Study Guide home with students. Later, students can quiz each other about dinosaurs, just as they did with family members.

- **Read** *Dinosaur Time Line* again.
- **Complete** the chart for each dinosaur. If you do not know an answer, write *do not know*. The first row is done for you.

| Dinosaur | How many million years ago did it live? | What did it eat? |
|---|---|---|
| **1.** Tyrannosaurus Rex | 100 | meat |
| **2.** Saltopus | | |
| **3.** Allosaurus | | |
| **4.** Archaeopteryx | | |
| **5.** Styracosaurus | | |
| **6.** Eoraptor | | |

## Family Link
Give your family members a quiz. Ask them questions about dinosaurs you know. Then give them the answers.

# Willie Dixon's Blues

by Robert Jackson

ELL Reader 5.3.4    Interview

## INTRODUCE THE BOOK

**Activate Prior Knowledge/Build Background** Read the title, and point to the photo. Tell students the photo shows Willie Dixon, a blues musician. Invite students to share what they know about the blues.

**Preview/Use Text Features** Preview the reader by talking about the photographs together and reading the captions.

**Preteach Vocabulary** Review the tested vocabulary words that appear in this book: **slavery** and **appreciate**. Introduce these key words from the book: **express** (p. 3), **performer** (p. 4), and **success** (p. 7). Discuss these words and add them to a Word Wall.

## READ THE BOOK

Choose among these options for reading to support students at all English proficiency levels.

**Read Aloud** Read the book aloud as students follow along. Pause to verify comprehension and to explain unfamiliar concepts.

**Monitored Reading** Have students read aloud a few pages at a time. Use the following questions to support comprehension:

- **Pages 2–5** What were Willie's talents? (He was a singer, songwriter, bass player, and arranger.)
- **Pages 6–9** Who are some other blues artists? (Memphis Slim, Mahalia Jackson, Koko Taylor)
- **Pages 10–12** How is Keshia like her grandfather? (She writes music and sings.)

**Reread** Have students reread the book with a partner, in small groups, or independently. Have them complete the Study Guide on page 239.

## RESPOND

Answers to the Reader's Inside Back Cover:

**Talk About It**
**1.** Possible responses: Willie performed for most of his life. He wrote more than 500 songs. He founded the Blues Heaven Foundation to help elderly blues musicians and teach young people. (Main Idea and Details)
**2.** Jazz, gospel, and rock 'n' roll are related to the blues.

**Write About It**
**3.** Answers will vary. Encourage students to elaborate on their responses.
Support writers at various English proficiency levels.
    **Beginning** Ask students about different expressive arts. For example: *Do you like to dance? Sing? Play music? Paint? Write poetry?* and so on. Invite students to draw and label a picture of themselves doing what they like to do to express themselves.
    **Intermediate** Ask similar kinds of questions, but invite students to write simple words or phrases describing what they like to do.
    **Advanced** Encourage students to respond in a paragraph. Invite them to write about two or three ways that they like to express themselves.

**Extend Language** Possible response: *Blues* refers to a color, but it is also a kind of music.

Answers to page 239:
**1.** He interviewed Marie Dixon, Willie's wife.
**2.** First they met at a club. Two years later, they met again at a drug store where Marie worked.
**3.** They could only play in small places, and a lot of people said they would make more money in Chicago.
**4.** Nobody was listening to his music in Chicago.
**5.** They are both about pain and disappointment.
**6.** Possible response: Her grandfather taught her music at an early age, and she has learned from many accomplished blues musicians.

**Family Link** Read aloud the Family Link activity on page 239 before sending copies of the Study Guide home with students. Later, students can share their family members' favorite kinds of music.

- **Read** *Willie Dixon's Blues* again.
- Use the information in the book to **answer** the questions.

pages 2–5

**1.** How did the author get the information for this book?

_____

_____

**2.** How did Marie and Willie meet?

_____

_____

_____

pages 6–7

**3.** Why did many musicians leave the South in the 1930s?

_____

_____

**4.** Why did Willie go to Paris in 1960?

_____

_____

_____

pages 8–12

**5.** What do gospel and the blues have in common?

_____

_____

**6.** Why do you think Keshia is so good at music?

_____

_____

## Family Link

Tell your family what you learned about the blues. Talk to your family members about their favorite kinds of music.

# Virtual Actors on the Screen

by Annette Pry

ELL Reader 5.3.5   Nonfiction

## INTRODUCE THE BOOK

**Activate Prior Knowledge/Build Background** Read the title, and talk about the illustration on the cover. It shows television screens with computer-animated characters on them. Ask students to talk about films they have seen with animated characters.

**Preview/Use Text Features** Preview the reader by talking about the photographs together and reading the captions.

**Preteach Vocabulary** Review the tested vocabulary words that appear in this book: **backgrounds** and **landscapes**. Introduce these key words from the book: **cartoon** (p. 2) and **movement** (p. 3). Discuss these words and add them to a Word Wall.

## READ THE BOOK

Choose among these options for reading to support students at all English proficiency levels.

**Read Aloud** Read the book aloud as students follow along. Pause to verify comprehension and to explain unfamiliar concepts.

**Monitored Reading** Have students silently read a few pages at a time. Use the following questions to support comprehension:

- **Pages 2–3** How is the movement seen in animation created? (A sequence of pictures is shown very quickly.)
- **Pages 4–5** How have computers changed animation? (They can do much of the work that artists used to do, and they can do it much faster.)
- **Pages 6–8** Besides movies, where else is animation used? (in computer games and video games)

**Reread** Have students reread the book with a partner, in small groups, or independently. Have them complete the Study Guide on page 241.

## RESPOND

Answers to the Reader's Inside Back Cover:

**Talk About It**
**1.** Possible response: The places on page 6 look more real. (Compare and Contrast)
**2.** backgrounds and landscapes

**Write About It**
**3.** Answers will vary. Remind students to support their opinions with details. (Fact and Opinion) Support writers at various English proficiency levels.

  **Beginning** Write the following statement on the board: *It is/is not a good idea to use VActors in movies because* _____. Have students circle the form of the verb that shows their opinion. Then have them dictate a reason to you to complete the sentence.
  **Intermediate** Provide the sentence frame shown above and encourage these students to complete the sentence on their own.
  **Advanced** Encourage students to complete the activity without assistance. Ask them to include at least two different reasons and/or examples to support their opinion.

**Extend Language** flying, walking, talking, fighting

Answers to page 241:
Possible responses: *What is special or unique about animated characters?* They can do things real actors cannot do. They do not get hurt. They do not have to be people at all. *What is special or unique about real actors?* They have feelings. They are more expressive than animated characters. Movie watchers know the difference between a real actor and an animated character.

**Family Link** Read aloud the Family Link activity on page 241 before sending copies of the Study Guide home with students. Later, students can vote on the most popular animated film, based on their own preferences and those of their family members.

- **Read** *Virtual Actors on the Screen* again.
- **Complete** the chart. Use information from the text. You may also include your own ideas.

| What is special or unique about animated characters? | What is special or unique about real actors? |
|---|---|
| | |

## Family Link

Tell your family what you learned about computer animation. Talk with family members about their favorite animated movie.

# The Anasazi: The Ancient Builders

by Zeke G. Ato                    ELL Reader 5.4.1    Expository Nonfiction

## INTRODUCE THE BOOK

### Activate Prior Knowledge/Build Background
Read the title, and talk about the photo on the cover. Tell students that it shows a cliff dwelling. It was built by the Anasazi, a group of Native Americans from the Southwest.

### Preview/Use Text Features
Preview the reader by talking about the photographs together and reading the captions. Point out the *Did You Know?* box on page 2.

### Preteach Vocabulary
Review the tested vocabulary words that appear in this book: **civilization**, **complex**, and **inspired**. Introduce these key words from the book: **ancient** (p. 2), **structures** (p. 3), and **dwellings** (p. 7). Discuss these words and add them to a Word Wall.

## READ THE BOOK

Choose among these options for reading to support students at all English proficiency levels.

### Read Aloud
Read the book aloud as students follow along. Pause to verify comprehension and to explain unfamiliar concepts.

### Monitored Reading
Have students read aloud a few pages at a time. Use the following questions to support comprehension:
- **Pages 2–3** Where did the Anasazi live? (in the area now known as the Four Corners, where Colorado, New Mexico, Utah, and Arizona meet)
- **Pages 4–8** How were the pueblos organized? (Rooms and apartments were built into the sides of cliffs. They surrounded a local meeting area called a *plaza*. People did their cooking in the courtyards.)
- **Pages 9–12** How were pueblos connected to other pueblos? (They were connected by straight, wide roads.)

### Reread
Have students reread the book with a partner, in small groups, or independently. Have them complete the Study Guide on page 243.

## RESPOND

Answers to the Reader's Inside Back Cover:

### Talk About It
**1.** They had to survive heavy snows, strong winds, drought, and possibly with enemy attack. They had to manage with little water nearby.
**2.** First, they lived in caves, which gave them protection. They used rock and mud to enhance their dwellings. These resources were available nearby. They built roads in order to travel easily between pueblos. (Draw Conclusions)

### Write About It
**3.** Possible responses: *Kinds of Buildings:* Cliff dwellings were high and grouped together. They provided protection from the wind and possibly from enemies. *Roads:* The roads were straight. They were strong and could withstand a heavy rain. *Farming Methods:* The Anasazi built channels to water their crops. This allowed them to stay in one place much longer. (Draw Conclusions)
Support writers at various English proficiency levels.

**Beginning** Help students locate and reread the appropriate section of the book for each part of the chart.
**Intermediate** Suggest that students look through the book for words and phrases to complete the chart.
**Advanced** Ask students to respond in complete sentences.

### Extend Language
Possible answers: skyscraper, apartment building, highway, freeway

Answers to page 243:
Drawings will vary, but check to be sure that students have drawn and labeled a mesa, cliff dwelling, kiva, plaza, and courtyard.

### Family Link
Read aloud the Family Link activity on page 243 before sending copies of the Study Guide home with students. Later, students can share their family members' comparisons of Anasazi cliff dwellings and cities.

Name _____

- **Read** *The Anasazi: The Ancient Builders* again.
- **Draw** a picture of an Anasazi pueblo. **Include** and **label** a mesa, plaza, kiva, and courtyard. Use the pictures in the book for help.

## Family Link

Share your drawing with family members. Talk with them about Anasazi dwellings. How are the dwellings like cities today?

# Strength of Spirit

by Halima Hadavi

## INTRODUCE THE BOOK

**Activate Prior Knowledge/Build Background** Read the title, and point to the two photos on the cover. Tell students the photos show two famous Americans who had disabilities: Franklin Delano Roosevelt and Helen Keller.

**Preview/Use Text Features** Preview the reader by talking about the photographs together and reading the captions.

**Preteach Vocabulary** Review the tested vocabulary word that appears in this book: **wheelchair**. Introduce these key words from the book: **deaf** (p. 3), **blind** (p. 3), and **disabled** (p. 11). Discuss these words and add them to a Word Wall.

## READ THE BOOK

Choose among these options for reading to support students at all English proficiency levels.

**Read Aloud** Read the book aloud as students follow along. Pause to verify comprehension and to explain unfamiliar concepts.

**Monitored Reading** Have students silently read a few pages at a time. Use the following questions to support comprehension:
- **Pages 2–8** How did Helen overcome her obstacles? (with determination and the help of her teacher, Annie Sullivan)
- **Pages 9–12** What did Franklin do for the United States? (He helped people when the country was going through difficult financial times. He was a strong leader during World War II.)

**Reread** Have students reread the book with a partner, in small groups, or independently. Have them complete the Study Guide on page 245.

## RESPOND

Answers to the Reader's Inside Back Cover:

**Talk About It**
**1.** She realized that there was a connection between words and things. That was when she learned how to communicate.
**2.** Answers will vary.

**Write About It**
**3.** *Helen:* blind and deaf, teacher, writer; *Franklin:* had polio, couldn't walk, U.S. President; *Both:* disabled, accomplished great things, raised money to help disabled (Compare and Contrast) Support writers at various English proficiency levels.
  **Beginning** Create a Venn diagram on the board. Guide by asking questions such as: *Where would I write* disabled? *Was Helen disabled? Was Franklin disabled? Were they both?* Continue with other possible entries. Have students copy the results.
  **Intermediate** Guide students as above, but have students fill in the diagram.
  **Advanced** Tell students to look at pages 3–8 for the left circle and pages 9–12 for the right circle. They can then fill in the overlapping section.

**Extend Language** *disability*: inability to do something; *disagree*: not agree; *disinfect* remove infectants; *disconnect*: take apart

Answers to page 245:
Keller: *Childhood:* screamed and broke things; Annie Sullivan taught her how to spell words with her hands.
*Challenges:* could not hear or see
*Achievements:* learned to read Braille; went to college; wrote books; raised money for the blind
Roosevelt: *Childhood:* active and healthy; liked sports
*Challenges:* got polio; couldn't walk
*Achievements:* became senator and then President; led the United States during World War II; started the March of Dimes

**Family Link** Read aloud the Family Link activity on page 245 before sending copies of the Study Guide home with students. Later, students can share what they learned about other people living with disabilities.

Name _____

- **Read** *Strength of Spirit* again.
- **Complete** the chart. **Write** about the childhood, challenges, and achievements of Helen Keller and Franklin Delano Roosevelt.

|  | Childhood | Challenges | Achievements |
|---|---|---|---|
| **Helen Keller** |  |  |  |
| **Franklin Delano Roosevelt** |  |  |  |

## Family Link
Share what you learned with your family. Ask family members about other people they know about who live with a disability.

# Masters of Disguise

by Amanda Adams

ELL Reader 5.4.3   Expository Nonfiction and a Poem

## INTRODUCE THE BOOK

**Activate Prior Knowledge/Build Background** Read the title, and ask students if they know the name of the insect in the photo. Tell students they will learn about this and other interesting insects in the book.

**Preview/Use Text Features** Preview the reader by talking about the photographs together and reading the captions. Point out the *Extend Language* feature on page 7.

**Preteach Vocabulary** Review the tested vocabulary words that appear in this book: **enable** and **critical**. Introduce these key words from the book: **disguise** (p. 2), **creatures** (p. 2), and **confusion** (p. 7). Discuss these words and add them to a Word Wall.

## READ THE BOOK

Choose among these options for reading to support students at all English proficiency levels.

**Read Aloud** Read the book aloud as students follow along. Pause to verify comprehension and to explain unfamiliar concepts.

**Monitored Reading** Have students read aloud a few pages at a time. Use the following questions to support comprehension:

- **Pages 2–3** Why do some insects look like things that are different from what they really are? (It helps them to hide from predators or to catch prey.)
- **Pages 4–6** What is the difference between *mimicking* and *using a disguise?* (*Mimicking* means looking like another insect. *Using a disguise* means looking like a completely different object.)
- **Pages 7–8** Do Viceroys use camouflage, or disguises, or do they imitate another insect? (Viceroys imitate Monarchs.) What about leafhoppers? (Leafhoppers use camouflage.)

**Reread** Have students reread the book with a partner, in small groups, or independently. Have them complete the Study Guide on page 247.

## RESPOND

Answers to the Reader's Inside Back Cover:

### Talk About It
**1.** Some have camouflage to blend into backgrounds, some look like other insects, and some look like different things altogether.
**2.** The Monarch and Viceroy look very similar. (Compare and Contrast)

### Write About It
**3.** Answers will vary. Allow students to do research. Possibilities include: polar bears and other arctic mammals, chameleons, rattlesnakes, various kinds of fish.
Support writers at various English proficiency levels.
   **Beginning** Have students draw a picture of an animal using its camouflage to blend into its background. Help students label the animal and elements of the background.
   **Intermediate** Have students choose the animal they want to write about. Write a model on the board with a different animal. For example: *Tigers have orange and black stripes. The stripes look like shadows. That helps the tiger to hide in the forest.* Have students use the model to write about their chosen animal.
   **Advanced** Ask students to write a detailed paragraph about their chosen animal.

**Extend Language** many leaves

Answers to page 247:
**2.** A praying mantis looks like a twig.
**3.** A katydid looks like leaves and stems.
**4.** A syrphid fly looks like a wasp or a bee.
**5.** A walking stick looks like a branch.

**Family Link** Read aloud the Family Link activity on page 247 before sending copies of the Study Guide home with students. Later, students can share their family members' experiences.

- **Read** *Masters of Disguise* again.
- **Write** about these insects. **Tell** what they look like. Follow the example.

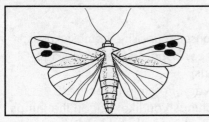

### 1. Moth
A moth looks like a scary animal.

_____

_____

### 2. Praying Mantis

_____

_____

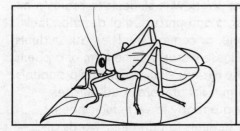

### 3. Katydid

_____

_____

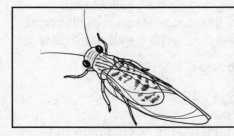

### 4. Syrphid Fly

_____

_____

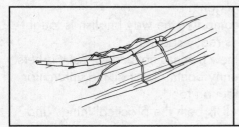

### 5. Walking Stick

_____

_____

## Family Link
Describe how the insects are disguised in nature. Ask family members if they have ever seen one of the insects named on this page.

# In This New Place

by Linda Marino

## INTRODUCE THE BOOK

**Activate Prior Knowledge/Build Background** Read the title, and tell students that this book is a collection of poems about moving to a new place.

**Preview/Use Text Features** Preview the reader by talking about the photographs and illustrations together, naming the labeled items, and reading the captions. Point out the *Extend Language* feature on page 7.

**Preteach Vocabulary** Review the tested vocabulary words that appear in this book: **episode** and **combination**. Introduce these key words from the book: **perfect** (p. 5), **courage** (p. 8), and **hope** (p. 8). Discuss these words and add them to a Word Wall.

## READ THE BOOK

Choose among these options for reading to support students at all English proficiency levels.

**Read Aloud** Read the book aloud as students follow along. Pause to verify comprehension and to explain unfamiliar concepts.

**Monitored Reading** Have students silently read a few pages at a time. Use the following questions to support comprehension:
- **Pages 2–5** What does the poet miss about her old home? (She misses her room, the language she used to speak, and her old friends.)
- **Pages 6–8** Do you think the poet will adjust to her new home? Why or why not? (Possible response: It seems as though she will adjust because she has a positive attitude and a sense of humor.)

**Reread** Have students reread the book with a partner, in small groups, or independently. Have them complete the Study Guide on page 249.

## RESPOND

Answers to the Reader's Inside Back Cover:

**Talk About It**
**1.** Possible responses: curiosity, homesickness, confusion, patience, hope, bravery/courage (Draw Conclusions)
**2.** Answers will vary. Possible responses: Focusing on the things you like, not on the things you don't like. Join groups that do activities you already enjoy. Make friends.

**Write About It**
**3.** Responses will vary. Tell students that their poem does not need to have complete sentences and that it does not need to rhyme.
Support writers at various English proficiency levels.
   **Beginning** Work with students to brainstorm a list of words and phrases that describe their school, home, or community. Then ask students to arrange these words into the form of a poem.
   **Intermediate** In a similar way, help students to brainstorm a list of words and phrases. When they are ready to write their poem, encourage students to add other words and phrases to expand on their initial ideas.
   **Advanced** Encourage students to memorize their poems and to recite them for the class.

**Extend Language** full, quiet, bright

Answers to page 249:
Possible responses:
**1.** The poet wonders what her old place is like now that she's gone.
**2.** The poet compares the way English is taught to the way it is really spoken.
**3.** The poet's new home is not perfect, but it is hers.
**4.** This is a funny poem about all the unfamiliar names of American food.
**5.** This poem lists both the practical things and the character traits you need when you move to a new school.

**Family Link** Read aloud the Family Link activity on page 249 before sending copies of the Study Guide home with students. Later, students can share the poems that they learned from their family members.

- **Read** *In This New Place* again.
- **Write** one or two sentences about each poem. **Tell** what the poem is about.

### 1. Questions
_____
_____

### 2. Where Am I From?
_____
_____

### 3. In This New Place
_____
_____

### 4. Cafeteria Menu, First Time Around
_____
_____

### 5. Supply List for a New Student
_____
_____

## Family Link
Read one of these poems for your family. Ask family members to tell you other poems that they know. Read or recite one of these poems for your classmates.

# Fast as Lightning

by Rani Patel

ELL Reader 5.4.5    Biography

## INTRODUCE THE BOOK

**Activate Prior Knowledge/Build Background** Read the title, and ask students if they know what the expression *fast as lightning* means. Explain that it describes the woman in the picture, Betty Robinson.

**Preview/Use Text Features** Preview the reader by talking about the illustrations and photographs together and reading the captions.

**Preteach Vocabulary** Review the tested vocabulary words that appear in this book: **hesitation** and **limelight**. Introduce these key words from the book: **amazing** (p. 2), **compete** (p. 5), and **champion** (p. 12). Discuss these words and add them to a Word Wall.

## READ THE BOOK

Choose among these options for reading to support students at all English proficiency levels.

**Read Aloud** Read the book aloud as students follow along. Pause to verify comprehension and to explain unfamiliar concepts.

**Monitored Reading** Have students read aloud a few pages at a time. Use the following questions to support comprehension:
- **Pages 2–5** Who was Charles Price, and why was he important in Betty's life? (He was one of Betty's teachers. He first noticed her abilities. He coached her and helped her join a women's running club in Chicago.)
- **Pages 6–7** Who were Betty's main competitors at the 1928 Olympics? (Helen Filkey and Fanny Rosenfeld)
- **Pages 8–12** What was Betty's greatest accomplishment? (Possible response: winning a gold medal even though she had suffered a serious injury)

**Reread** Have students reread the book with a partner, in small groups, or independently. Have them complete the Study Guide on page 251.

## RESPOND

Answers to the Reader's Inside Back Cover:

**Talk About It**
**1.** She was in an airplane crash in 1931 and was injured. (Cause and Effect)
**2.** Responses will vary. Possible responses: She had accomplished her goal. Running was painful after the injury. She could no longer compete with the greatest runners. (Make Inferences)

**Write About It**
**3.** Answers will vary.
Support writers at various English proficiency levels.

  **Beginning** Tell students to close their eyes and to "make a movie in their minds" as you verbalize: *You are in a race. You are running very fast. You cross the finish line first. Congratulations! You are the winner!* Ask students how they feel and write the words on the board. Have them copy the words.
  **Intermediate** On the board, write words such as *tired, proud, excited, happy,* and so on. Tell students to circle the words that describe how they would feel and to write sentences in this pattern: *I would feel excited.*
  **Advanced** Ask students to give reasons for their feelings. For example: *If I were Betty Robinson, I would be proud because I worked so hard.*

**Extend Language** A *winner* is a person who wins.

Answers to page 251:
*1928:* Betty joins a running club and goes to the Olympics. She wins a gold medal.
*1931:* Betty is injured in a plane crash.
*1932:* Betty is unable to go to the Olympic games.
*1936:* Betty goes to the Olympics and helps her team win a relay.

**Family Link** Read aloud the Family Link activity on page 251 before sending copies of the Study Guide home with students. Later, students can share what they learned about other famous athletes.

Name _____

- **Read** *Fast as Lightning* again.
- **Look** at the time line. These are important dates in the life of Betty Robinson. **Write** what happened in each of these years.

1925

1928 _____
_____

1930

1931 _____
_____

1935

1932 _____
_____

1936 _____
_____

1940

## Family Link

Tell family members what you learned about Betty Robinson. Ask them to tell you about another famous athlete.

# My Great-Grandpa Collins

by Jimmy Keating

ELL Reader 5.5.1    Historical Fiction

## INTRODUCE THE BOOK

**Activate Prior Knowledge/Build Background** Read the title, and talk about the photo. Tell students that the photo shows a police officer in the early 1900s. Say: *This book tells about a man who came to the United States from Ireland. It is a fictional story, but it uses photos as illustrations.*

**Preview/Use Text Features** Preview the reader by talking about the photographs together, naming the labeled items, and reading the captions. Point out the Did You Know box on page 4.

**Preteach Vocabulary** Review the tested vocabulary words that appear in this book: **spectacles** and **eerie**. Introduce these key words from the book: **researched** (p. 2), **married** (p. 4), **relatives** (p. 6), and **homesick** (p. 7). Discuss these words and add them to a Word Wall.

## READ THE BOOK

Choose among these options for reading to support students at all English proficiency levels.

**Read Aloud** Read the book aloud as students follow along. Pause to verify comprehension and to explain unfamiliar concepts.

**Monitored Reading** Have students silently read a few pages at a time. Use the following questions to support comprehension:

- **Pages 2–4** What kind of person was Great-Grandpa Collins? (He was tall. He loved to tell stories and jokes, to dance and sing. He was brave.)
- **Pages 4–5** What did Great-Grandpa Collins do in America? (He got married and lived in Boston for the rest of his life. He had three children. He was a policeman.)
- **Pages 6–8** What has Jimmy learned about his family? (He has learned how his family came to America and about his extended family in Ireland.)

**Reread** Have students reread the book with a partner, in small groups, or independently. Have them complete the Study Guide on page 253.

## RESPOND

Answers to the Reader's Inside Back Cover:

**Talk About It**
**1.** He has his great-grandpa's spectacles, police badge, and hat. They are important because Jimmy is interested in his great-grandpa's life. (Main Idea and Details)
**2.** All her friends loved him. She thought he was the best policeman in Boston. (Character)

**Write About It**
**3.** Answers will vary. Circulate as students work and provide assistance as necessary.
Support writers at various English proficiency levels.

**Beginning** Allow students to draw a picture of a favorite family dish. Help them label the picture.
**Intermediate** Provide a model for students to use. For example: *My family loves to eat tamales. We always have tamales on holidays. They are delicious!*
**Advanced** Read students' work and provide feedback, making suggestions for ways to expand on their description and add details.

**Extend Language** Irish people are from Ireland. Answers will vary.

Answers to page 253:
Possible responses: In 1915, he immigrated to the United States. He lived in Boston and became a policeman. He married Claire and had three children, fourteen grandchildren, and thirty-six great-grandchildren. He went back to Ireland twice.

**Family Link** Read aloud the Family Link activity on page 253 before sending copies of the Study Guide home with students. Later, students can tell the class what they learned about their extended families.

- **Read** *My Great-Grandpa Collins* again.
- **Write** a summary of Great-Grandpa Collins's life. Use the pictures as a guide. The first and last sentences are written for you.

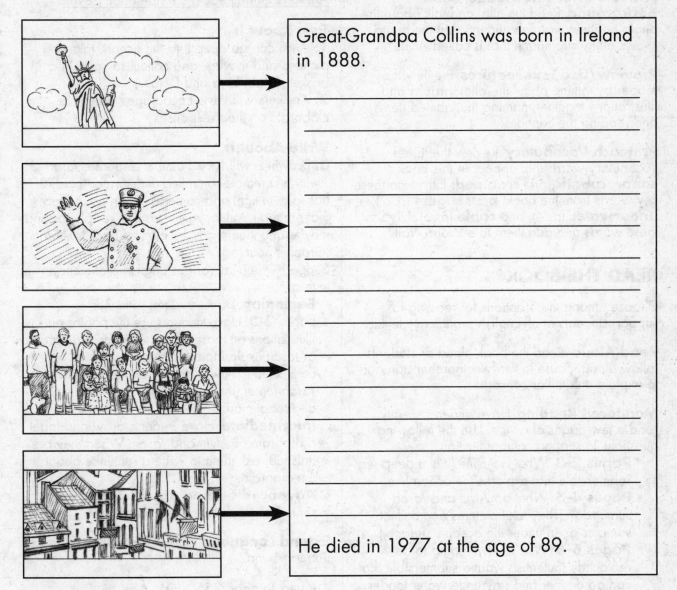

Great-Grandpa Collins was born in Ireland in 1888.

_____

_____

_____

_____

_____

_____

_____

_____

_____

_____

_____

_____

_____

_____

_____

He died in 1977 at the age of 89.

## Family Link

How many people are in your family? Do you know all their names? Where do they live? Talk to your family members. Learn about your relatives.

# Exploring the Oceans with *Alvin*

by Alice Cary

ELL Reader 5.5.2   Expository Nonfiction

## INTRODUCE THE BOOK

**Activate Prior Knowledge/Build Background** Read the title, and talk about the photo on the cover. Tell students that the photo shows a tiny submarine that is called *Alvin*.

**Preview/Use Text Features** Preview the reader by talking about the photographs and illustrations together, naming the labeled items, and reading the captions.

**Preteach Vocabulary** Review the tested vocabulary words that appear in this book: **sonar**, **robotic**, and **cramped**. Introduce these key words from the book: **passengers** (p. 2), **underwater** (p. 4), and **cable** (p. 5). Discuss these words and add them to a Word Wall.

## READ THE BOOK

Choose among these options for reading to support students at all English proficiency levels.

**Read Aloud** Read the book aloud as students follow along. Pause to verify comprehension and to explain unfamiliar concepts.

**Monitored Reading** Have students silently read a few pages at a time. Use the following questions to support comprehension:
- **Pages 2–3** What is *Alvin*? (It is a deep-sea submersible that explores the ocean.)
- **Pages 4–5** What do *Alvin* and *Jason Junior* do? (They take pictures and collect samples deep under the ocean's surface.)
- **Pages 6–8** Why is *Alvin* going to be replaced? (Scientists want a submersible that can go deeper and stay underwater longer than *Alvin*.)

**Reread** Have students reread the book with a partner, in small groups, or independently. Have them complete the Study Guide on page 255.

## RESPOND

Answers to the Reader's Inside Back Cover:

**Talk About It**
**1.** *Alvin* can go deep into the ocean, take pictures and movies, and collect samples in a basket. (Main Idea and Details)
**2.** Answers will vary. Encourage students to elaborate on their responses.

**Write About It**
**3.** Drawings will vary. Possible response: *Jason Junior* is a remote-controlled underwater robot. It has its own light and cameras. It can go in places that are too small for *Alvin*. *Jason* takes photos and movies and then sends the pictures back to *Alvin*. (Graphic Sources)
Support writers at various English proficiency levels.

**Beginning** Direct students' attention to pages 2–5. Have students use the photos and illustrations on those pages to sketch a diagram of *Jason* exploring the ocean floor while connected to *Alvin*. Help students label *Alvin*, *Jason Junior*, the lights, cameras, basket, sonar, and robotic arms.
**Intermediate** Have students draw and label a diagram of *Alvin* and *Jason*. When they are finished, ask them to write a sentence about the diagram.
**Advanced** Students can write a few sentences describing their diagrams.

**Extend Language** *Subway* means *a railway under ground.*

Answers to page 255:
*1967: Alvin* finds a U.S. Navy plane that crashed into the ocean in 1944.
*1968 Alvin* sinks to the bottom of the ocean.
*1969: Alvin* is rescued.
*1971: Alvin* makes its first dive since 1968.
*1977: Alvin* finds strange new creatures near an underwater hot spring.

**Family Link** Read aloud the Family Link activity on page 255 before sending copies of the Study Guide home with students. Later, students can share what family members knew about the ocean.

- **Read** *Exploring the Oceans with* Alvin again.
- **Complete** the time line. **Write** one thing that happened to *Alvin* in each year. The first fact has been provided for you.

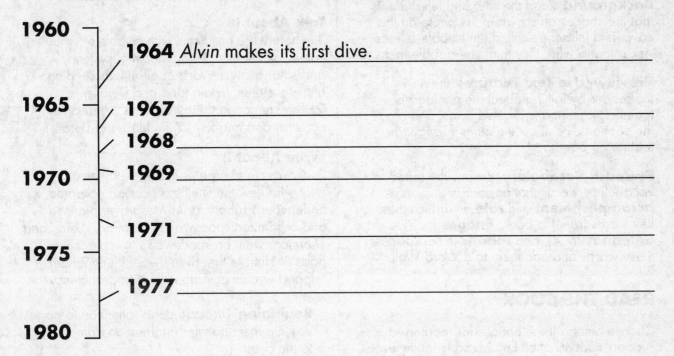

**1960**

**1964** *Alvin* makes its first dive. _____

**1965**

**1967** _____

**1968** _____

**1970**

**1969** _____

**1971** _____

**1975**

**1977** _____

**1980**

## Family Link

Tell your family members what you learned about *Alvin.* Ask them to tell you what they know about the ocean.

# Fixing Hubble's Troubles

by Philip Stewart

ELL Reader 5.5.3    Nonfiction

## INTRODUCE THE BOOK

**Activate Prior Knowledge/Build Background** Read the title, and tell students that the spacecraft shown in the photo on the cover is a telescope called the Hubble Telescope. Ask students what they think the Hubble looks at.

**Preview/Use Text Features** Preview the reader by talking about the photographs together, naming the labeled items, and reading the captions. Point out the *Extend Language* feature on page 5.

**Preteach Vocabulary** Review the tested vocabulary words that appear in this book: **accomplishment** and **role**. Introduce these key words from the book: **images** (p. 2), **antennas** (p. 4), and **robotic** (p. 8). Discuss these words and add them to a Word Wall.

## READ THE BOOK

Choose among these options for reading to support students at all English proficiency levels.

**Read Aloud** Read the book aloud as students follow along. Pause to verify comprehension and to explain unfamiliar concepts.

**Monitored Reading** Have students silently read a few pages at a time. Use the following questions to support comprehension:
- **Pages 2–4** What are some parts of the Hubble telescope? (mirrors, cameras and other instruments, communication antennas, solar arrays, control systems)
- **Pages 5–6** Why was it so difficult to fix Hubble? (All the repairs had to be done in outer space.)
- **Pages 7–11** What did the astronauts have to do in order to work on Hubble? (train for a year; fly to the telescope; grab it with a robotic arm; place it in the shuttle payload bay; then go on spacewalks)
- **Page 12** Was the trip worthwhile? (Possible response: Yes: Hubble was fully repaired.)

**Reread** Have students reread the book with a partner, in small groups, or independently. Have them complete the Study Guide on page 257.

## RESPOND

Answers to the Reader's Inside Back Cover:

### Talk About It
**1.** There were problems with Hubble's communications antennas, control systems, and solar arrays. Worst of all, it was sending blurry pictures. (Main Idea and Details)
**2.** They replaced the gyroscopes, solar arrays, camera, and mirrors. (Main Idea and Details)

### Write About It
**3.** *Covey:* in charge of mission; *Bowersox:* pilot who flew the shuttle; *Nicollier:* operated Endeavour's robotic arm; *Musgrave:* planned and organized spacewalks; *Hoffman, Akers, and Thornton:* went on spacewalks to replace the parts of Hubble that didn't work (Summarize) Support writers at various English proficiency levels.

**Beginning** Direct students' attention to page 7. Help them transfer information from the text to the chart.
**Intermediate** Tell students to look at page 7 while working on their chart.
**Advanced** Tell students to look at pages 8–12 to confirm the information on page 7 and to add details.

### Extend Language Best

Answers to page 257:
Possible responses:
**2.** What did Hubble carry?
**3.** When did scientists discover problems with Hubble?
**4.** Why did scientists decide to build new instruments?
**5.** How long did the astronauts train?
**6.** How many spacewalks did it take to repair Hubble?

**Family Link** Read aloud the Family Link activity on page 257 before sending copies of the Study Guide home with students. Later, students can share what family members told them about outer space.

Name _____

- **Read** *Fixing Hubble's Troubles* again.
- **Read** the answers. **Write** a question for each answer. Follow the example.

| Page | Question | Answer |
|------|----------|--------|
| 2 | **1.** Why did scientists decide to put a giant telescope in orbit around the Earth? | They wanted clear images from outer space. |
| 3 | **2.** | It carried cameras and other instruments. |
| 4 | **3.** | They discovered problems soon after the launch. |
| 5 | **4.** | because it wasn't possible to replace the mirror |
| 7 | **5.** | They trained for more than a year. |
| 12 | **6.** | It took five spacewalks to fix Hubble. |

## Family Link

Tell your family what you learned about the Hubble telescope. What do your family members know about outer space? Take notes so that you can tell your classmates what you learned.

# Jules Verne's Imagination

by Yoshi Fukuda

ELL Reader 5.5.4    Expository Nonfiction

## INTRODUCE THE BOOK

**Activate Prior Knowledge/Build Background** Read the title, and point to the photograph on the cover. Tell students that the picture shows Jules Verne, the author of *Journey to the Center of the Earth.*

**Preview/Use Text Features** Preview the reader by talking about the illustrations together and reading the captions.

**Preteach Vocabulary** Review the tested vocabulary words that appear in this book: **armor** and **plunged**. Introduce these key words from the book: **spacecraft** (p. 4), **helicopters** (p. 6), and **satellites** (p. 12). Discuss these words and add them to a Word Wall.

## READ THE BOOK

Choose among these options for reading to support students at all English proficiency levels.

**Read Aloud** Read the book aloud as students follow along. Pause to verify comprehension and to explain unfamiliar concepts.

**Monitored Reading** Have students read aloud a few pages at a time. Use the following questions to support comprehension:
- **Pages 2–3** How did Verne get started as a science fiction writer? (He went to the library and took notes on scientific discoveries. Then he took his notes home and created stories.)
- **Pages 4–5** How are Verne's imaginary trip to the Moon and the real trip alike? (They were both launched off the coast of Florida and landed in the ocean on their return. The two spacecraft looked alike.)
- **Pages 6–12** Why do you think people still read books by Jules Verne? (Possible responses: He made many predictions about the future that came true. He wrote about exciting adventures.)

**Reread** Have students reread the book with a partner, in small groups, or independently. Have them complete the Study Guide on page 259.

## RESPOND

Answers to the Reader's Inside Back Cover:

**Talk About It**
**1.** Both were flying machines that used propellers. Verne's helicopter had thirty-seven propellers to keep it in the air and two propellers to move it forward. A real helicopter needs only two rotors to fly. (Compare and Contrast)
**2.** It was like staying in a luxury hotel.

**Write About It**
**3.** Responses will vary.
Support writers at various English proficiency levels.
> **Beginning** Help students to label their drawings. Encourage them to demonstrate how the invention is used or what it can do through pantomime.
> **Intermediate** Ask students to answer two questions about their invention: *What is it called? What can it do?*
> **Advanced** If students need a model to help them get started, have them reread the descriptions of the imaginary helicopter on page 6 and of *Nautilus* on pages 8–9.

**Extend Language** *Television* comes from Greek and Latin. It means *to see from far away. Computer* is also from Latin. It means *a thing that makes calculations. Auto-* means *self* (Greek) and *mobile* means *able to move* (Latin).

Answers to page 259:
Possible responses:
**2:** Captain Hatteras explores the polar region.
**3:** A man travels around the world on ships and trains.
**4:** Captain Nemo explores the ocean in his luxury submarine.
**5:** In the Paris of 1960, people are unhappy.

**Family Link** Read aloud the Family Link activity on page 259 before sending copies of the Study Guide home with students. Later, students can share the stories that family members told them.

Name _____

- **Read** *Jules Verne's Imagination* again.
- **Write** a summary of each of these books by Jules Verne.

---

pages 4–5
## 1. From the Earth to the Moon
Space travelers go to the Moon with a dog and battle Moon men.

_____

_____

---

page 7
## 2. Voyages and Adventures of Captain Hatteras

_____

_____

---

page 7
## 3. Around the World in Eighty Days

_____

_____

---

pages 8–9
## 4. 20,000 Leagues Under the Sea

_____

_____

---

pages 10–11
## 5. Paris in the Twentieth Century

_____

_____

---

## Family Link
Tell family members about these stories. Ask them to tell you about
other science fiction stories.

# Gold in the American River

by Ferris James

ELL Reader 5.5.5   Expository Nonfiction

## INTRODUCE THE BOOK

**Activate Prior Knowledge/Build Background** Read the title. Explain that the American River is near San Francisco, California.

**Preview/Use Text Features** Preview the reader by talking about the illustrations together, naming the labeled items, and reading the captions. Point out the *Extend Language* feature on page 9.

**Preteach Vocabulary** Review the tested vocabulary words that appear in this book: **overrun** and **vacant**. Introduce these key words from the book: **gold** (p. 2), **dream** (p. 2), and **miners** (p. 9). Discuss these words and add them to a Word Wall.

## READ THE BOOK

Choose among these options for reading to support students at all English proficiency levels.

**Read Aloud** Read the book aloud as students follow along. Pause to verify comprehension and to explain unfamiliar concepts.

**Monitored Reading** Have students silently read a few pages at a time. Use the following questions to support comprehension:

- **Pages 2–5** James Marshall did not want anyone to know about the gold. Why not? (He did not want people coming onto his ranch.)
- **Pages 6–8** How did Native Americans feel about the Gold Rush? (Possible response: They did not like it. Their land was overrun by miners.)
- **Pages 10–12** Why do so many people still move to California? (People think it is a good place to live and work.)

**Reread** Have students reread the book with a partner, in small groups, or independently. Have them complete the Study Guide on page 261.

## RESPOND

Answers to the Reader's Inside Back Cover:

**Talk About It**
**1.** The Gold Rush made the population of California grow quickly with people from many lands. (Main Idea and Details)
**2.** Possible responses: People move to be with family members, take a job, go to school, or start a new life. (Generalize)

**Write About It**
**3.** Explain that students should use their imaginations and what they learned in the book to create their journal entries.
Support writers at various English proficiency levels.
  **Beginning** Write a journal entry on the board. For example: *We have just arrived in San Francisco. Everyone in the town seems excited. But I am too tired to start looking for gold yet.* Ask students to verbalize another sentence for the entry.
  **Intermediate** Have students work in pairs to brainstorm and write one or two journal entries.
  **Advanced** Have students look at the journal entry on the board. Suggest that they write the entry for the day before or after.

**Extend Language** cars, airplanes, buses

Answers to page 261:
Possible responses:
**2.** News about the gold rush spread around the world. People came from far away, even though travel was difficult.
**3.** Travelers overran John Sutter's ranch and set up camps along the American River.
**4.** The Gold Rush caused a lot of pollution and destruction, but it also brought people together and inspired new businesses.
**5.** The Gold Rush has ended, but California is still a place of opportunity for newcomers.

**Family Link** Read aloud the Family Link activity on page 261 before sending copies of the Study Guide home with students. Later, students can tell the class about things that are made of gold.

- **Read** *Gold in the American River* again.
- **Summarize** each section of the book. Follow the example.

---

pages 3–5
## "Gold in the American River!"

**1.** James Marshall finds gold at Sutter's sawmill. Sam Brannan runs through the streets telling everybody about it. Everyone runs to the river.

---

pages 6–7
## The Gold Rush

**2.** _____

_____

---

page 8
## Reaching California

**3.** _____

_____

---

pages 9–10
## Impact of the Gold Rush

**4.** _____

_____

---

pages 11–12
## The Gold Rush Spirit Lives On

**5.** _____

_____

---

# Family Link
Share what you learned about the Gold Rush with your family. Ask family members to tell you about things that are made out of gold.

# Nighttime Under the Sea

by Camilla Dacier

ELL Reader 5.6.1   Nonfiction

## INTRODUCE THE BOOK

**Activate Prior Knowledge/Build Background** Read the title, and look at the cover illustration with students. Ask students whether they can name the sea animals shown. Then have students confirm their guesses by looking at the key on page 5.

**Preview/Use Text Features** Preview the reader by talking about the illustrations and photographs together, naming the labeled items, and reading the captions.

**Preteach Vocabulary** Review the tested vocabulary words that appear in this book: **sea urchins** and **algae**. Introduce these key words from the book: **aquarium** (p. 2), **creatures** (p. 4), and **habitats** (p. 4). Discuss these words and add them to a Word Wall.

## READ THE BOOK

Choose among these options for reading to support students at all English proficiency levels.

**Read Aloud** Read the book aloud as students follow along. Pause to verify comprehension and to explain unfamiliar concepts.

**Monitored Reading** Have students read aloud a few pages at a time. Use the following questions to support comprehension:
- **Pages 2–3** When and where does this story take place? (at the Monterey Bay Aquarium at night)
- **Pages 4–5** What is an ocean zone? (It is a different environment or habitat within the ocean.)
- **Pages 6–8** Where do the girl and her mother go to sleep? (on the floor, under a tank attached to the ceiling)

**Reread** Have students reread the book with a partner, in small groups, or independently. Have them complete the Study Guide on page 263.

## RESPOND

Answers to the Reader's Inside Back Cover:

**Talk About It**
**1.** Responses will vary. Encourage students to elaborate on their answers.
**2.** They are being overfished.

**Write About It**
**3.** Model how to describe one of the animals shown in this book. Verbalize as you fill in a row of the chart, saying, for example: *A barracuda is long and skinny. It has sharp teeth. It is silver in color.*
Support writers at various English proficiency levels.

> **Beginning** Allow beginning students to simply draw and label a picture of an animal from the book.
> **Intermediate** Have students draw a picture of a sea animal. In addition to the animal's name, students can label the drawing by writing words and phrases, such as *dark spots, red stripes, hard shell, sharp teeth*, and so on.
> **Advanced** Ask students to write a short paragraph that describes one of the sea animals using words and phrases from a completed chart.

**Extend Language** In Spanish, the names of these sea animals are: *tortuga* (sea turtle), *tiburón* (shark), *cangrejo* (crab), and *estrella de mar* (sea star).

Answers to page 263:
*Rocky Shore or Tide Pool*: **2.** sea urchin **3.** sea star **6.** sea turtle
*Coral Reef/Kelp Forest or Open Water*:
**1.** jellyfish **4.** barracuda **5.** sunfish

**Family Link** Read aloud the Family Link activity on page 263 before sending copies of the Study Guide home with students. Later, students can teach classmates the names of these animals in their home languages.

- **Read** *Nighttime Under the Sea* again.
- **Label** each of the animals shown. Then **draw** a line to the habitat where that animal lives.

1. _____

2. _____

**Rocky Shore or Tide Pool**

3. _____

4. _____

**Coral Reef/Kelp Forest or Open Water**

5. _____

6. _____

## Family Link
Teach your family the names of these animals. Ask your family if they know the names of any of these animals in another language.

# All Things in Balance

by Tamara Jasmine Burrell

## INTRODUCE THE BOOK

**Activate Prior Knowledge/Build Background** Read the title, and direct students' attention to the photo on the cover. Ask students to guess what the book is going to be about, based on the title and photo.

**Preview/Use Text Features** Preview the reader by talking about the photographs and illustrations together, naming the labeled items, and reading the captions.

**Preteach Vocabulary** Review the tested vocabulary words that appear in this book: **scrawny** and **starvation**. Introduce these key words from the book: **herbivore** (p. 2), **carnivore** (p. 3), and **omnivore** (p. 6). Discuss these words and add them to a Word Wall.

## READ THE BOOK

Choose among these options for reading to support students at all English proficiency levels.

**Read Aloud** Read the book aloud as students follow along. Pause to verify comprehension and to explain unfamiliar concepts.

**Monitored Reading** Have students read aloud a few pages at a time. Use the following questions to support comprehension:
- **Pages 2–3** What is the difference between herbivores and carnivores? (Carnivores eat animals and herbivores eat only plants.)
- **Pages 4–5** Why are there fewer animals at the top of a food chain? (because it takes many things at the bottom of a food chain to support the living things at the top)
- **Pages 6–7** What causes the balance of nature to get upset? (Sometimes it is a natural disaster such as a flood, storm, or drought; sometimes humans can do something that upsets the balance.)

**Reread** Have students reread the book with a partner, in small groups, or independently. Have them complete the Study Guide on page 265.

## RESPOND

Answers to the Reader's Inside Back Cover:

**Talk About It**
**1.** A food chain is a chain of living things that provide food for each other. (Main Idea and Details)
**2.** The balance of nature is the correct balance among the plants and animals in an environment. (Main Idea and Details)

**Write About It**
**3.** *Herbivores:* giraffes, antelopes, zebras, elephants, buffalo, wildebeests; *Carnivores:* lions, hyenas, leopards, cheetahs (Students may also include additional animals.) (Classify) Support writers at various English proficiency levels.
> **Beginning** Direct students' attention to pages 2–3. Verbalize as you complete the chart on the board. Have students copy the chart.
> **Intermediate** Have students dictate to you as you complete the chart.
> **Advanced** Have students help beginning students to complete the chart.

**Extend Language** An omnivore eats both meat and plants. *Carni* means meat.

Answers to page 265:
Answers will vary. Sample answer:
**1.** An eagle eats a fox.
**2.** A fox eats mice.
**3.** The mice eat small plants.
**4.** The plants take nutrients from the ground.

**Family Link** Read aloud the Family Link activity on page 265 before sending copies of the Study Guide home with students. Later, students can share the food chains that they created at home.

Name _____

- **Read** *All Things in Balance* again.
- **Draw** a food chain.
- **Write** a sentence about each level of the food chain.

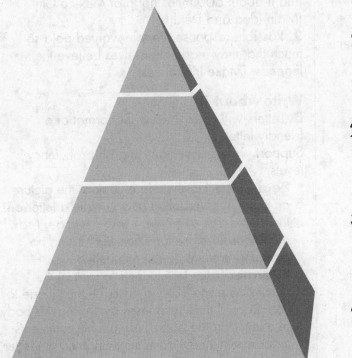

1. _____

_____

2. _____

_____

3. _____

_____

4. _____

_____

## Family Link

Share the food chain with your family. Ask family members to help you create another food chain.

# A Tale of Gold and Glory

by Elizabeth Hines

ELL Reader 5.6.3   Nonfiction

## INTRODUCE THE BOOK

**Activate Prior Knowledge/Build Background** Read the title, and talk about the cover illustration. Tell students it shows people from Spain looking for gold in the New World. The person in front is a Native American guide.

**Preview/Use Text Features** Preview the reader by talking about the illustrations together and reading the captions. Point out the *Did You Know?* box on page 12.

**Preteach Vocabulary** Review the tested vocabulary words that appear in this book: **precious** and **adorn**. Introduce these key words from the book: **explored** (p. 2), **conquer** (p. 2), and **jewelry** (p. 4). Discuss these words and add them to a Word Wall.

## READ THE BOOK

Choose among these options for reading to support students at all English proficiency levels.

**Read Aloud** Read the book aloud as students follow along. Pause to verify comprehension and to explain unfamiliar concepts.

**Monitored Reading** Have students read aloud a few pages at a time. Use the following questions to support comprehension:

- **Pages 2–3** Why did the Spanish sail to the New World? (They wanted to reach India and China. They were looking for gold.)
- **Pages 4–10** How did the Spanish treat Native Americans? (They conquered Native American groups and took their land.)
- **Pages 11–12** Did the Seven Cities of Gold really exist? (Probably not. Nobody ever found them.)

**Reread** Have students reread the book with a partner, in small groups, or independently. Have them complete the Study Guide on page 267.

## RESPOND

Answers to the Reader's Inside Back Cover:

**Talk About It**
**1.** The Spanish conquerors thought they would find it about 600 miles north of Mexico City. (Main Idea and Details)
**2.** Possible response: People wanted gold so much that they made themselves believe the legends. (Make Inferences)

**Write About It**
**3.** Letters will vary. Review the format of a friendly letter.
Support writers at various English proficiency levels.

> **Beginning** Have students look at the picture on page 10. Verbalize as you write a letter on the board. For example: *I saw a village. I saw many houses close together. But I found no gold.* Have students copy the letter.
> **Intermediate** Tell students to look at the picture on page 10 and describe the village to you. Record their responses by writing the body of a letter on the board, using their comments to form sentences. Have students copy the letter.
> **Advanced** Have students use one of the letters you created as a model for their own original letters.

**Extend Language** *Golden* means *made of gold.*

Answers to page 267:
**1.** He sailed to find an easy way to get to India and China. Instead he found the New World. He went there four times.
**2.** He was a Spanish monk. He traveled north from Mexico City almost 600 miles. Near a city, he became fearful and turned back.
**3.** In 1540, he left New Spain with many people. They conquered a Zuni village. He sent scouts east and west, but returned without finding the Cities of Cíbola.

**Family Link** Read aloud the Family Link activity on page 267 before sending copies of the Study Guide home with students. Later, students can share what they learned at home about Native Americans.

Name _____

- **Read** *A Tale of Gold and Glory* again.
- What did you learn about Christopher Columbus, Marcos de Niza, and Francisco Vasquez de Coronado? **Complete** the chart.

| Pages | Person | What I Learned About Him |
|---|---|---|
| 2–3 | **1. Christopher Columbus** | |
| 5–9 | **2. Marcos de Niza** | |
| 9–11 | **3. Francisco Vasquez de Coronado** | |

## Family Link
Tell your family what you have learned. Ask your family members what they know about Native Americans.

# Lighter Than Air

by Bernice Dodge

ELL Reader 5.6.4    Nonfiction

## INTRODUCE THE BOOK

**Activate Prior Knowledge/Build Background** Read the title, and talk about the illustration on the cover. Tell students it shows a hot-air balloon. Invite students to tell about any hot-air balloons they have seen.

**Preview/Use Text Features** Preview the reader by talking about the photographs and illustrations together and reading the captions.

**Preteach Vocabulary** Review the tested vocabulary words that appear in this book: **hydrogen**, **era**, and **explosion**. Introduce these key words from the book: **airships** (p. 2), **steer** (p. 3), and **passengers** (p. 6). Discuss these words and add them to a Word Wall.

## READ THE BOOK

Choose among these options for reading to support students at all English proficiency levels.

**Read Aloud** Read the book aloud as students follow along. Pause to verify comprehension and to explain unfamiliar concepts.

**Monitored Reading** Have students silently read a few pages at a time. Use the following questions to support comprehension:
- **Pages 2–5** What was the problem with the first airships? (They were slow and difficult to steer.)
- **Pages 6–8** How are airplanes and airships different? (Airplanes can go much faster and they are much smaller than airships.)
- **Pages 9–12** Why aren't airships so popular today? (People think they are too dangerous.)

**Reread** Have students reread the book with a partner, in small groups, or independently. Have them complete the Study Guide on page 269.

## RESPOND

Answers to the Reader's Inside Back Cover:

**Talk About It**
**1.** *Airships were beautiful:* opinion; *Hydrogen is lighter than air:* fact. (Fact and Opinion)
**2.** so that the airplanes couldn't shoot them (Detail)

**Write About It**
**3.** To prepare students for this activity, show them aerial photos of cities and landscapes, if available.
Support writers at various English proficiency levels.
**Beginning** Encourage students to draw their own aerial view. Help them write labels for their drawings, such as *Los Angeles from the Air.*
**Intermediate** Encourage students to label their drawings on their own, using a few words or phrases.
**Advanced** Ask students to write a description of a view from a hot-air balloon. Allow them to draw a picture if that will help them to get started.

**Extend Language** *Kindergarten* is the first year of school for American children. A *hamburger* is a kind of sandwich. A *dollar* is an amount of money.

Answers to page 269:
*LZ10:* one of Count Zeppelin's improved airships; It made more than 100 flights in 1911.
USS *Macon:* a "mother ship" for the U.S. Navy that could carry airplanes
*R34:* the first airship to cross the Atlantic Ocean, in 1919
*Graf Zeppelin:* a grand airship that had ten sleeping rooms and a fancy dining room; It went around the world in 1929.
*The Hindenburg:* one of the largest airships ever built; It exploded over New Jersey in 1937.

**Family Link** Read aloud the Family Link activity on page 269 before sending copies of the Study Guide home with students. Later, students can tell the class about their family members' experiences flying in airplanes and/or other kinds of aircraft.

Name _____

- **Read** *Lighter Than Air* again.
- **Tell** about each of these airships. **Write** the most important facts you learned about each one.

---

page 5
**LZ1:** The first airship built by Count Zeppelin. It was only a little faster than other airships. _____

---

page 6
**LZ10:** _____

---

page 8
**The USS *Macon*:** _____

---

page 9
**R34:** _____

---

pages 9–10
**Graf Zeppelin:** _____

---

page 11
**The *Hindenburg*:** _____

---

## Family Link

Tell your family what you learned about airships. Ask them whether they have ever flown. Did they fly in an airplane, airship, or something else? Ask them to tell you about it.

# What Do You See, James Van Der Zee?

by Patricia Wheeler

ELL Reader 5.6.5    Narrative Nonfiction and Poetry

## INTRODUCE THE BOOK

**Activate Prior Knowledge/Build Background** Read the title, and talk about the photograph on the cover. Ask: *When do you think this photo was taken? Why do you think so?*

**Preview/Use Text Features** Preview the reader by talking about the photographs together and reading the captions.

**Preteach Vocabulary** Review the tested vocabulary words that appear in this book: **nighttime** and **jammed**. Introduce these key words from the book: **photographs** (p. 2), **portraits** (p. 2), and **renaissance** (p. 3). Discuss these words and add them to a Word Wall.

## READ THE BOOK

Choose among these options for reading to support students at all English proficiency levels.

**Read Aloud** Read the book aloud as students follow along. Pause to verify comprehension and to explain unfamiliar concepts.

**Monitored Reading** Have students read aloud a few pages at a time. Use the following questions to support comprehension:

- **Pages 2–5** How was James Van Der Zee a part of the Harlem Renaissance? (He lived and worked in Harlem at the time of the Harlem Renaissance, photographing African Americans.)
- **Pages 6–9** How are the poems "Heroes" and "Come Along!" alike? (They both describe African American achievement in the early 1900s.)
- **Pages 10–12** How would you sum up the work of Van Der Zee? (Possible response: He took many beautiful photographs over a long period of time.)

**Reread** Have students reread the book with a partner, in small groups, or independently. Have them complete the Study Guide on page 271.

## RESPOND

Answers to the Reader's Inside Back Cover:

**Talk About It**
**1.** Possible response: Van Der Zee thought the people in his photos were beautiful, dignified, and proud. (Draw Conclusions)
**2.** The Harlem Renaissance was a time of creativity that happened in Harlem during the 1920s. (Summarize)

**Write About It**
**3.** Model the activity by talking about one of the photos, telling what you like about it.
Support writers at various English proficiency levels.
   **Beginning** Have students dictate their ideas to you.
   **Intermediate** Provide the following sentence frames to students: *I like the photo called ____. I like the way the photo shows ____. I like that because ____.* Encourage students to elaborate on these sentence frames.
   **Advanced** Provide the same sentence frames to students, and encourage them to elaborate on their responses.

**Extend Language** A *masterpiece* is a work of art; *nighttime* is the evening; *daytime* is the morning and afternoon; a *headline* is the title of an article.

Answers to page 271:
**2.** A young woman in a dress smiles happily.
**3.** African American soldiers march through New York City. They are proud and dignified.
**4.** A couple poses for the camera by their Cadillac. They look proud and happy.
**5.** A little girl and her mother share a quiet moment.

**Family Link** Read aloud the Family Link activity on page 271 before sending copies of the Study Guide home with students. Later, students can tell the class about photos they have at home.

Name _____

- **Read** *What Do You See, James Van Der Zee?* again.
- **Write** about the photographs in the book. **Describe** the people in each photograph.

---

page 2
## 1. "Future Expectations"

A man and woman are in their house on their wedding day. A little girl sits by their feet. The girl is a "picture" of their future.

---

page 3
## 2. "Do Tell"

_____

_____

---

page 6
## 3. "Victory Parade of the 369th Regiment"

_____

_____

---

pages 8–9
## 4. "A Couple With Raccoon Fur Coats"

_____

_____

---

page 11
## 5. "Mother and Daughter"

_____

_____

## Family Link
Tell your family members about the photos in this book. Then, look at a family photo album with someone in your family and talk about the pictures.

# Multilingual Lesson Vocabulary
## Unit 1

| English | Spanish | Chinese | Vietnamese | Korean | Hmong |
|---------|---------|---------|------------|--------|-------|
| **Week 1: Frindle** | | | | | |
| **acquainted** | conocer (gente) | 習慣 | đã quen | 알고 있는 | sib paub |
| **assignment** | trabajo | 任務 | bài làm | 과제 | dej num |
| **essential** | esencial | 必需的 | quan trọng, chủ yếu | 필수의 | tseem ceeb |
| **expanded** | ampliado | 擴展 | đã mở rộng | 전개하다 | thuav loj tuaj |
| **guaranteed** | garantiza | 保證 | đã bảo đảm | 보장하다 | guaranteed |
| **procedures** | procedimientos | 程序 | thủ tục | 진행 절차 | cov lus qhia |
| **reputation** | reputación | 名譽 | danh tiếng | 평판 | koob meej |
| **worshipped** | adoraba | 崇拜 | đã tôn thờ | 존경하다 | pe hawm |
| **Week 2: Thunder Rose** | | | | | |
| **branded** | marcados | 烙印 | được đóng dấu | 상표를 붙이다, 낙인을 찍다 | ci npe, ntau npe |
| **constructed** | construyó | 修建 | đã xây dựng | 세우다 | txiav |
| **daintily** | con elegancia | 精緻 | một cách xinh đẹp | 우아하게 | ntxim nyiam |
| **devastation** | devastación | 破壞 | sự tàn phá | 황폐하게 함 | tu siab |
| **lullaby** | nana | 催眠曲 | bài hát ru em | 자장가 | zaj nkauj rau me nyuam ab |
| **pitch** | brea | 瀝青 | mức giọng | 던지다 | lub suab |
| **resourceful** | ingeniosa | 機智勇敢 | tháo vát | 자원이 풍부한 | muaj tswv yim heev |
| **thieving** | (hábitos de) robar | 竊取 | trộm cắp | 도둑질의 | nyiag |
| **veins** | venas | 靜脈 | những đường gân, tĩnh mạch | 성질, 경향 | leeg |

| English | Spanish | Chinese | Vietnamese | Korean | Hmong |
|---------|---------|---------|------------|--------|-------|
| **Week 3: Island of the Blue Dolphins** | | | | | |
| **gnawed** | royeron | 咬 | gặm nhấm | 갉아먹다 | tom, xov |
| **headland** | promontorio | 陸岬 | mũi đất | 돌출부 | pob tsuas |
| **kelp** | algas | 海帶 | loại rong biển lớn | 켈프 | nroj hiav txwv |
| **lair** | guarida | 穴 | hang ổ | 짐승의 굴 | tsiaj chaw sov |
| **ravine** | barranco | 山溝 | khe núi | 협곡 | qhov dej |
| **shellfish** | mariscos | 貝類 | động vật có vỏ như cua, tôm, sò, hào, chem chép | 갑각류 동물 | pias deg |
| **sinew** | tendón | 精力 | sợi gân nối cơ với xương | 힘줄 | leeg |
| **Week 4: Satchel Paige** | | | | | |
| **confidence** | confianza | 信心 | sự tin tưởng | 자신감 | muaj peev xwm |
| **fastball** | bola rápida | 快球 | quả bóng thần tốc | 속구 | pob txawb muaj zog heev |
| **mocking** | burlón | 嘲笑 | chế giễu | 비웃는 | thuam |
| **outfield** | jardines | 外野 | khu vực cách xa người ném hoặc bắt bóng nhất trên sân chơi bóng chày/dã cầu | 외야 | tshav ntau pob |
| **unique** | único | 獨特 | đặc biệt nhất, độc nhất vô nhị | 독특한 | zoo txawv |
| **weakness** | debilidad | 弱點 | khuyết điểm | 약함 | tsis muaj zog |
| **windup** | movimiento para lanzar | 纏繞 | mưu toan khiêu khích | 종결, <야구> 와인드업 | thaj thaum tus neeg yuav txawb baseball |

| English | Spanish | Chinese | Vietnamese | Korean | Hmong |
|---------|---------|---------|------------|--------|-------|
| **Week 5: Shutting Out the Sky** | | | | | |
| **advice** | consejos | 忠告 | lời khuyên | 충고 | lus ntuas |
| **advised** | aconsejó | 勸告 | đã khuyên | 충고하다 | ntuas |
| **circumstances** | circunstancias | 情況 | các tình huống | 상황 | tej lub sij hawm |
| **elbow** | ábrete paso | 手肘 | khuỷu tay | 팔꿈치 | lauj tshib |
| **hustled** | estafaba | 催促 | đã xô đẩy | 재촉하다, ~를 척 척 해내다 | mos |
| **immigrants** | inmigrantes | 移民 | người di dân | 이민 | tus neeg tsiv teb tsaws chaw rau ib qhov chaw tshiab |
| **luxury** | lujo | 豪華 | sự xa hoa | 호화로운 | tau zoo nyob |
| **newcomer** | recién llegado | 新來者 | người mới đến | 새로 온 사람 | neej tuaj tshiab |
| **peddler** | mercachifle | 小販 | người bán hàng rong | 행상인 | neej thov khawv |

# Unit 2

| English | Spanish | Chinese | Vietnamese | Korean | Hmong |
|---------|---------|---------|------------|--------|-------|
| **Week 1: Inside Out** | | | | | |
| **caterpillar** | oruga | 小毛蟲 | con sâu | 애벌레 | kab ntsig |
| **cocoon** | capullo | 繭 | cái kén | 고치 | tsev rau npauj npaim |
| **disrespect** | falté el respeto | 不尊敬 | không kính nể | 경멸 | saib tsis taus |
| **emerge** | emerger | 湧現 | ra khỏi | 나타나다 | tawm tuaj |
| **migrant** | migratorio | 移居 | người di cư | 이동성의 | tus tsiv teb tsaws chaw |
| **sketched** | esbocé | 速寫 | đã vẽ | 스케치하다 | kos |
| **unscrewed** | desenrosqué | 鬆開 | đã mở nút | 나사가 빠지다 | ntswj rov qab |
| **Week 2: Passage to Freedom: The Sugihara Story** | | | | | |
| **agreement** | acuerdo | 協議 | sự thỏa thuận | 협정 | pom zoo |
| **cable** | cable | 電報 | điện tín | 케이블 | hlua |
| **diplomat** | diplomático | 外交官 | nhà ngoại giao | 외교관 | tus sawv cev ntawm ib tug nom mus rau lwm tus nom |
| **issue** | asunto | 簽發 | cấp phát | 쟁점 | teeb meem |
| **refugees** | refugiados | 難民 | người tị nạn | 난민 | neeg poob teb poob chaw |
| **representatives** | representantes | 代表 | đại biểu, người đại diện | 대표 | neeg sawv cev |
| **superiors** | superiores | 長官 | quan chức cấp trên | 윗사람, 상위의 | tus hlob |
| **visa** | visa | 護照 | giấy chiếu khán | 비자 | visa |
| **Week 3: Ch'i-lin Purse** | | | | | |
| **astonished** | asombrada | 吃驚 | kinh ngạc | 놀라다 | ceeb |
| **behavior** | comportamiento | 行為 | hành vi | 행동 | yeeb yam |
| **benefactor** | benefactora | 恩人 | người được hưởng | 은인 | tus pab nyiaj txiag |
| **distribution** | distribución | 分配 | việc phân phát | 배급 | faib |

| English | Spanish | Chinese | Vietnamese | Korean | Hmong |
|---|---|---|---|---|---|
| **gratitude** | gratitud | 謝意 | lòng biết ơn | 감사 | (nyiaj) tshav ntuj |
| **procession** | procesión | 隊伍 | đoàn người, đám rước | 행진, 행렬 | mus (tom ntej) |
| **recommend** | recomendar | 推薦 | giới thiệu | 추천하다 | qhuas |
| **sacred** | sagrado | 神聖 | thiêng liêng, sùng kính | 신성한 | muaj nuj nqis |
| **tradition** | tradición | 傳統 | truyền thống | 전통 | ib txwm ua dhau los |

## Week 4: Jane Goodall's 10 Ways to Help Save Wildlife

| | | | | | |
|---|---|---|---|---|---|
| **conservation** | conservación | 保護 | sự bảo tồn | 보존, 보호 | tu tsiaj kom txhob ploj mus |
| **contribute** | contribuyen | 貢獻 | đóng góp | 기부하다, 공헌하다 | ntxiv rau |
| **enthusiastic** | entusiastas | 熱心 | hăng hái | 열광적인 | zoo siab |
| **environment** | medio ambiente | 環境 | môi trường | 환경 | ib puag cig |
| **investigation** | investigación | 調查 | sự điều tra | 조사 | soj ntsuam, nrhiav |

## Week 5: The Midnight Ride of Paul Revere

| | | | | | |
|---|---|---|---|---|---|
| **fate** | destino | 命運 | định mệnh | 운명 | txoj hmoo |
| **fearless** | intrépido | 無畏的 | can đảm | 용감한 | tsis ntshai |
| **glimmer** | destello | 微光 | le lói | 깜박이는 빛, 반짝거리다 | ci |
| **lingers** | se entretiene | 徘徊 | chần chừ, nán lại | 꾸물거리다, 오래 끌다 | nyob luj loos |
| **magnified** | ampliado | 放大 | được phóng đại | 확대하다 | ua kom loj tuaj |
| **somber** | sombrías | 微暗 | nghiêm nghị | 어두컴컴한, 흐린 | tsaus ntuj |
| **steed** | corcel | 駿馬 | con ngựa hùng dũng | 말 | nees |

# Unit 3

| English | Spanish | Chinese | Vietnamese | Korean | Hmong |
|---------|---------|---------|------------|--------|-------|
| **Week 1: Wings for the King** | | | | | |
| **admiringly** | con admiración | 讚賞地 | một cách thán phục | 탄복할 만하게 | ntshaw |
| **permit** | permítame | 許可 | cho phép | 허락하다 | pub, cia |
| **scoundrel** | canalla | 歹徒 | tay côn đồ | 악당, 천한, 불명예스러운 | neeg phem |
| **subject** | súbdita | 目標 | đề tài | 주제, 화제 | zwm |
| **worthless** | inútiles | 無價值的 | không có giá trị | 하찮은 | tsis muaj nuj nqis |
| **Week 2: Leonardo's Horse** | | | | | |
| **achieved** | logrado | 達到 | đạt được | 이룩하다 | ua tau |
| **architect** | arquitecto | 建築師 | kiến trúc | 건축가 | ua vaj ua tsev |
| **bronze** | bronce | 古銅 | (về kim loại) đồng | 청동 | tooj liab |
| **cannon** | cañón | 大炮 | súng đại bác | 대포 | phom loj |
| **depressed** | deprimido | 壓平的 | buồn trầm uất | 낙담한 | nyuj siab |
| **fashioned** | elaboró | 塑造 | đã làm theo mẫu | ~을 만들다 | ua raws li |
| **midst** | (en) medio (de) | 中間 | ở giữa | 한가운데 | nruab nrab |
| **philosopher** | filósofo | 哲學家 | triết gia | 철학자 | tus neeg soj tsum neeg lub leej |
| **rival** | rival | 對手 | đối thủ | 경쟁자 | tus neeg nyiam sib tw |
| **Week 3: The Dinosaurs of Waterhouse Hawkins** | | | | | |
| **erected** | erigió | 豎起 | dựng lên | 직립하다 | sawv tseg |
| **foundations** | cimientos | 基礎 | nền tảng | 토대 | qhov txheem |
| **mold** | molde | 模具 | khuôn | 틀, 뼈대 | puab |
| **occasion** | ocasión | 場合 | dịp | 경우 | sij hawm |

| English | Spanish | Chinese | Vietnamese | Korean | Hmong |
|---------|---------|---------|------------|--------|-------|
| **proportion** | proporción | 比例 | tỷ lệ, cân xứng | 비율 | sib txig |
| **tidied** | ordenó | 整理 | đã dọn gọn gàng | 정돈된 | huv |
| **workshop** | taller | 工場 | xưởng nhỏ | 연수회 | hoob sib tham |

## Week 4: Mahalia Jackson

| English | Spanish | Chinese | Vietnamese | Korean | Hmong |
|---------|---------|---------|------------|--------|-------|
| **appreciate** | apreciar | 讚賞 | hiểu và biết ơn, thưởng thức | 감사하다 | saib muaj nuj nqis |
| **barber** | barbero | 理髮師 | thợ hớt tóc | 이발사 | tus txiav plaub hau |
| **choir** | coro | 唱詩班 | ban hợp ca | 합창단 | ib pab hu nkauj |
| **released** | se publicó | 釋放 | đã phát hành | 해방하다 | tso ntawm |
| **religious** | religiosa | 宗教 | sùng đạo | 종교적인 | ntseeg ntuj |
| **slavery** | esclavitud | 奴隸 | chế độ nô lệ | 노예의 | ua qhev |
| **teenager** | adolescente | 少年 | thanh thiếu niên tuổi từ 13 đến 19 | 10대의 청소년 | tub ntxhais hluas |

## Week 5: Special Effects in Film and Television

| English | Spanish | Chinese | Vietnamese | Korean | Hmong |
|---------|---------|---------|------------|--------|-------|
| **background** | fondo | 背景 | nền, hậu cảnh | 배경 | nyob tom qab |
| **explosions** | explosiones | 爆炸 | sự bùng nổ | 폭발 | tawg |
| **landscape** | paisaje | 場景 | cảnh vật | 풍경 | toj roob hauv pes |
| **miniature** | miniatura | 縮影 | hình, vật được rút nhỏ | 소형 모형 | tej yam me me |
| **prehistoric** | prehistórico | 史前 | tiền sử | 선사 시대의 | puag thaum ub |
| **reassembled** | reensamblados | 重新組裝 | lắp ráp lại | 다시 모으다 | rov sib dhos |

# Unit 4

| English | Spanish | Chinese | Vietnamese | Korean | Hmong |
|---------|---------|---------|-----------|--------|-------|
| **Week 1: Weslandia** | | | | | |
| **blunders** | tropezones | 錯誤 | những sai lầm vụng về | 큰 실수 | dig muag, tsis kag siab |
| **civilization** | civilización | 文明 | nền văn minh | 문명 | cov neeg muaj txuj ci tsim kho lub neej |
| **complex** | complejo | 複雜 | phức tạp | 복잡한 | ib pawg |
| **envy** | envidia | 妒嫉 | ghen ty | 부러워하다 | khib |
| **fleeing** | huir | 逃走 | chạy trốn | 벗어나는 | khiav |
| **inspired** | inspiró | 啟發 | được gợi cảm | 영감을 주다, 고무하다 | ua rau yus xav heev |
| **rustling** | susurrando | 沙沙聲 | xào xạc | 바스락 소리나는 | txav ub no |
| **strategy** | estrategia | 策略 | kế hoạch, chiến lược | 전략, 방법 | tswv yim |
| **Week 2: Stretching Ourselves: Kids With Cerebral Palsy** | | | | | |
| **abdomen** | abdomen | 腹部 | bụng | 복부 | plab mog |
| **artificial** | artificial | 人工的 | nhân tạo, giả | 인공의 | khoom yas |
| **gait** | manera de caminar | 步態 | dáng đi | 걸음걸이 | taug kev |
| **handicapped** | discapacitado | 缺陷者 | bị khuyết tật | 장애가 있는 | xiam hoob khab |
| **therapist** | terapeuta | 治療師 | bác sĩ chuyên khoa | 치료사 | tus kho mob |
| **wheelchair** | silla de ruedas | 輪椅 | xe lăn | 휠체어 | tog laub |
| **Week 3: Exploding Ants: Amazing Facts About How Animals Adapt** | | | | | |
| **critical** | críticos | 重要 | quan trọng, then chốt | 비판적인 | nyaum, tseem ceeb |
| **enables** | permite | 使能夠 | làm cho có thể | 가능하게 하다 | ua tau |
| **mucus** | mucus | 黏液 | đờm dãi | 점액 | quav ntswg |
| **scarce** | escaso | 缺乏 | khan hiếm | 부족한 | tsawg tsawg |

| English | Spanish | Chinese | Vietnamese | Korean | Hmong |
|---------|---------|---------|------------|--------|-------|
| **specialize** | se especializan | 專門研究 | chuyên môn về | 특수화하다 | ua ib yam khoom kaws xwb |
| **sterile** | estériles | 不育 | vô trùng | 불임의, 살균한, 헛된 | muaj tsis tau me nyuam |

## Week 4: The Stormi Giovanni Club

| English | Spanish | Chinese | Vietnamese | Korean | Hmong |
|---------|---------|---------|------------|--------|-------|
| **cavities** | caries | 洞 | sâu răng | 구멍 | qhov |
| **combination** | combinación | 組合 | sự phối hợp | 결합 | ob peb yam los ua ke |
| **demonstrates** | demuestra | 展示 | biểu diễn | 증명, 설명하다 | ua piv txwv |
| **episode** | episodio | 情節 | một giai đoạn | 에피소드 | ib zag |
| **profile** | (mantenerse en) segundo plano | 外形 | tiểu sử sơ lược | 특성 | sab ntsej muag |
| **strict** | estricto | 嚴密 | nghiêm khắc, gắt gao | 엄격한 | nkhaws |

## Week 5: The Gymnast

| English | Spanish | Chinese | Vietnamese | Korean | Hmong |
|---------|---------|---------|------------|--------|-------|
| **bluish** | azulados | 帶藍色的 | có chút màu xanh da trời | 푸르스름한 | xiav loos |
| **cartwheels** | volteretas laterales | 側手翻 | lộn nhào | 옆으로 재주넘기 | tis lis kas |
| **gymnastics** | gimnástica | 體操 | môn thể dục | 체조의 | txawj siv tes taw |
| **hesitation** | duda | 猶疑 | sự do dự | 주저 | ua ob peb lub siab, ua siab deb |
| **limelight** | centro de atención | 石灰光 | ánh đèn pha | 조명, 스포트라이트 | teem ci ntsa |
| **skidded** | patinó | 滑動 | trượt | 미끄러지다 | kiv, ya |
| **somersault** | dar saltos mortales | 筋斗 | lộn mèo | 공중제비 | somersault |
| **throbbing** | latía | 跳動 | nhức nhối | 두근두근하는, 떨리는 | od od |
| **wincing** | haciendo una mueca de dolor | 畏縮 | nhăn mặt | 주춤하는 | quaj txhawj |

# Unit 5

| English | Spanish | Chinese | Vietnamese | Korean | Hmong |
|---------|---------|---------|------------|--------|-------|
| **Week 1: The Three-Century Woman** | | | | | |
| **eerie** | escalofriante | 令人毛骨悚然 | bí hiểm | 무시무시한, 기묘한 | yam txawv txawv txaus ntshai |
| **intersection** | intersección | 交叉點 | điểm cắt nhau, ngã tư đường | 교차점 | kev sib tshuam |
| **pondered** | reflexionó | 考慮 | đã suy gẫm | 숙고하다 | xav |
| **severe** | serio | 嚴厲 | nghiêm trọng | 심한 | nyaum |
| **spectacles** | gafas | 眼鏡 | mắt kính | 광경 | tej yam rau neeg sawv daws saib |
| **withered** | marchita | 凋枯 | nhăn nheo, héo úa | 쇠약해진 | ua kom me zog thiab laus zog |
| **Week 2: The Unsinkable Wreck of the R. M. S. Titanic** | | | | | |
| **cramped** | estrecho | 侷促 | đã nhét vào; chật chội | 답답한 | ti |
| **debris** | restos | 殘骸 | mảnh vỡ | 파편 | khib nyiab |
| **interior** | interior | 內部 | nội thất, bên trong | 내부의 | sab hauv tsev |
| **ooze** | limo | 滲流 | chảy rỉ | 배어 나오다, 새다 | av nkos |
| **robotic** | robótico | 機器人的 | về người máy | 로봇의 | raws li robots |
| **sediment** | sedimento | 沉積 | đất sạn ở dưới đáy | 침전물 | tej yam khoom tog rau qab deg |
| **sonar** | sonar | 聲波導航測距儀 | về mặt trời | 수중 음파 탐지기 | sonar |
| **Week 3: Talk With an Astronaut** | | | | | |
| **accomplishments** | logros | 成就 | sự thành công | 성취 | yam ua tau |
| **focus** | atención | 焦點 | tiêu điểm | 초점 | saib meej |
| **gravity** | gravedad | 重力 | trọng lực | 중력 | gravity |

| English | Spanish | Chinese | Vietnamese | Korean | Hmong |
|---------|---------|---------|------------|--------|-------|
| **monitors** | monitores | 顯示器 | theo dõi | 모니터 | saib |
| **role** | ejemplo | 角色 | vai trò | 역할 | yus txoj hauj lwm |
| **specific** | específico | 特殊的 | đặc biệt, cụ thể | 특정한 | meej, tseeb |

## Week 4: Journey to the Center of the Earth

| English | Spanish | Chinese | Vietnamese | Korean | Hmong |
|---------|---------|---------|------------|--------|-------|
| **armor** | armadura | 裝甲 | áo giáp | 갑옷 | tub rog cev khaub ncaws hnav thaib ib ce |
| **encases** | reviste | 裝箱 | bao bọc | 싸다 | ntim |
| **extinct** | extintas | 絕種 | tiệt chủng | 멸종하다 | tuag tag |
| **hideous** | horrorosas | 醜陋 | xấu xí | 무서운 | dab tuag |
| **plunged** | sumergido | 浸入 | lao vào | 밀어 넣다 | dhia rau |
| **serpent** | serpiente | 大蛇 | con rắn | 큰 뱀 | nab |

## Week 5: Ghost Towns of the American West

| English | Spanish | Chinese | Vietnamese | Korean | Hmong |
|---------|---------|---------|------------|--------|-------|
| **economic** | económico | 經濟 | về kinh tế | 경제의 | kev nrhiav nyiaj txiag |
| **independence** | independencia | 獨立 | sự độc lập | 독립 | nyob ib leeg (tsis tso leej twg) |
| **overrun** | rebosante | 超出量 | chạy nhanh hơn | 침략하다 | khiav tshaj |
| **scrawled** | garabateó | 潦草地寫 | vẽ nguệch ngoạc | 낙서하다 | sau ntawv nyeem tsis tau |
| **vacant** | vacantes | 空置 | bỏ trống | 공허한 | chav khoom |

# Unit 6

| English | Spanish | Chinese | Vietnamese | Korean | Hmong |
|---------|---------|---------|------------|--------|-------|
| **Week 1: At the Beach** | | | | | |
| **algae** | algas | 海藻 | rong rêu | 조류 | nroj tsuag hauv dej hiav txwv |
| **concealed** | ocultos | 隱瞞 | bị che giấu | 숨기다 | zais |
| **driftwood** | madera flotante | 漂流木頭 | gỗ trôi dạt trên nước | 쓰레기 | ntoo ua dej tshoob los |
| **hammocks** | hamacas | 吊床 | những chiếc võng | 해먹 | txaj hlua pw |
| **lamented** | lamentó | 哀嘆 | đã than khóc | 유감스러운 | los yas tshooj |
| **sea urchins** | erizos de mar | 海膽 | các con nhím biển | 성게 | yam ntsev nyob dej hiav txwv |
| **sternly** | severamente | 嚴厲地 | nghiêm nghị | 엄격하게 | nyaum li |
| **tweezers** | pinzas | 鑷子 | cây nhíp | 족집게, 핀셋 | rab koob nrho pos |
| **Week 2: The Mystery of Saint Matthew Island** | | | | | |
| **bleached** | decolorados | 漂白 | bị bạc màu | 탈색되다 | ntxhua tshuaj dawb |
| **carcasses** | animales muertos | 屍體 | những bộ xương | 시체 | lub cev |
| **decay** | descomposición | 腐朽 | hư thối | 부식하다 | lwj |
| **parasites** | parásitos | 寄生生物 | ký sinh trùng | 기생충 | kab mob uas nyob hauv |
| **scrawny** | escuálido | 骨瘦如柴 | ốm khẳng khiu | 수척한 | nka tawv |
| **starvation** | inanición | 飢餓 | sự đói khát | 기아 | tshaib plab |
| **suspicions** | sospechas | 懷疑 | những nghi ngờ | 의심 | tsis ntseeg lwm tus |
| **tundra** | tundra | 寒帶草原 | bình nguyên ở vùng bắc cực hoặc vùng núi; lãnh nguyên | 툰드라 | toj |

| English | Spanish | Chinese | Vietnamese | Korean | Hmong |
|---------|---------|---------|------------|--------|-------|
| **Week 3: King Midas and the Golden Touch** | | | | | |
| **adorn** | adornar | 裝飾 | làm tăng vẻ đẹp | 꾸미다 | ua rau zoo nkauj |
| **cleanse** | (te) bañas | 洗滌 | làm sạch | 깨끗이 하다 | ntxuav kom hu |
| **lifeless** | inanimada | 無生命 | không có sinh lực | 생명이 없는 | tsis muaj sia |
| **precious** | precioso | 珍貴 | quý báu | 귀중한 | muaj nuj nqis |
| **realm** | reino | 領土 | vương quốc | 범위 | lub vaj loog |
| **spoonful** | cucharada | 一匙 | đầy một muỗng | 소량 | diav puv nkaus, diav puv npo |
| **Week 4: The Hindenburg** | | | | | |
| **criticizing** | criticando | 批評 | chỉ trích | 비판하는 | hais taus |
| **cruised** | navegó | 巡航 | đã bay ở tốc độ hiệu quả về nhiên liệu | 유람 항해하다 | caij cig |
| **drenching** | empapándolo | 脫灰 | ướt sũng | 가득 채운 | ntub dej tag, tsau dej |
| **era** | era | 時代 | thời kỳ | 시대 | lub sij hawm |
| **explosion** | explosión | 爆炸 | sự bùng nổ | 폭발 | tawg |
| **hydrogen** | hidrógeno | 氫 | khí hy-đrô | 수소 | pa hydrogen |
| **Week 5: Sweet Music in Harlem** | | | | | |
| **bass** | bajo | 低音 | đàn bass | 저음의 | lub suab laus |
| **clarinet** | clarinete | 單簧管 | kèn clarinet | 클라리넷 | raj nplaim |
| **fidgety** | inquieto | 坐立不安的 | bồn chồn | 안절부절 못하는 | nti nti |
| **forgetful** | olvidadizo | 健忘 | hay quên | 잊기 쉬운 | hnov qab heev, hnov qauj heev |
| **jammed** | improvisé | 阻塞 | bị ép chặt; đầy ních người | [장소 따위를] 메운 | daig |
| **nighttime** | noche | 夜間 | ban đêm | 야간에 | hmo ntuj |
| **secondhand** | de segunda mano | 第二手的 | cũ, đã có người dùng trước | 중고의 | tus tes ntev nyob ntawm lub moos |